AF776129

Critical theory and Independent Living

Manchester University Press

Critical theory and contemporary society

Series editors:

David M. Berry, Professor of Digital Humanities, University of Sussex
Darrow Schecter, Professor of Critical Theory and Modern European History, University of Sussex

The *Critical Theory and Contemporary Society* series aims to demonstrate the ongoing relevance of multi-disciplinary research in explaining the causes of pressing social problems today and in indicating the possible paths towards a libertarian transformation of twenty-first century society. It builds upon some of the main ideas of first-generation critical theorists, including Horkheimer, Adorno, Benjamin, Marcuse and Fromm, but it does not aim to provide systematic guides to the work of those thinkers. Rather, each volume focuses on ways of thinking about the political dimensions of a particular topic, which include political economy, law, popular culture, globalisation, feminism, theology and terrorism. Authors are encouraged to build on the legacy of first-generation Frankfurt School theorists and their influences (Kant, Hegel, Kierkegaard, Marx, Nietzsche, Weber and Freud) in a manner that is distinct from, though not necessarily hostile to, the broad lines of second-generation critical theory. The series sets ambitious theoretical standards, aiming to engage and challenge an interdisciplinary readership of students and scholars across political theory, philosophy, sociology, history, media studies and literary studies.

To buy or to find out more about the books currently available in this series, please go to: https://manchesteruniversitypress.co.uk/series/critical-theory-contemporary-society/

Critical theory and Independent Living

Teodor Mladenov

MANCHESTER UNIVERSITY PRESS

Copyright © Teodor Mladenov 2024

The right of Teodor Mladenov to be identified as the author of this work has been asserted in accordance with the Copyright, Designs and Patents Act 1988.

Published by Manchester University Press
Oxford Road, Manchester, M13 9PL

www.manchesteruniversitypress.co.uk

British Library Cataloguing-in-Publication Data
A catalogue record for this book is available from the British Library

ISBN 978 1 5261 7515 1 hardback

First published 2024

The publisher has no responsibility for the persistence or accuracy of URLs for any external or third-party internet websites referred to in this book, and does not guarantee that any content on such websites is, or will remain, accurate or appropriate.

Typeset by Newgen Publishing UK

To Kapka

Contents

Foreword

As a non-academic, I am honoured to be asked to write this foreword to what must be a truly critical account of Independent Living. My own background in Independent Living began within the development of the movement in England. There, I created a network of local telephone information and advice services run by and for disabled people throughout the UK called DIAL UK (Davis and Woodward, 1981). This network developed from 8 local services around the Midlands of England in 1981–1992 and from Aberdeen to Truro in 1984.

By 1984, the then Strathclyde Regional Council in Scotland had published a report titled *Living in a Hostile Environment*. One of the recommendations was to establish a 'Disabled People's Forum' by using the principles and practices of community development. With my experience of creating DIAL UK, Strathclyde's social work department employed me to establish the Glasgow Disability Forum. This has eventually metamorphosised into the Glasgow Disability Alliance, with a membership of over 5,000 disabled people.

During the latter part of my career in social work, I was involved in the provision of community support for those affected by the closure of the Young Chronic Sick Units within the then Glasgow Health Board. At the outset of the project, the estimate was that 95 per cent of the patients would be placed in nursing homes, with only 5 per cent receiving support in the community. A group of disabled people already living in the community helped interact with the patients and discuss with them the value of community living. There were also discussions of the principles and practices of Independent Living with our social work team. As a result, nearly 75 per cent of the patients (many of whom had been hospitalised for decades) were provided with their own accommodation in the community, assisted by individual packages of support.

From their inception in 1968, social work departments in Scotland were not allowed to give clients money to resolve their personal and social issues. Therefore, with the upsurge of the demand from the fledgling Independent Living movement, I was involved in developing a system of 'indirect payments' (via a third party) to allow people across most of the West of Scotland, which was then covered by Strathclyde Regional Council, to employ their own personal assistants. This anomaly was rectified when the Community Care (Direct Payments) Act 1996 allowed local authorities to make payments directly to people requiring personal care and social support.

Alongside a number of other disabled people, I also established a Centre for Independent Living in Glasgow in 1995, which we now call the Glasgow Centre for Inclusive Living (GCIL). This Centre eventually developed into the biggest in Scotland, supporting people in Glasgow and its surrounding local authorities. It has been run by disabled people to assist those who have been given a direct payment to engage an agency or employ their own personal assistant(s). GCIL has also provided support with seeking housing and employment – two of the other vital pillars of Independent Living.

On my retiral from social work and while assisting a large charity in England to redirect their institutional residential care to community-based services, I turned my attention to the development of the Independent Living movement in Scotland. It is within this context that I met Teodor Mladenov. Although I was conversant in the principles and practices of Independent Living, he has helped in my understanding of the wider philosophical issues around Independent Living and personal assistance. With his recent encouragement, I have returned to writing articles about the Independent Living movement, following a period of uncertainty. His vast experience of the European scene, especially in postsocialist Eastern Europe, has been of immense help to the movement not only in Europe, but here in Scotland as well, including to the Scottish government in their attempts to bring personal assistants into the workforce planning of the new National Care Service.

This is Mladenov's second title in the Critical Theory and Contemporary Society series. His first, *Critical Theory and Disability: A Phenomenological Approach*, was welcomed as a powerful exposure of the existential-ontological dimensions of disablism. Opening up a space for re-imagining and revaluing different ways of being human, this previous title showed the relevance of activism to theoretical discussion. I anticipate there will be a similar positive reaction to Mladenov's new book. Here, he has examined the current debates around Independent Living, this time in terms of psychopower, decommodification, careification, deinstitutionalisation, defamilialisation, deétatisation, and decolonialisation. Although these terms may sound complicated, each is admirably defined and discussed in the following chapters.

I would commend this book to any student, teacher, or researcher interested in the political or socio-economic position of disabled people. Reading it has surely deepened my knowledge and thinking around Independent

Living and the lived experience of disabled people. I will now take up a couple of points covered by the author to explain what I mean.

Mladenov argues that contemporary critical theory can clarify the often diverse and sometimes internally contradicting elements within the Independent Living paradigm, while critical-theoretical ideas and practices can assist the understanding of the ontology, deontology, and axiology of Independent Living. Disabled people's activism is seen as a viable source of intellectual production. Here, Mladenov gives a glancing reference to Antonio Gramsci – a point that I would like to discuss further. Gramsci (1971) considered that all men (sic) are intellectuals, in that all have intellectual and rational faculties, but not all men have the social opportunities to be intellectuals. He saw modern intellectuals not as talkers but as practice-minded directors and organisers who produced hegemony through ideological apparatuses such as education and the media. Furthermore, he distinguished between traditional intelligentsia, which sees itself as a class apart from society, and the thinking groups that every class produces from its own ranks organically. Such 'organic intellectuals' do not simply describe social life in accordance with scientific rules but instead articulate, through the language available in their culture, the feelings and experiences which the masses could not express for themselves. To Gramsci, it was the duty of organic intellectuals to speak to the obscured precepts of folk wisdom, or common sense (*senso comune*). These intellectuals would represent excluded social groups of a society, or what Gramsci referred to as the 'subaltern'.

Within critical theory, Gramsci's term 'subaltern' has been used to designate the colonised populations who have been socially, politically, and geographically excluded from the colonial centres of power and from the metropolitan homeland of the empire. These are people and social groups prevented from accessing the socio-economic institutions of society, which denies their agency and silences their voices in colonial politics. The resultant situation is akin to Giorgio Agamben's (2005) 'state of exemption', in which a sovereign or state can place a person or group outside the realm of customary law in times of emergency, or just because the powerful do not know what to do with them. Judith Butler (2004) used the concept to discuss the state of detainees within Camp Delta, Guantanamo Bay, during the war in Afghanistan.

Such critical theorising similarly highlights the lived experience of disabled people and their Independent Living movement, erased under the hegemony of professionals and their political masters who dominate disabled people's socio-medical world. The movement's mantra 'Nothing about us without us' gives voice to this 'organic', bottom-up, practical wisdom of the Independent Living activists, which contains important social-collectivist elements, a powerful critique of self-sufficiency, and the intimate knowledge of living in a hostile world. As Mladenov explains, this organic knowledge and lived experience are often unheard or rather dismissed by the more advantaged and powerful listeners. Such instances of 'epistemic injustice' (Fricker, 2007) have been highlighted in the interactions between patients and their doctors around the patients' treatment and lifestyles (Carel and Kidd, 2017). The argument has been developed further in my own work (Elder-Woodward, 2014) by emphasising that the advantaged not only disregard the testimony of the disadvantaged but also speak for them. I have identified this as 'epistemic displacement' that not only discolours the thinking and needs of the organic yet disadvantaged thinker but further disempowers them and their group, by speaking about them in their absentia.

At a time when the UN Convention on the Rights of Persons with Disabilities is urging states to include disabled people and their directly accountable organisations in policy and practice developments at all levels (international, national, and local), discussions on how to make effective the involvement of organic thinkers are particularly germane. As these intellectuals, including the thinkers involved in the Independent Living movement, experience kickbacks from hegemonic groups, particularly within the fields of social care support and healthcare, I'm reminded of Vic Finkelstein, a major driver of the movement in Britain. Finkelstein (cited in Campbell and Oliver, 1996: 100) once made the following statement:

> My position was that in a representative democracy where people organise and present their views, you take those views to represent the group they say they're representing until other organisations emerge to challenge them. That's what democracy is about. Inasmuch as there is no other reflection of their views, these are the views. The fact that it's a minority membership is true, but the question then is 'Who speaks for the majority?' I once gave a talk to a medical disability group and they raised this issue. They said, 'These views you're putting forward are interesting, but they only represent a minority of disabled people.' So I said, 'Who represents the majority? You?' Of course, they just became embarrassed, because if it isn't us it's them, the doctors.

This debate is still prevalent today. In a study of a major disabled people's organisation in Sweden, Disability Human Rights, Krantz *et al.* (2023) interviewed 171 members, both disabled and non-disabled. Using qualitative analysis, they found two main dimensions in the arguments around who should represent disabled people – the ideological dimension, which legitimised representation through lived experience or a human rights approach, and the pragmatic dimension, which legitimised representation through relational claims or organisational necessities. Further analysis revealed a paradox. When a representative is required to have a body with certain characteristics, other knowledge-related aspects risk devaluation. The authors conclude that, paradoxically, the organisation has a goal of rendering impairment irrelevant in society, while rendering impairment a main issue when electing representatives. Their most pertinent argument from the perspective of today's movement is:

> The fundamental battle for the modern disability movement may not even be about defining 'us', but rather about maintaining its members, as they are crucial for the local chapters. There needs to be an active local level where representatives can be recruited if the movement is not to be reduced to an academic debate, or again, run by professionals. After all, if the movement is to make claims and fill the 'about' with content, legitimate representatives are required. Daring to discuss undoubtedly sensitive questions about who is disabled and who has the right to make claims on their behalf is crucial if the disability movement is to evolve, expand and have an impact. (Krantz *et al.*, 2023: 209)

The tension around who represents disabled people and their views on the services which support them in the community continues to this day, particularly in the case of those who have speech and/or cognitive impairments, where others often assume they know what is needed and speak on disabled people's behalf. In fact, after over a decade of fiscal and organisational abrasion, I have encouraged the Independent Living movement in Scotland to reflect on its position and take stock of its policies and strategies: 'Perhaps it is time to think about [the movement's] balance between participating in civic pluralism, and its grass-roots of political resistance' (Elder-Woodward, 2016: 12).

But the underpinning oppositions can be viewed in a positive light when we consider the world and its political spheres in terms of Chantal Mouffe's (2013) 'agonistic pluralism'. Agonism, as opposed to antagonism, implies a deep respect and concern for the other. Indeed, as Samuel Chambers (2001) points out, the Greek *agon* refers most directly to an athletic contest oriented not merely toward victory or defeat but emphasising the importance of the struggle itself – a struggle that cannot exist without the opponent. An agonistic discourse will therefore be one marked not merely by conflict but, just as importantly, by mutual admiration. In terms of Mouffe's theory, agonism reflects that we live in a pluralistic world in which we should value the stance of our opponents in their thinking and lived experience. The voice and agency of Gramsci's 'organic type' should not dominate that of the 'traditional type' – instead, both should be working together, as equal contestants in the struggle to achieve an outcome through which all can prosper. This is truly important to the lives of disabled people. Working together, in a respectful manner, will facilitate the struggle to achieve the positive objective we all want.

A practical example of agonistic pluralism can be found in the work of the British Social Care Institute for Excellence (SCIE). Drawing on insights from several social care recipient groups, SCIE (2022) explains the philosophical and practical implications of 'co-production', in which public services are delivered in an equal and reciprocal relationship between professionals, people using services, their families, and their neighbours. Where activities are co-produced in this way, both services and neighbourhoods become far more effective agents of change (Boyle and Harris, 2009).

The other idea that I would like to discuss briefly is Mladenov's bifurcation of care into 'paternalist' and 'egalitarian'. In 'paternalist care', the carer stands in or serves as a deputy for the cared-for person – in effect, the latter becomes dominated and dependent. Paternalist care is manifested in today's social care system in Britain. The commodification of care is not only present in its commissioning and procurement, but in its operation. Time and task limitations depersonalise the relationship between the carer and the cared-for person. The latter not only feels objectified but is often charged for the 15-minute slot, while they may get fewer minutes of care because the home carer is always in a rush to get to the next client. As a result, people often have to choose between going to the toilet and having a cup of tea: 'I'd be fully washed and dressed by 8.00am then sit there with nothing to do and nowhere to go' (disabled person cited in Witcher, 2014: 22).

With 'egalitarian care', on the other hand, the carer intervenes not to take control of the care but to give it back to the cared-for person. Drawing on existential philosophy, Mladenov points out that egalitarian care enables people to realise themselves as 'world-disclosers' instead of being reduced to objects. Becoming a world-discloser provides an opportunity to preserve and create meaning, including the meaning of one's own life and the meaning of being. In essence, the egalitarian care made possible by the pillars of Independent Living – including personal assistance – has enabled disabled people to become fully human and equal citizens by avoiding the objectification effected by paternalist care. This reminds me of what the personal assistant employer Jack shares with Jenny Morris (1993b: 125) – the freedom Independent Living and personal assistance give to people can be transformative: 'I'm a husband, a father and a breadwinner. And ten years ago I was in an institution where I couldn't even decide when to go to the toilet ... You know, you can't really understand it if you haven't done it ... your whole life changes'.

In the introduction to her book *Make Them Go Away: Clint Eastwood, Christopher Reeve and the Case Against Disability Rights*, Mary Johnson (2003: xvii) writes:

> Public discussion has still not gotten around to the new ideas that underpin the disability rights vision. Reasonable accommodation, demedicalization, universal design, customization and integration are simple enough concepts to understand, but hard to implement when the society you live in continues to see people with disabilities as having something wrong with them, needing cure

> or charitable help, or as sly malcontents trying to get some special rights they don't deserve, creating nothing but problems and extra costs for the rest of us.

I would submit that critical discourses such as those within Mladenov's book and those which will undoubtedly flow from it will promote the principles and practices of Independent Living and the rights disabled people have as equal citizens. I am hopeful that other 'organic thinkers' within the movement – together with those living academic, professional, and political lives – will similarly endorse such critical thinking and embed it within the public discussion of Independent Living and disability rights.

Jim Elder-Woodward, OBE DUniv PhD BA(Hons)
Glasgow, November 2023

Acknowledgements

I dedicate this book to the memory of the Independent Living activist Kapka Panayotova (1956–2021).

Other people who have helped me understand Independent Living through conversations and joint work are my colleagues in the European Network on Independent Living: Ines Bulic Cojocariu, Jamie Bolling, Kamil Goungor, Nadia Hadad, and Natasa Kokic; the founder Adolf Ratzka; my partner, Lilia Angelova-Mladenova; and the Scottish Independent Living pioneer Jim Elder-Woodward. Thank you all!

I am also grateful to the School of Humanities, Social Sciences and Law at the University of Dundee for a three-month research leave, which enabled me to lay the foundations of the book.

I have used, in a revised form, material from the following articles: Mladenov, T., Bulic Cojocariu, I., Angelova-Mladenova, L., Kokic, N., and Goungor, K. (2023) 'Independent Living in Europe and beyond: past, present, and future', *International Journal of Disability and Social Justice*, 3:1, 4–23; Mladenov, T. (2022) 'Independence and its meaning: ENIL's monitoring of Article 19 as a struggle for hermeneutical justice', in M. H. Rioux, J. Viera, A. Buettgen, and E. Zubrow (eds) *Handbook of Disability: Critical Thought and Social Change in a Globalizing World*. Singapore: Springer, 1–16; Mladenov, T. (2021) 'The social model of disability, the independent living and the idea of "care"', *Critique and Humanism Journal*, 55:2, 9–24; and Mladenov, T. and Petri, G. (2019) 'Independent living in Central and Eastern Europe? The challenges of postsocialist deinstitutionalisation', in I. Fylling, L. Baciu, and J. Breimo (eds) *EU Social Inclusion Policies in Post-Socialist Countries: Top-Down and Bottom-Up Perspectives on Implementation*. London: Routledge, 16–34.

List of tables

List of abbreviations

CEE	Central and Eastern Europe
CIL	Centre for Independent Living
COVID-19 DRM	COVID-19 Disability Rights Monitor
CRPD	Convention on the Rights of Persons with Disabilities
EASPD	European Association of Service Providers for Persons with Disabilities
ECCL	European Coalition for Community Living
EEG	European Expert Group on the Transition from Institutional to Community-based Care
ENIL	European Network on Independent Living
ESIFs	European Structural and Investment Funds
GIL	Gothenburg Cooperative for Independent Living
ILI	Independent Living Institute
LSS	Act Concerning Support and Services for Persons with Certain Functional Impairments
NHS	National Health Service
PA	personal assistance
PAA	Personal Assistance Act
PDA	Persons with Disabilities Act
SFBT	Solution Focused Brief Therapy
STIL	Stockholm Cooperative for Independent Living
STS	Science and Technology Studies
ULOBA	Independent Living Norway
UPIAS	Union of the Physically Impaired against Segregation
WHO	World Health Organization
YHD	Association for the Theory and Culture of Handicap

Introduction

Like most critical-theoretical analyses, this book is about freedom, but unlike most critical theory, it approaches freedom from a disability perspective by drawing on the wisdom of the disabled people's Independent Living movement. Following the latter's lead, I regard freedom as implying independence. But how can something usually understood (including by critical theorists) as intrinsically restricting independence – something like disability – be used as a ground for understanding it? Or, to ask the same question from a critical disability studies perspective, is not independence an intrinsically ableist and, by intersectional extension, also classist, racist, androcentric, heteronormative, and ageist concept?

What makes the Independent Living movement a source of insight for critical theorising on freedom-as-independence is that Independent Living realises independence as a specific form of *inter*dependence rather than as self-sufficiency. Moreover, Independent Living realises independence as both an individual and a collective achievement. Independent Living, therefore, incorporates relations of dependence, although not every dependence is commensurate with Independent Living. Independent Living is about (re)gaining control over one's life by limiting professional and parental intervention, but also by acquiring access to specific supports and adequate means. Independent Living is inextricably entangled with power, and particularly with professional power, biopower, psychopower, and parental authority.

Most critical theorists are profoundly concerned about freedom but do not understand disability and, even less so, disability advocacy. If they consider disability, it is usually as an argument against capitalism, following the logic that the profit imperative injures human bodies and minds, producing impairments. As an example, for Jonathan Crary (2014: 86, original emphasis), autism is a pathology created by techno-capitalism through the medium of television that 'might have a catastrophic *physical* impact on the developing human being … it could produce extreme, permanent impairments in the acquisition of language and in the capacity for social interaction'. Similarly, Bernard Stiegler (2010: 42) makes recourse to various impairments to expose the dangers of late capitalist consumerism:

> The generational confusion inherent in consumerism destroys any shared concern for taking care of the world and of oneself, self-care as opposed to a consumption resulting in obesity and other 'sedentary' problems (such as cardiovascular pathologies): addiction, cognitive overflow syndrome, attention deficit disorder, depression, impotence, and, finally, the collapse of desire.

In these accounts, impairments are unambiguously negative – they are reduced to unwanted results of contemporary capitalist developments. A similar negation results from Jasbir Puar's (2017) seminal analysis of capitalist 'debilitation' and 'slow death' – a critique of systemic violence that simultaneously 'increases ableism and sanism, which are of course also forms of violence' (Ben-Moshe, 2020: 266). The alternative is to look at physical, cognitive, or mental health 'disorders' as (potentially) positive differences, as grounds for individual and collective identity and organising, and/or as sources of enlightenment (Goodley *et al.*, 2019). Such an alternative is promoted by the psychiatric survivors movement, the neurodiversity movement, and the Independent Living movement, among others. This book follows the latter's lead by embracing the disability perspective as a positive epistemic resource for critical theorising about freedom-as-independence.

My way into Independent Living

In 1997–1998, for 12 months, I worked part-time as a ward attendant in a closed psychiatric hospital in Bulgaria. I did night shifts, seven or eight per month, which enabled me to work while studying full-time – I was pursuing a combined Bachelor's/Master's degree in Psychology at Sofia University, which I completed in 2000. While working in the psychiatric hospital, I witnessed first-hand, and I was a (reluctant) participant in, the reproduction of professional power and the ableist violence emanating from it.

It was routine to restrain some of the patients by fixing them to their beds with straps tied to their wrists and ankles, to have them immobilised during the night. I also witnessed the practice of locking people up in an isolation room in the men's ward that included a bed (fixed to the floor) and a camera to observe the inmate through a monitor in the staff room. Some patients hid from the camera by sleeping under the bed. On several occasions, I was called upon to help with holding patients so that they could be forcibly medicated. Most of the nurses and ward attendants seemed relieved when the psychiatrist on duty over-medicated the patients – this meant that the staff would be able to have a quieter night. Having keys for the locked doors was a material token of power – a colleague told me on my first night shift that the person who has the keys is the person who is in control.

I felt uncomfortable with these manifestations of institutional violence. I was just encountering the ideas of anti-psychiatry, as I was part of a group of like-minded students who were studying the psychotherapeutic approach of Solution Focused Brief Therapy (SFBT). SFBT challenges professional power by treating the person who seeks help with mental health issues as an equal partner in constructing the solutions to their problems (de Shazer, 1994) – the opposite of what I witnessed in the psychiatric hospital. I resisted institutional culture and practices by conversing with the patients and by striving to take their words at face value (rather than as 'symptoms'). I doggedly avoided wearing a medical gown, but, ironically, it was some of the patients (rather than the psychiatrists or nurses) who insisted that I did – I guess, to be more easily identifiable as belonging to those on the other side of the institutional divide.

I remember one occasion when the psychiatrist on duty admitted a new patient and shared with me the intention to take away the woman's pencils (she had brought with her a set of colouring pencils, as she was keen on drawing). Knowing that I was a psychology student, the psychiatrist used the opportunity to teach me a lesson about the intricacies of wielding professional power: 'When you go to someone else's house, you take off your shoes, don't you? That is why I am taking away her pencils – to make her understand that she is not at home.' 'Will you let her keep her shoes?' I retorted. Later, I noticed that the patient was allowed to keep her pencils.

In Bulgaria, the second half of the 1990s was a time of scarcity, austerity, and sheer chaos. As elsewhere in the postsocialist region, psychiatric and other institutions in the country were badly hit by the neoliberal restructuring and retrenchment that characterised this period. Ironically, from the perspective of the struggling psychiatry, these reforms were branded as 'shock therapy' (Murrell, 1993). We did not have enough personal protective equipment, so sometimes I had to clean the corridors and toilets (night-shift ward attendants did not clean the patients' rooms) without gloves. I used an old rag and a bucket. Sometimes, there was no cleaning liquid, so I used plain water. Now and then, I also had to recycle the plastic bags that we used to collect rubbish by emptying them in the container outside the building, then bringing them back to be reused. For a brief period, the dinner that we served was so meagre (a slice of bread and a piece of white cheese) that the patients must have gone to bed hungry. Cigarettes were always in high demand – the patients constantly solicited cigarettes from each other and from the staff.

Postsocialist austerity exacerbated the violence of institutionalisation by worsening the working conditions of the staff and the living conditions of the residents. However, it was the cultures and practices of institutionalisation (inherited from state socialist social policy) that created this violence in the first place. My engagement with SFBT and anti-psychiatry, as well as my experience of working in the psychiatric hospital, helped me understand this and prepared me for my subsequent involvement with the Independent Living movement. In 2000, I started working with the Centre for Independent Living–Sofia (CIL–Sofia), a Bulgarian disability rights organisation founded and led by the disabled activist Kapka Panayotova. Ever since, I have been an ally, although I have not (yet) identified as disabled.

My attachment to the movement was strengthened in 2017–2019, when I did research at the European Network on Independent Living (ENIL), supported by funding from the European Commission in the framework of a Marie Curie Individual Fellowship. As I write this book in 2023, I am based in Scottish academia, at the University of Dundee, where I have been a member of the academic faculty since 2019. Still, I continue to identify with the activists. I am also an Eastern European, and my analyses are influenced by my state socialist upbringing and postsocialist experience (including higher education and 10 years of working in the Bulgarian civil society sector). This position in the gap between state socialism and postsocialist neoliberalisation has informed my scepticism towards both the state and the market, which underpins much of the analysis that follows.

The views presented here are my own and I take responsibility for them, but they have been shaped and underpinned by my engagement with CIL–Sofia and ENIL. Moreover, I intentionally seek to ground my critical-theoretical analyses in the work of the activists. Thus, I regard disabled people's activism as a viable source of knowledge production – an epistemic intervention of an 'organic' type, in Gramscian terms. This bottom-up, practical wisdom of the Independent Living movement has often been misrepresented by academics and caring professionals (such as physicians, rehabilitators, nurses, psychologists, social workers, special teachers, and therapists) as being overwhelmingly liberal-individualist, but it contains equally important social-collectivist elements, together with a powerful critique of self-sufficiency. It also has a prominent transnational dimension that has so far remained underexplored. The conceptual tools of contemporary critical theory will help clarify these diverse and sometimes internally contradicting elements of the Independent Living paradigm, in their inherent complexity and dialectical richness. For their part, Independent Living ideas and practices will help rethink critical-theoretical constructs.

A specific contradiction that this book seeks to overcome boils down to the tension between the anti-intellectualism of disability advocacy and the depoliticisation of disability within contemporary academic research. Anti-intellectualism has found apt expression in Michael Oliver's (1992b) charge of 'intellectual masturbation' targeted at disability studies scholars. In turn, depoliticisation has been addressed by Dan Goodley and his co-authors (2019: 980) in a recent seminal paper – as the field of disability studies becomes more diverse and theoretically sophisticated, it tends to get alienated from the everyday concerns of disabled people and to undermine their leading role in research. Goodley *et al.*'s (2019: 980) advice is that to understand disability, 'one must draw on the expertise of disabled people as active subjects of intellectual endeavour'. This is exactly what I intend to do.

Critical theory, disability studies, and disability activism

In terms of method, the book will combine critical theorising with development of case study vignettes that focus on ENIL's work and kindred advocacy initiatives. What I identify as 'critical theory' goes beyond the Frankfurt School thinkers to include the critical philosophies of Michel Foucault (1978, 1988, 1991; Fraser, 2003; Rose, 1999), Gilles Deleuze (1992; Deleuze and Guattari, 2004; Han, 2017), and Bernard Stiegler (2010). It also includes Nancy Fraser's theory of social justice (Fraser, 1996, 2005; Fraser and Honneth, 2003), analyses of epistemic injustice epitomised in the work of Miranda Fricker (2007), and (neo)Marxist critiques of neoliberal marketisation (Fraser, 2013; Harvey, 2005). In addition, I make use of welfare state theory (Esping-Andersen, 1990, 1999; Fraser, 1987, 1997; Offe, 1984; Orloff, 2009; Titmuss, 1974).

From the perspective of this book, critical theorising also includes the work of disability activists and scholars. This, I hope, will help overcome the erasure of disability from critical-theoretical analyses, thus continuing the work started with my previous contribution to the Critical Theory and Contemporary Society series (Mladenov, 2015a). But whereas in my 2015 book I looked at the mutually reinforcing (and sometimes contradictory) relations between disability studies, activism, and phenomenology, here my specific intention is to highlight and explore in depth the links between critical theorising and the disabled people's Independent Living movement and analytic paradigm.

Indeed, disability studies has from its very inception in the 1980s incorporated socio-political critique. In these early days, the emerging discipline was informed by Marxism and neo-Marxism in Britain (Finkelstein, 1980; Oliver, 1990), whereas in North America, functionalism (Stone, 1984) and critiques of stigma, prejudice, and discrimination constituted the dominant underpinning frameworks (Bagenstos, 2000; Hahn, 1990). Thus, (neo) Marxism provided the theoretical context for the emergence of the social model of disability in its influential British version (Oliver, 2009), whereas the Independent Living paradigm was originally informed by the ideas of American civil rights activists, anti-discrimination, consumerism, and deinstitutionalisation (DeJong, 1979). That said, both the social model of disability and Independent Living were grounded in peer support (DeJong, 1979; Oliver, 2009; UPIAS, 1976a) and, accordingly, have been strongly critical of professional power – a critique rendered in terms of challenging the medical model of disability (Brisenden, 1986), medicalisation (Oliver, 2009), or the 'rehabilitation paradigm' (DeJong, 1979).

In the 1990s and the 2000s, there was a new wave of disability theorising that sought to incorporate concepts from poststructuralism, feminism, queer studies, phenomenology, and critical realism into disability studies. In this period, disability studies scholars turned to critical philosophers such as Judith Butler, Gilles Deleuze, Jacques Derrida, Michel Foucault, Donna Haraway, and Maurice Merleau-Ponty to (re)articulate their arguments (Corker and Shakespeare, 2002; Davis, 2002; Garland-Thomson, 1997; Michalko, 2002; Paterson and Hughes, 1999; Shakespeare, 2006, 2014; Thomas, 1999; Tremain, 2005). The 2010s witnessed the intensification and further development of these differentiating trends, together with the rise of decolonial and intersectional analyses of disability (Altermark, 2018; Bell, 2011; Ben-Moshe, 2020; Erevelles, 2011; Goodley, 2017; Goodley *et al.*, 2019; Grech, 2009; McRuer, 2006; Meekosha, 2011; Meekosha and Soldatic, 2011; Musengi, 2023; Soldatic, 2013).

The approaches seeking to revise the original tenets of disability studies since the 1990s eventually came to be identified as *critical* disability studies (Goodley *et al.*, 2019; Meekosha and Shuttleworth, 2009) – a somewhat misleading term, considering that disability studies has been self-reflexively critical since its inception. Moreover, the critical value of the recognitive turn, as reflected in the enhanced attention to discourse and culture that has characterised much of the post-1990s disability theorising – a shift eloquently defended by Shakespeare (1994) in a seminal paper defining the trend – could nevertheless be questioned due to its crowding out of redistributive issues. This shift of attention from economic redistribution to cultural recognition amidst neoliberal globalisation has been criticised as undermining the critical potential of kindred emancipatory disciplines such as feminism (Fraser, 2013). Nowadays, the political-economic analysis of capital and capitalism is back on the critical theorists' agenda, enriched by feminist, anti-racist, ecological, and decolonial insights (Fraser, 2022: 1–2). Disability studies scholars and activists are important (although often marginalised) stakeholders in this renewal of critical political economy.

The 2010s were also a time when *postsocialist* disability studies started to make a mark in both Europe and North America, combining ethnographic and historical detail with a reinvigorated critique of statism, professional power, productivism, and neoliberal marketisation (Dimitrova, 2020; Hartblay, 2014; Kolářová, 2014; Kolářová and Winkler, 2021; Mladenov, 2015a, 2018; Phillips, 2010; Rasell and Iarskaia-Smirnova, 2014). In hindsight, postsocialist disability studies constituted a mixture of disparate concepts and frameworks, drawing on several generations of disability theorising and combining social modellist insights and Independent Living influences with ideas from (neo)Marxism, poststructuralism, phenomenology, queer studies, intersectionality, and decolonial critique.

Institutionally and geographically positioned on the margins, postsocialist scholars have remained less affected by the factional affiliations and tensions characterising Western European and North American disability studies. This has allowed conceptual experimentation, albeit with much more limited resources than have been available in the centres of knowledge production in the Global North. Postsocialist scholarship has also unsettled the opposition between the North and the South due to the hybridity of the knowledge production emerging out of a third, intermediary, and therefore doubly erased, region (Dimitrova and Mladenov, 2023).

I will return to these points in Chapter 7, in my discussion of the links between Independent Living and the critiques of coloniality and decoloniality. For now, it suffices to say that I will draw on concepts, frameworks, and data generated in the domain of postsocialist disability studies to construct and support some of my key arguments about Independent Living. The situation of disabled people in the postsocialist countries of Central and Eastern Europe (CEE) reflects in a condensed form the 'postsocialist condition' diagnosed by Fraser (1997) as the global transition from state-managed to market-based societies since the 1980s. Nowadays, we all live in postsocialism, while disabled people in CEE experience some of the worst excesses of the state-socialist legacies and more recent neoliberal trends.

A brief history of Independent Living

The ideas and practices of Independent Living emerged in the late 1960s in the United States. They originated from the activism of Ed Roberts and other disabled students at the University of California, Berkeley, who were seeking alternatives to their institutional, restrictive, and medicalised living arrangements on the university campus. Eventually, this activism resulted in the formal establishment of the first Centre for Independent Living (CIL) in Berkeley in 1972. The pioneers of Independent Living 'became aware of the degree to which control over their lives had been taken over by medical and rehabilitation professionals. They thus came to realize that the concerns about self-determination raised by the black and student movements had considerable relevance to their own lives as disabled people' (Zukas, 1975: n.p.).

For many who fight for empowerment, equality, and social inclusion of disabled people, the founding of the first CIL in Berkeley marks the symbolic birth of the disability rights movement. It was influenced by the struggle of Black Americans for civil rights, as well as by other liberation movements that defined the 1960s (Charlton, 1998: Ch. 8). Eventually, the Independent Living movement gave rise to an analytic paradigm (DeJong, 1979) reflecting disabled people's fight for self-determination and embodying the 'nothing about us without us' principle (Charlton, 1998).

In Europe, the ideas of Independent Living were introduced in the 1970s and 1980s by disability activists such as Adolf Ratzka in Sweden and John Evans in the UK. This was a time of fervent activity and international exchange. John Evans (2002: 10) recounts how, in 1983, British activists attended the first Conference on Independent Living in Sweden:

> This was reciprocated in the UK with its first Conference on Independent Living and attended by Adolf Ratzka and Judy Heumann, who was then the Director of the CIL from Berkeley, California. After these two Conferences there was a very close liaison and relationship between the UK and Swedish Independent Living developments, which would form the basis for the beginnings of a European movement. (Evans, 2002: 10; see also Ratzka, 1996)

In Britain, the movement received a decisive boost in 1979 from a group of disabled people confined to a residential institution in Hampshire, England – the Le Court Cheshire Home (Evans, 2002). The Le Court residents sought ways to live independently in the community, similar to their CIL–Berkeley peers. This led to the establishment in 1984 of one of the first CILs in the UK, the Hampshire CIL (a detailed history of the Independent Living movement in the UK is provided by Hunt, 2019: Ch. 8). In Sweden, the Stockholm Cooperative for Independent Living (abbreviated as STIL) was conceived in 1984 but started activity later, first as a pilot project in 1987 and then permanently in 1989, after overcoming 'massive resistance from some political parties, the labor unions, traditional service providers and the established disability organizations' (Ratzka, 1996).

Both John Evans, a founding member of the Hampshire CIL, and Adolf Ratzka, founder of STIL, were involved in the establishment of the European Network on Independent Living (ENIL) in 1989. ENIL was conceived as a membership organisation, a pan-European heir of CIL–Berkeley, similarly led and controlled by disabled people. The establishment of ENIL has been described by Evans (2002: 13–14) as

> one of the most significant events in Europe for the Independent Living Movement. ... It started when over 80 disabled people, most of whom were

> personal assistance users, from 14 different European countries, congregated at the European Parliament in Strasbourg to discuss issues of concern on Independent Living. This ended up being an historic event because the main outcome of this meeting of minds was the establishment of ENIL and hence for the first time there was a co-ordinated approach for Independent Living at a European level.

Indeed, since its founding in 1989, ENIL has been at the forefront of campaigning for Independent Living in Europe. The organisation's work is based on the principles of solidarity, peer support, self-representation, cross-impairment, and self-determination (ENIL, n.d.-a). More recently, ENIL's work has become increasingly intersectional by incorporating the neurodiversity perspective and by considering the overlaps between disability and older age, gender, poverty, and locality. In this, ENIL has been following (but also shaping) the contemporary trend in global disability rights advocacy and disability studies.

Independent Living has been strong not only in Western Europe, but also in Southern and Eastern Europe. The movement has been growing in Spain (viandalucia.org) and Portugal (vidaindependente.org), where successful links with academics have been established. In the 1990s, organisations fighting for Independent Living, including Centres for Independent Living, were established in postsocialist countries such as Bulgaria (cil.bg), Serbia (www.cilsrbija.org), Slovenia (yhd-drustvo.si), and Poland (niezaleznezycie.pl). Independent Living has also spread beyond North America and Europe. Centres for Independent Living have been founded in Cambodia (www.facebook.com/phnompenh.cil), Costa Rica (www.facebook.com/mvicr), Japan (www.j-il.jp), Korea (www.kcil.or.kr), Mongolia (www.facebook.com/MILC.TugeemelKhugjil), Nepal (www.cil.org.np), Palestine (www.facebook.com/ILC.Pal), and the Philippines (www.lifehaveninc.org), among other countries.

Independent Living theory and practice

The Independent Living theory that this book reconstructs and draws upon starts from practice and remains firmly grounded in practice. The realisation of Independent Living requires a system of interrelated supports and accommodations controlled or overseen by disabled people. The pioneers at CIL–Berkeley promoted 'a holistic, integrated approach by providing a comprehensive array of services' designed and monitored by the people who use them (Zukas, 1975: n.p.). Originally, these user-led and user-controlled services included support with finding and managing personal assistants, advocacy and advice concerning benefits and services, and help with maintaining assistive devices such as wheelchairs (Zukas, 1975). Hunt (2019: n.p.) describes the first CILs as

> facilitators, trying to provide support, information and advice, so that people could make better use of existing resources for themselves. At times, this might mean becoming negotiators with other service-providers to highlight the absence of services, such as tackling a local housing department to provide accessible housing where none existed or engaging with local transport providers where no accessible transport existed. At other times, it could be about providing support to individuals to achieve more for themselves.

More recently, ENIL (2023d: 14) has defined a CIL as

> a cross-disability organisation controlled by disabled people with a mission to promote social inclusion and mainstreaming of disabilities in all public policies. CILs should focus on personal assistance, peer support and building inclusive communities, information and training activities for both disabled and non-disabled people, policy research from the perspective of the UN CRPD and legal representation for disabled people who want to live independently but have no opportunities to do so.

The supports considered key for Independent Living, sometimes conceptualised as the '12 Basic Rights' (Spectrum CIL, n.d.) or the '12 Pillars of Independent Living' (Disability Rights UK, n.d.; ENIL, 2023d: 11), include accessible environment, accessible transport, accessible and affordable housing, accessible information, appropriate assistive technology, personal assistance, inclusive education and training, adequate income, access to employment, independent advocacy, peer support/counselling, and accessible and appropriate healthcare. We should add to this list support with decision making (discussed in Chapter 7) that is needed to make Independent Living possible for some people with intellectual and psychosocial impairments (Gooding, 2018).

The pillars of Independent Living are summarised in Article 19 of the UN Convention on the Rights of Persons with Disabilities (CRPD) and detailed in General Comment No. 5 of the Committee on the Rights of Persons with Disabilities (2017), while supported decision making is addressed in Article 12 and General Comment No. 1 (Committee on the Rights of Persons with Disabilities, 2014). It is the simultaneous and coordinated presence of all these supports and accommodations, as well as their user-led and user-controlled management and development, that constitute the holistic and integrated approach envisioned by the Independent Living pioneers.

This international consensus notwithstanding, the Independent Living movement has not been homogeneous. Jim Elder-Woodward (2016: 254) points out that the movement has incorporated diverse political philosophies, including liberal, communitarian, and civic-pluralist ones. Accordingly, there are people within the movement who are more supportive of the market (and marketisation), and those who are more supportive of the state (and welfarism). Some emphasise individual agency and responsibility, while others emphasise collective forms of being through peer support and organised advocacy. There are also those who see activation as a necessary component of the Independent Living paradigm, and those who criticise activation as an expression of neoliberal responsibilisation. In addition, some activists see the family as a key source of support, while others stress the family's oppressive dimension. There are even those who defend small institutions, and those who think that Independent Living is not for people with intellectual impairments.

Independent Living is itself part of the wider and internally fragmented disability movement, which includes the big, nationally representative organisations that are often ideologically and politically at odds with the smaller and more radical initiatives such as the ones affiliated with Independent Living. Organisations *for* disabled people are sometimes opposed to organisations *of* disabled people, with the latter seen as more representative based on the 'nothing about us without us' principle. Parental organisations have a particularly uneasy presence in disability politics. Moreover, organisations *of* disabled people may be acting as organisations *for* disabled people by defending the status quo of professional power and, by extension, paternalism, segregation, institutionalisation, and ableist othering.

The Independent Living paradigm reconstructed in this book based on the work of ENIL is steeped in my own ideological preferences, activist attachments, and theoretical commitments. But I have learned most of what I know about Independent Living from activists. This work is an attempt to systematise and deepen this knowledge rooted in practice and protest and therefore unavoidably partial, partisan, and agonistic.

Summary of the key arguments and contributions

The central critical-theoretical argument of the book is that freedom is grounded in specific relations of *inter*dependence. I contend that this is a major lesson to be learned from the Independent Living movement, whose wisdom is deep, strong, and enduring due to being 'organic', by which I mean practical rather than abstract, everyday rather than institutional, and bottom-up rather than top-down. It is a wisdom accumulated by using, on an everyday basis, support from others – including environmental, cultural, and technological accommodations – to get out of bed, go to the toilet, eat a sandwich, put on a jacket, get on a bus, read a sign, express a preference, have a drink, remember a name, buy a ticket, send an email, cast a vote. It is also a wisdom that comes from lacking assistance and adjustments for these everyday activities, and therefore from having to fight for them; a wisdom articulated in self-help and peer-support encounters, during marches, in efforts to convince or challenge powerholders; a radical, organically critical wisdom – one that insists on independence amidst relations of conspicuous dependence.

Let me now unpick this central argument, highlighting the links of its constitutive elements to the Independent Living paradigm. This will also help outline some of the contributions that the book makes to critical theory, disability studies, and disability rights advocacy.

First, I argue that individual, everyday freedom is relational – it is grounded in relations of *inter*dependence. This insight stems from exploring the supports provided by the Centres for Independent Living – most prominently personal assistance, but also help with finding accessible and affordable housing, choosing and using assistive devices, talking to peers, organising workplace adjustments, understanding entitlements, claiming benefits, monitoring policies, organising protests, and so forth. An organically developed, bottom-up framework for understanding the fundamental role of these different forms of support for individual freedom – as well as for grasping their interrelations – is found in the concept of the 'pillars of Independent Living'.

I ground the insight that freedom is relational in the Independent Living movement's more general (and *qualified*) defence of the welfare state, critique of marketisation (and particularly of neoliberal restructuring), and affirmation of familial relationships and supports. This conceptualisation helps me facilitate a mutually productive exchange between the Independent Living paradigm and welfare state theory by exploring the relationships between Independent Living and the three organising principles of social welfare – the state, the market, and the family (Esping-Andersen, 1990; 1999). I explore in parallel the relationships between Independent Living and the main welfare regimes discussed in the comparative analyses of social welfare – liberal, social democratic, conservative, and post/socialist. This type of analysis, first presented in Mladenov *et al.* (2023) and developed further here, constitutes a novelty in both welfare state theory and what can be called 'Independent Living Studies' – a subfield of disability studies that is still in the process of emergence despite the half-century history of the movement.

However, second, I also argue that not every *inter*dependence enables freedom – on the contrary, many relations of *inter*dependence actually hinder freedom. To distinguish between freedom-enabling and freedom-disabling *inter*dependence, I identify two forms of care – paternalist and egalitarian. This distinction is another novelty, which I derive from the critique of care voiced by Independent Living activists and thinkers, the centrality of 'choice and control' in the Independent Living paradigm, its links with consumerism, and its advocacy for deinstitutionalisation. Egalitarian care also resonates with the 'nothing about us without us' principle, as reflected in the structure of the Centres for Independent Living – organisations that, when genuine, are run and controlled by disabled people.

In terms of the state–market–family nexus, I argue that the movement's critique of freedom-hindering *inter*dependence has entailed a critique of professional power and statism, a qualified embrace of the market, and a certain discord with familialism that overlaps with some strands of feminist theorising. Against this background, Independent Living's defence of the welfare state, decommodification, and familial support is presented as dialectically related to Independent Living's advocacy for deétatisation, quasi-marketisation, and defamilialisation. Only by understanding these contradictions can one appreciate the depth of Independent Living's contribution to social welfare and its critical theorising. It also helps explain the vicissitudes of Independent Living's fate in liberal, social democratic, conservative, and post/socialist contexts – a topic that has so far remained unexplored and that this book pioneers. The reconciliation of the Independent Living contradictions has therefore been circumstantial and context dependent, and I show how the movement has diversified to accommodate different welfare regimes.

The analysis of the state and the market is aided by Foucaultian studies of power – specifically, of the biopower of welfarism, and of the psychopower of marketisation. In its turn, the family is discussed through a feminist lens that helps deconstruct familialism. On this basis, I show that the Independent Living paradigm can be a fertile ground for further developments of the critical-theoretical analyses of biopower, psychopower, and parental authority. More specifically, I argue that the Independent Living perspective helps bring agency back in those critiques of biopower and psychopower that overemphasise its decentring or deconstruction. In turn, my analysis of parental authority leads to positing a 'universal caregiver/care-receiver' model of equity. I thus build on Nancy Fraser's (1997) concept of 'universal caregiving' by arguing that in addition to enabling differently gendered humans to become equal in providing care, equity requires enabling differently abled humans to become equal when receiving care.

The book also engages with metatheoretical issues concerning knowledge creation and voice. To this end, I discuss evidence suggesting that the practical wisdom of the Independent Living movement has been routinely marginalised or, worse, appropriated and misrepresented by the powerholders. I use the critical-theoretical toolkit of 'epistemic injustice' to conceptualise these relations of knowledge and power that provide the background conditions for affirming freedom as a specific kind of *inter*dependence. But the book does not only interpret. It also seeks to join forces with Independent Living activists in their definitional struggles, hoping to contribute to the activists' attempts at (re)appropriating key terms such as 'disability', 'independence', 'personal assistance', and 'deinstitutionalisation', while also creating an archive. As already explained, this partisanship is grounded in my way into Independent Living, which reflects my positionality.

Based on all these considerations, the book asserts that the organic insights of the Independent Living movement can revitalise critical theory. Thus, the Independent Living paradigm helps understand better and eventually reconcile the dialectical tensions between the individual and the state–market–family nexus; develop a normatively anchored critique of power; and reshape the relations of knowledge production and exchange to make them epistemically just. When taken seriously, this approach to challenging injustice overcomes the pessimism, normative deficiency, and ableism that characterise much contemporary critical theorising, including poststructuralist critiques of biopower and psychopower. I show how Independent Living's embodied, grounded, and relational understanding of autonomy and freedom charts ways towards reconciling the oppositions between positive and negative liberty, structure and agency, theory and practice, individual and collective, private and public, mind and body. In addition, the paradigm's policy-oriented and normative critique makes it possible to advance critical-theoretical analyses towards transforming real lives (in addition to academic ones).

I also argue that the insights of the Independent Living movement tell us something fundamental about the human condition – something elusive that I have been trying to articulate in my previous work, something related to the aporia of being one. Put succinctly, the being of the one is enabled by the being of the others, although the underpinning relations of *inter*dependence usually remain hidden in the background of familiarity – until they get disrupted by an uninvited guest, an equipmental breakdown, a state of exception, or an injury creating impairment. Critical studies of disability reveal that not only disabled people, but all humans are enabled by others and by the attendant collectively created and maintained accommodations to get out of bed, eat a sandwich, get on a bus, and so forth. Independent Living corroborates this insight, adding that the underlying relations of *inter*dependence are enabling (as opposed to enforcing) only when they enhance one's self-determination.

Overview of the chapters

Following this introduction, Chapter 1 outlines prominent definitional struggles concerning the meanings of disability and independence. Considering definitions in terms of 'struggle' is underpinned by the critical-theoretical insight that definitions are political. As such, definitional struggles around disability and independence are key elements of disabled people's fight for epistemic justice.

Chapter 2 builds on this insight by introducing ENIL's work in epistemic terms. The idea guiding this account is that the organisation fights to change the world by subverting hegemonic understandings of major terms in contemporary social policy such as independence, inclusion, care, and capacity. This epistemic work is political and is part of the definitional struggles introduced in Chapter 1.

Chapters 3, 4, and 5 discuss Independent Living in its relation to three key organising principles of social welfare – the state, the market, and the family. This structure of the presentation is derived from welfare state theory and requires a brief explanation.

Strictly speaking, the state, the market, and the family are institutions rather than 'principles' because they are more 'material' and rigid than principles, but I identify them as principles to avoid confusion with my critique of institutional care and institutionalisation. Gøsta Esping-Andersen (1990: 21), a key figure in contemporary welfare state theory, similarly regards the state, the market, and the family as 'the three main principles that need to be fleshed out prior to any theoretical specification of the welfare state'. They underpin the three key types of welfare regimes identified by Esping-Andersen (1999: 5): liberal regimes are market biased because they seek to derive social welfare from the functioning of the (labour) market; conservative (including Southern European) regimes are family biased because they tend to rely on the family to deliver social welfare; and social-democratic regimes are state biased because they rely on state intervention to create social welfare. Thus, a 'welfare regime can be defined as the combined, interdependent way in which welfare is produced and allocated between state, market, and family' (Esping-Andersen, 1999: 34–35). I discuss Esping-Andersen's typology in Chapter 3.

The relationships of the Independent Living paradigm with the state, the market, and the family are complex but, overall, critical. In Chapters 3, 4, and 5, I show how this criticality feeds into central debates in contemporary critical theory concerning professional power (and biopower), neoliberalism (and psychopower), and familialism (and parental authority). This helps outline the contributions of Independent Living to critical theorising and praxis, as these contributions have developed organically over five decades of campaigning for self-determination.

There is arguably a fourth organising principle of social welfare – community or civil society (see Esping-Andersen, 1999: 35–36, n. 2 and 5) – which is implied throughout the analysis, although not explicitly thematised. It is reflected in the fact that Independent Living is not only an analytic paradigm, but also a social movement. This is embodied in ENIL's work, in the significance of peer support and self-organising for Independent Living, in the roles of charity and the Church, and in the tensions between Independent Living initiatives and traditional disability organising. Self-organising is a collective expression of the struggle for individual independence, understood here as a specific kind of *inter*dependence that enables re/gaining control over one's life: 'Modern expert systems and health care practices failed disabled people and "self-organisation" is a response to that historical failure' (Hughes, 2009: 682). That said, the self-organising of Independent Living activists remains largely dependent on state or private funding, as is the case with many civil society initiatives – in this sense, they may be conceived as 'extensions' of the state and the market even when they criticise these institutions (see Esping-Andersen, 1999: 36, n. 5).

Chapter 6 explores the practical realisation of the Independent Living critique through the medium of collective self-organising by discussing ENIL's advocacy for deinstitutionalisation and personal assistance. This analysis shows how ENIL's epistemic struggle for redefining independence, inclusion, care, and capacity (Chapter 2) is part of the more general Independent Living critique of the state, the market, and the family (Chapters 3, 4, and 5).

Chapter 7 discusses some concepts and trends that have been implied throughout the book but not considered in depth until that point. More specifically, I look at the links between the Independent Living paradigm and recent developments in disability studies and advocacy regarding mental capacity, de/coloniality, and technology. These areas of concern are singled out because they enhance the understanding and practice of Independent Living, but also because they are likely to define the future of both Independent Living advocacy and disability studies. The conclusion finishes with a brief reflection on this future.

1

Disability and independence

Considering meaning as political reflects a key critical-theoretical intuition. It was Michel Foucault (1980) who transformed the insight that knowledge and power are inseparable into a postmodern truism. More recently, analyses of 'epistemic injustice' have shown how people are oppressed and resist their oppression within specific epistemic practices of everyday communication. In her seminal book, tellingly titled *Epistemic Injustice – Power and the Ethics of Knowing*, Miranda Fricker (2007: 3) has reasserted that knowledge and power are intertwined but has criticised the postmodern tendency to reduce knowledge to power because it may lead to a normative cul-de-sac, where power is omnipresent (therefore normal), reason is power (therefore an illusion), and justice is unattainable.

Within this critical tradition but looking specifically at social welfare, Nancy Fraser (1987) has explored the 'politics of need interpretation'. Fraser's (1987) argument is that human needs are never merely given but always interpreted, and that this interpretation is intrinsically political. However, the welfare state transforms the identification, measuring, and satisfying of its citizens' needs from political matters to juridical, administrative, and therapeutic ones. This prevents the citizens from contesting interpretations of their needs imposed by legal, managerial, and medical professionals. Fraser (1987) develops this analysis as part of a wider critique of the 'juridical–administrative–therapeutic state', which positions its members as legal subjects (juridical dimension), as purchasing consumers or 'dependent' clients (administrative dimension), and as deviant individuals in need of normalising interventions (therapeutic dimension). Thus, the juridical–administrative–therapeutic state

> individualizes [its members] as 'cases' and so militates against collective identification. It imposes monological, administrative definitions of situation and need and so preempts dialogically achieved self-definition and self-determination. It positions its subjects as passive client or consumer recipients and not as active co-participants involved in shaping their life-conditions. Lastly, it construes

> experienced discontent with these arrangements as material for adjustment-oriented, usually sexist therapy and not as material for empowering processes of consciousness-raising. (Fraser, 1987: 115)[1]

It is therefore hardly surprising that definitional struggles have always been at the heart of disabled people's fight for dignity, emancipation, and self-determination. They have entailed challenges to pathologising, individualising, and restrictive definitions created and maintained by caring professionals and disabling societies. Along the way, disabled people have shifted the meaning of disability from individual deficiency to restrictions imposed on people with impairments by the way societies are organised. This 'social model of disability' has been widely regarded as the 'big idea' (Hasler, 1993: 280) of the disabled people's movement. I will first discuss the social model's contribution to disabled people's definitional struggles. I will then focus on Independent Living's role in the latter, paying special attention to the ways in which the Independent Living paradigm has challenged liberal understandings of autonomy and freedom. I will finish the chapter by exploring a potential alignment between the social model and Independent Living that could bolster disabled people's attempts at realising epistemic justice.

Definitional struggles and the social model of disability

One of the formulations that founded the social model of disability was provided in the middle of the 1970s by the members of the Union of the Physically Impaired against Segregation (UPIAS), a British organisation of disabled people advocating for a radical change in the dominant understandings and practices concerning disability:

> We define impairment as lacking part of or all of a limb, or having a defective limb, organ or mechanism of the body; and disability as the disadvantage or restriction of activity caused by a contemporary social organisation which takes no or little account of people who have physical impairments and thus excludes them from participation in the mainstream of social activities. (UPIAS, 1976a: 14)

This definition has been among the most discussed, criticised, and revised statements in disability studies. It makes a sharp distinction between 'impairment' and 'disability' that has later been used to articulate the social model of disability in its influential British version (Oliver, 2009). In both formulations, the term 'impairment' refers to bodily differences, but later its scope has been expanded to include mental and behavioural differences (see, for example, Beresford, 2005; Beresford *et al.*, 2010). For its part, the term 'disability' denotes the restrictions imposed by society on people who have 'impairments'. From the perspective of the social model, the problems faced by disabled people are not *caused* by their physical, mental, or behavioural differences but by the way society is organised. This also means that the social model does not deny the value of therapeutic interventions and medical care but presupposes that medical procedures and technologies can only treat impairments, whereas the treatment of disability requires political means and approaches.

Disability studies scholars have criticised the social model on both realist and constructionist grounds (Mladenov, 2015a: Ch. 2). Critical realists such as Tom Shakespeare (2006, 2014) have reproached the social model for neglecting the intrinsically restrictive materiality of impairment, whereas social constructionists such as Bill Hughes and Kevin Paterson (1997; Paterson and Hughes, 1999) have done so for neglecting its sociality. Realists have sought a compromise in relational models of disability such as the one promoted by the World Health Organization, or the one that has informed the UN Convention on the Rights of Persons with Disabilities. For their part, constructionists have insisted that (political) sociality is primary, and (non-political) materiality comes second: 'the materiality of the body ... is constructed through the ritualised repetition of norms' (Altermark, 2018: 45). Along these lines, 'crip theory' (McRuer, 2006) has challenged the norm (of able-bodiedness) to liberate bodily/mental difference. A strongly argued recent constructionist contribution that aligns with 'crip theory' has come from the work of Niklas Altermark (2018: 50, original emphasis):

> we *ought* to consider what a world would look like when help systems, answering to the fluctuating abilities of human beings, were not premised on diagnoses and classifications of disabilities, that is, a world in which the normative devaluation of disability was crossed over and where the norm of the able body and brain was replaced with something else.

Notwithstanding criticisms, the social model has exercised an immense impact on contemporary disability policy formulations, whose most important instance is currently the UN Convention on the Rights of Persons with Disabilities (CRPD). The CRPD is an international, legally binding human rights instrument that entered into force in 2008, reflecting nearly four decades of struggle of disabled people and their organisations for equality, self-determination, and social inclusion (Moriarity and Dew, 2011: 686). The states that have ratified the document have committed to amending their legislation in accordance with the provisions of the CRPD and to implementing relevant policies. The CRPD has already been ratified by most countries in the world. It has been regarded by the UN as epitomising a paradigmatic shift in disability policy,

> from viewing persons with disabilities as 'objects' of charity, medical treatment and social protection towards viewing persons with disabilities as 'subjects' with rights, who are capable of claiming those rights and making decisions for their lives based on their free and informed consent as well as being active members of society. (United Nations, n.d.)

The CRPD states in its Preamble that 'disability results from the interaction between persons with impairments and attitudinal and environmental barriers that hinders their full and effective participation in society on an equal basis with others'. In this formulation, the CRPD accepts the distinction between 'impairment' and 'disability' asserted by the social model, but it also modifies this distinction along critical realist lines by stating that the restrictions faced by disabled people result from the interaction between the impairments and the barriers in the environment, rather than being directly caused by the barriers, as is the case in UPIAS's earlier and more radical formulation.

That said, most of the CRPD's provisions clearly focus on the socially constructed barriers rather than on individual impairments. But although the social understanding of disability has been incorporated in international human rights legislation, definitional struggles around the term have continued. As Altermark (2018: 78) has argued in his analysis of the 'post-institutional' treatment of people with intellectual impairments, the very idea of progress, of a transition from the past of objectification to the present and future of emancipation, has masked ongoing disempowerment. Moreover, the meaning of legislative acts is not given but constantly recreated through interpretations saturated with epistemic injustices.

A recent example is the Bulgarian Persons with Disabilities Act (PDA, in force since 1 January 2019), which includes many elements of the CRPD. However, it does this tokenistically and essentially retains the status quo of the medical assessment of disability and, accordingly, the domination of the medical model and the paternalist approach in Bulgarian disability policy.[2] This becomes clear when reading closely the definition of disability included in the act. At first sight, the legislation adopts unreservedly the formulation of Article 1 of the CRPD by defining 'people with disabilities' as 'persons with physical, mental, intellectual and sensory impairments which in interaction with their environment could hinder their full and effective participation in public life' (PDA, Additional Provisions, §1). However, this ostensibly progressive move gets immediately negated in the next provision, which makes the meaning of the term 'people with *permanent* disabilities' dependent on the decision of the medical assessment:

> 2. 'People with permanent disabilities' [*Хора с трайни увреждания*] are persons with permanent physical, mental, intellectual and sensory impairments

> [*недостатъчност*] which in interaction with their environment could hinder their full and effective participation in public life, and for whom the medical expert assessment has established a type and degree of disability or degree of permanently reduced ability to work of 50 and over 50 percent. (PDA, Additional Provisions, §1)

It must be emphasised that it is the term 'people with *permanent* disabilities' rather than 'people with disabilities' that determines the access to basic rights and benefits for disabled Bulgarians. Therefore, the definition of the term 'people with disabilities' provided in the PDA functions tokenistically, without making any difference to the actual practices of defining needs and providing support.

The very translation of legislative provisions between languages is an inherently political interpretive activity (Mladenov, 2013). Translation is interpretation (Müller, 2007), therefore potentially a site of struggle for epistemic justice. As an example, the Bulgarian translation of the CRPD, available on the website of the Bulgarian Social Assistance Agency (asp.government.bg), disregards the distinction between 'impairment' and 'disability' by substituting both terms with the Bulgarian word *увреждане* (corresponding to the English 'disability'). This disregard reflects the epistemic inertia that characterises the field of disability policy more generally. In the context of the definitional struggle outlined above, it is also an instance of epistemic injustice.

Anticipating the discussion on coloniality in Chapter 7, it is important to underline that there is nothing specifically 'British', 'Western', or 'liberal' about the social model of disability as conceptualised by Oliver (2009). The founding statements underpinning Oliver's work were formulated for UPIAS (1976a) by Vic Finkelstein (2005) based on his experience of fighting against apartheid in South Africa, as well as his Marxist convictions (I am grateful to Mark Priestley for drawing my attention to this genealogy of the social model during a seminar in 2021). It seems safe to assume that whatever their culture, people who understand the social/structural conditioning of agency and who consider oppression before considering individual failings would feel the perspective of the social model as 'native'. More collectivist cultures and mindsets would actually be more inclined to see disablement from a social perspective. A similar point has been made by Martin Musengi (2023) in an article on decolonising disability policies through Indigenous theorisation in Zimbabwe. Musengi has argued that it has been the medical model of disability that has resulted from colonial influence, while the social model has been very much in line with Indigenous thinking, as reflected in *Ubuntu* philosophy.

However, it may seem that this argument could hardly be applied to Independent Living whose origins are more unambiguously American,

Western, or liberal. And yet, similar to the social model, Independent Living has a strong collectivist dimension and is firmly grounded in relations of *inter*dependence, as will be explained in the next section.

Definitional struggles and independence

Historically, the meaning of individual 'independence' has been as contested as the meaning of 'disability' since the very inception of the Independent Living movement. When social workers and other caring professionals talk about 'independence' and 'independent living', they usually mean living on one's own and/or having skills for coping without support with everyday tasks such as cooking, shopping, or cleaning the house. For example, the support workers interviewed by Altermark (2018) routinely render independence in terms of self-sufficiency:

> The idea is to make them [the group home residents] more independent. So I work to make myself redundant. You want as little support for them as possible. But, they live here for a reason, so it's not possible to make them accomplish what people such as you and I can do. But you can make them less dependent on support. (interviewee quoted in Altermark, 2018: 93)

This is also the way in which individual independence is understood in the wider society. Indeed, at first sight, the idea of the 'independent living' of disabled people may seem strange and even counterintuitive since impairments often lead to enhanced dependence on additional support in the form of family care, personal assistance, assistive devices, financial assistance, medical care, and so forth. Moreover, social scientists, and particularly feminist scholars, have asserted for decades that everyone, and not only disabled people, is *inter*dependent, because everyone needs care, support, technologies, and medical interventions (Watson *et al.*, 2004). Disability studies scholars have followed suit. Lennard Davis (2002: 31), for example, has argued that 'impairment is the rule, and normalcy is the fantasy. Dependence is the reality, and independence grandiose thinking'. With this formulation, Davis has sought to emphasise the universal nature of human *inter*dependence – a central claim in contemporary critical disability studies. In the words of Altermark (2018: 120), 'we all fall short of ideals of full ability and complete independence'. Ben-Moshe (2020: 79) has even gone as far as suggesting that 'concepts such as self-determination, normalization, autonomy, and independent living are colonial, white, masculine, Western constructs. Disability related policy relies on notions of autonomy and individualism, a form of self-reliance that is foreign to many indigenous and non-Western communities.' Independent Living and self-determination are here clearly equated with self-sufficiency.

However, the Independent Living movement understands the idea of 'independence' differently than Davis, Altermark, and Ben-Moshe. When Davis (2002: 31) argues that 'independence [is] grandiose thinking', or Altermark (2018: 16) that the feminist ethics of care 'challenges a moral ontology of self-sufficient individuals striving to be independent', or Ben-Moshe (2020: 79) that independent living is a 'colonial, white, masculine, Western' construct, they all use the term 'independence' in the conventional way, to mean ability to cope alone, without external support, to be self-sufficient. But from the perspective of the Independent Living movement, to be 'independent' does not mean to cope without support or to be self-sufficient – it means to have access to support that is organised in such a way so that the person who uses it has maximum choice and control in their everyday life.

Thus, the Independent Living advocate Jenny Morris (2006: 242) has identified three key elements in the activists' understanding of Independent Living: 'First, an assertion that disabled people should have the same opportunities for choice and control in their lives as non-disabled people; second, a challenge to the usual interpretations of the words "independent" and "independence"; and, finally, the aspiration that any assistance required should be under the control of disabled individuals themselves'. As an illustrative example, on the homepage of the website of the Swedish Independent Living Institute (ILI) – a leading research centre on Independent Living in Europe, led and controlled by disabled people – we read:

> Independent Living is a philosophy and a movement of people with disabilities who work for self-determination, equal opportunities and self-respect. Independent Living does not mean that we want to do everything by ourselves and do not need anybody or that we want to live in isolation. Independent Living means that we demand the same choices and control in our every-day lives that our non-disabled brothers and sisters, neighbors and friends take for granted. We want to grow up in our families, go to the neighborhood school, use the same bus as our neighbors, work in jobs that are in line with our education and interests, and start families of our own. (ILI, n.d.)

Other Independent Living pioneers have been similarly concerned about challenging the conventional meaning of independence:

> We believe fundamentally that all individuals have the right to live independently in the community regardless of their disability. But it is important to note the sense in which we use the word 'independence', because it is crucial to everything we are saying. We do not use the term 'independent' to mean someone who can do everything for themself, but to indicate someone who has taken control of their life and is choosing how that life is led. ... The most important factor is not the amount of physical tasks a person can perform, but the amount of control they have over their everyday routine. (Brisenden, 1986: 178)

Such definitional efforts at negating the equivalence between independence and self-sufficiency have been a central feature of seminal texts produced by Independent Living activists and scholars. An alternative approach, particularly prominent in Britain, has been to abandon the term 'independent', as Colin Barnes (2004: 9, original emphasis) has explained:

> In view of the dangers of mis-interpretation some disability activists, particularly in the UK where social model thinking is especially influential, have adopted the terms 'integrated' or 'inclusive' living rather than the original 'independent' living to characterise the philosophy on which their activities are based. Such terms have a far greater appeal to the left of centre elements within Britain's disabled peoples movement who recognise that humans are by definition 'social' beings, and that *all* humans, regardless of the degree and nature of impairment, are interdependent.

In my own work, instead of abandoning the term, I have sided with those who struggle to reclaim Independent Living from its misinterpretation as self-sufficiency. I capitalise the term to indicate that my use is in accordance with (my understanding of) the Independent Living movement and analytic paradigm, and that I am not following the everyday and caring professionals' discourse of 'independence' and 'independent living'.

I understand Independent Living to be about self-determination – 'being self-governing; free from outside control; not subject to another's authority' (Elder-Woodward, 2016: 253). Marie Sépulchre (2022) has theorised the form of freedom that underpins this understanding of independence as republican freedom or 'freedom as non-domination' – a third kind of freedom that differs from both negative (liberal) and positive (socialist) freedom. Freedom as non-interference (negative freedom) tends to prioritise self-sufficiency, while freedom as capacity to act (positive freedom) tends to be productivist (that is, to require contribution or 'active citizenship') and, moreover, fails to subject interferences to checks and balances. Freedom as non-domination is an alternative – interferences are needed, but they need to be subjected to individual and collective (democratic) checks and balances, while contribution is not a condition of full citizenship:

> The ideal of freedom as non-domination is valuable to find institutional arrangements that will be acceptable to citizens with contrasting political views. Indeed, founding a discussion on freedom as non-domination bypasses debates regarding equality of opportunity or outcome by stressing people's common desire to be free to live a good life, without being subjected to or fearing the arbitrary interference of other parties. (Sépulchre, 2022: 24)

The individual or psychopolitical dimension of this 'freedom as non-domination' is reflected in skills of expressing preferences, making choices, and managing support (Chapter 4). Only such skills can be regarded as properly Independent Living skills, but, importantly, they may also be – and most often are – exercised with support rather than in isolation (as in supported decision making and peer support). To put it slightly differently, from the perspective of the Independent Living paradigm, disabled people are independent when their *inter*dependence is organised or socially constructed in such a way that their opportunities to have choice and control in their everyday lives are maximised. If understood in this way, the idea of Independent Living does not negate but accepts, presupposes, and builds upon the idea of *inter*dependence, as also affirmed by ENIL:

> There is a continuous debate on independence vs. interdependence; *ENIL considers that all human beings are interdependent and that the concept of independent living does not contravene this*. Independent living does not mean being independent from other persons, but having the freedom of choice and control over one's own life and lifestyle. (ENIL, n.d.-d, emphasis added)

For example, if I can choose when to have breakfast and what to have for breakfast, I am independent in the sense intended by the Independent Living movement even if I need someone or something – a personal assistant or an assistive device – to help me with feeding.[3] However, if my support is organised in such a way that someone else – say, a home carer or a service provider – is enabled to impose on me their decisions about my breakfast, then my independence is hindered by a social barrier. It is clear that to be able to choose my breakfast, I need to have something to eat in the first place, but often the very access to basic goods such as food, shelter, and clothing depends on my opportunities for Independent Living. In turn, it is precisely the barriers to Independent Living that increase poverty and marginalisation, depriving disabled people of basic goods.[4]

Both Morris's (2006) and ILI's (n.d.) definitions of Independent Living call for measures that enable disabled people to be like nondisabled people. However, there is a problem with this vision. It overlaps with the approach of 'normalisation' stemming from the work of Bengt Nirje in Sweden and Wolf Wolfensberger in the United States, which has been important in early deinstitutionalisation reforms – as Ben-Moshe (2020: 73) points out, although the principle of normalisation 'is often perceived as the desire to normalize people, the goal was to aid those with disabilities, especially intellectual disabilities, enhance their quality of life so that it resembles the lives of those without disabilities'. And yet, the ideas of normalisation (later reformulated by Wolfensberger in terms of 'social role valorisation') eventually led to a shift from big to small, 'home-like' institutions – that is, to the *re*institutionalising form of deinstitutionalisation that I criticise in Chapter 6. Similar points are made by Altermark (2018) in his analysis of the 'post-institutional era' in Sweden. Notably, unlike Independent

Living, the reform of normalisation or social role valorisation was driven by caring professionals.

Another problem with attempts at normalisation is that they disregard the multiple forms of oppression that non-disabled people face in their everyday lives. In other words, trying to make disabled people like non-disabled people fails to change the world to make it accommodating for everyone. Since the status quo of exclusion in the Global North is white, middle-class, and patriarchal, a step further would be to argue that normalisation 'is based on white, settler, middle-class, nondisabled, heteronormative assumptions about what constitutes being on par with one's nondisabled peers' (Ben-Moshe, 2020: 179–180). Essentially, normalisation is about incorporation or assimilation, not inclusion. Many non-disabled people do not take choice and control for granted. They are subjected to different and mutually constitutive mechanisms of oppression, as illuminated by intersectional analyses. These mechanisms range from the 'hard' powers of exploitation, direct discrimination, and thanatopower, to the 'soft' powers of indirect discrimination, biopower, and psychopower. Real self-determination requires self-determination for all, and the latter requires addressing these diverse forms of power. Otherwise, disabled people would merely be incorporated into oppressive regimes instead of being included in a free society.

Independent Living and liberal autonomy

Considered as self-determination, Independent Living seems to be yet another term for 'maturity' in the Kantian sense. In his article 'An answer to the question: What is Enlightenment?', Kant (1991a: 54) defines Enlightenment as the moment in which humans become 'mature' or autonomous in their use of reason. The Kantian distinction between the private and the public spheres is underpinned by the principle that 'the individuals comprising the public are endowed with a rational will which is *independent of all empirically existing institutions and experience*' (Schecter, 2010: 190, emphasis added). It follows that 'maturity' would be difficult if not impossible for women because of their strong links with the private sphere that is inherently restricted by obligation, convention, and prejudice (Kant, 1991a: 54). Elsewhere, Kant (1991b: 77, original emphasis) also excludes propertyless people from full citizenship: 'the domestic servant, the shop assistant, the labourer, or even the barber, are merely labourers (*operarii*), not *artists* (*artifices*, in the wider sense) or members of the state, and are thus unqualified to be citizens'. This reasoning suggests that any form of dependency, including any reliance on formal and/or informal support systems, impairs the 'maturity' needed for self-governing:

> Kant openly excludes women, children and salaried workers from the public sphere because of their supposed lack of autonomy. In his estimation they are emotionally and economically dependent, which means that if allowed to participate in public affairs, they are likely to embrace a politics of irrational need rather than a juridical politics of freedom and rational cognition. If this happens, law is deprived of its epistemological dimension at the same time that the transcendence of natural and mechanical necessity is forfeited. (Schecter, 2010: 191)

Since this logic would also exclude disabled people from the public sphere because of their enhanced dependence on formal and informal supports, how could Independent Living promote self-determination without being exclusive? The hardest hit would be people with intellectual impairments, whose difference 'does not entail falling short of just any ideal but of the absolutely central ideal of humanity as characterised by reason and rationality' (Altermark, 2018: 8; see also Goodley *et al.*, 2019: 986). Of note here is that 'intellectual impairment' is itself a socially constructed and highly prescriptive or normative category. In his critique of Enlightenment humanism, Altermark (2018: 57) looks at ideas promoted by Locke, Hume, Stuart Mill, Taylor, Kant, and Rawls, concluding that 'the history of citizenship has been premised on the exclusion of people seen as lacking reason and rationality'. Similarly, Clifford Simplican (2015) has argued that there is an exclusionary 'capacity contract' that underlies Enlightenment inclusion, citizenship, and political membership.

In my previous work (Mladenov, 2012), I have defended Independent Living from this charge of reproducing exclusions generated by liberal autonomy. By analysing a prominent model of personal assistance developed by Independent Living advocates (Ratzka, 2004), I have shown that the 'maturity' embraced by Independent Living is grounded in specific relations of *inter*dependence. This point allows absolving Independent Living from the accusation of reinforcing the 'capacity contract', in which individuals are forced into a liberal-individualist model of citizenship. Independent Living presupposes a distributed or relational form of agency – it is about relational self-determination, also known in the feminist literature as 'relational autonomy' (Mackenzie and Stoljar, 2000). As we shall see in Chapter 4, this reframing of independence as a specific type of *inter*dependence is key for understanding the links between Independent Living and the market (and, by extension, psychopower), as well as the attendant critique of self-sufficiency that is integral to the Independent Living paradigm. It is also constitutive of the Independent Living's critique of austerity policies discussed in Chapter 3.

On the practical level, the relational understanding of agency implied by the Independent Living paradigm means that Independent Living

> is possible through the combination of various environmental and individual factors that allow disabled people to have control over their own lives. This includes the opportunity to make real choices and decisions regarding where to live, with whom to live and how to live. Services must be available, accessible to all and provided on the basis of equal opportunity, free and informed consent and allowing disabled people flexibility in our daily life. Independent living requires that the built environment, transport and information are accessible, that there is availability of technical aids, access to personal assistance and/or community-based services. It is necessary to point out that independent living is for all disabled persons, regardless of the gender, age and the level of their support needs. (ENIL, n.d.-c)

This definition of Independent Living has been a key resource in ENIL's fight for epistemic justice and will be discussed in detail in Chapter 2. Such definitional struggles have been far from trivial or scholastic – they have sought to create opportunities for full citizenship and freedom against the background of deeply ingrained epistemic intuitions inherited from the European Enlightenment. Other points of epistemic struggle have included the meaning of key Independent Living reforms such as deinstitutionalisation, or key supports such as personal assistance (both discussed in detail in Chapter 6). The global advance of the Independent Living movement has resulted in the mainstreaming of such reforms and supports through their incorporation in national legislation, strategies, guidelines, and professional practices. The CRPD has greatly contributed to this process – Independent Living has been codified as a human right in Article 19 of the CRPD, whose provisions have been explained in detail in General Comment No. 5, drafted by the Committee on the Rights of Persons with Disabilities (2017).

However, the mainstreaming of Independent Living has also meant intensification of epistemic injustices because of increasing misinterpretation and misuse of key Independent Living policies and supports (Angelova-Mladenova, 2017: 11). Currently, such epistemic appropriations of Independent Living ideas and terms constitute a major strategy for maintaining the status quo of keeping disabled people confined to residential institutions or at home – controlled and patronised by their carers, pathologised, undermined, neglected, or abused as in the early days of the movement. Moreover, as with the meaning of disability, the struggle for the meaning of individual independence and 'independent living' has been deployed on the terrain of translation of the CRPD between languages – for example, by translating 'independent' with terms connoting 'self-sufficient' (Mladenov, 2013). For this reason, activists have proposed creating mechanisms to oversee the translation between languages:

> The European Commission should monitor translations or appoint a European body to do so to avoid terms like 'personal help' or 'personal support'

> appearing in place of the term personal assistance. Moreover, they should ensure that government bodies responsible for misleading translations are educated on issues of independent living by organisations *of* disabled people. (Jolly, 2009: 10–11, original emphasis)

Concluding remarks

The Independent Living paradigm emerged and developed in parallel with the social model of disability. As argued in Chapter 1, the 1970s and 1980s were a time of intense exchanges between disabled activists from both sides of the Atlantic, which resulted in interpenetration of ideas. This becomes clear when looking at activist documents of the time – consider, for example, the *Policy Statement* of UPIAS:

> The Union aims to have all segregated facilities for physically impaired people replaced by arrangements for us to participate fully in society. These arrangements must include the necessary financial, medical, technical, educational and other help required from the State *to enable us to gain the maximum possible independence* in daily living activities, to achieve mobility, to undertake productive work, and *to live where and how we choose with full control over our lives*. (UPIAS, 1976b: n.p., emphases added)

Conceptually, the ideas underpinning the social model of disability and those that are part of the Independent Living paradigm are complementary. This complementarity reflects the dialectic between structure and agency in disability advocacy and disability studies. The emphasis on structure tackles external barriers. Recall that the social model directs attention towards the socially constructed barriers faced by disabled people, and away from their individual 'impairments'. In the same way, the advocates of Independent Living explain the restrictions on self-determination experienced by disabled people with the socially created and maintained barriers rather than with people's 'impairments'. Therefore, 'the philosophy of the social model of disability underpins the aims of the independent living movement' (Jolly, 2009: 5).

There is influence in the opposite direction as well, when the focus on agency highlights the importance of self-determination. The latter enriches the social model by emphasising that it is not enough to remove the barriers to the participation of disabled people in social life. What is also needed is to organise this participation in such a way that disabled people have opportunities to exercise choice and control. In other words, social justice requires combining structural-collectivist with relational-autonomist strategies in disability policy. The impact of Independent Living on social model theorising has been highlighted by Colin Barnes (2007: 349, original emphasis), who has argued that 'disabled people's self-organization and the thinking behind the concept of independent living provided Mike Oliver (1981) with the inspiration for the development of the *social model of disability*'.

Independent Living has also influenced the approach to disability embraced by the CRPD. Thus, CRPD's Preamble recognises 'the importance for persons with disabilities of their individual autonomy and independence, including the freedom to make their own choices'. Moreover, in its Article 19 titled 'Living independently and being included in the community', the CRPD affirms Independent Living as a universal human right and obliges its States Parties to take positive measures to ensure that it is exercised:

> States Parties to the present Convention recognize the equal right of all persons with disabilities to live in the community, with choices equal to others, and shall take effective and appropriate measures to facilitate full enjoyment by persons with disabilities of this right and their full inclusion and participation in the community.

The meaning of Article 19 is further clarified in General Comment No. 5 of the Committee on the Rights of Persons with Disabilities (2017: para. 4) that states: 'Independent living and inclusive life in the community are ideas that historically stemmed from persons with disabilities asserting control over the way they want to live by creating empowering forms of support such as personal assistance and requesting that community facilities be in line with universal design principles.'

To summarise, both the Independent Living paradigm and the social model of disability have emerged and have been developed as a result of disabled people's struggle against socially created disablement, including juridically, administratively, and therapeutically imposed interpretations of their needs. The Independent Living paradigm asserts that disabled people should have choice and control in their lives – in other words, Independent Living is about self-determination. The social model conceptualises disability as restrictions of activity imposed by society upon people with impairments. The two frameworks align productively when researchers and activists criticise restrictions imposed by society on disabled people's self-determination. The synergies thus created make both ideas stronger.

There is no need to abandon the discourse of Independent Living for its resonance with liberal individualism and Enlightenment rationalism. What is needed is to continue reclaiming the terms 'independence' and 'independent living' as part of the ongoing fight of Independent Living activists and their allies for epistemic justice. This, however, has become an increasingly difficult task. Article 19 of the CRPD has been widely misinterpreted and misused in the states that have ratified the CRPD. A survey on Independent Living, conducted by ENIL in 2020, received 143 responses from 43 European countries – the respondents from 31 of them assessed the implementation of Article 19 as 'inadequate', while the rest assessed it as 'requiring improvement' (ENIL, 2022a: 9). The mainstreaming of disability rights has intensified rather than alleviated definitional struggles around Independent Living. The interpretations of disabled people's needs have never been more settled on paper yet more contested in practice.

Notes

1 Fraser has criticised the welfare state from a democratic-socialist perspective. For a similar critique but from a right-libertarian perspective, see Szasz (2001). The analyses in this book are aligned with Fraser's approach.

2 Bulgaria ratified the CRPD in 2012 but the translation of its principles into effective and sustainable practices still fails in making a real difference to the lives of disabled people in the country. In Bulgaria, disability continues to be heavily medicalised – the medical expert assessment that embodies the approach of paternalist care in its pure form still dominates the identification of the needs of disabled Bulgarians. Bulgarian deinstitutionalisation has been reduced to moving disabled children and adults from large to small institutions – a process that leaves the practices and attitudes of paternalist care unscathed. The great majority of disabled Bulgarians who use personal assistance are forced to rely on their relatives for providing this type of support, which reinforces the attitudes, roles, habits, and rituals of paternalism in both parties. Bulgarian educators still perceive disabled children overwhelmingly through the lens of their individual 'defects' that have to be 'corrected' by specially trained experts, following the individual-paternalist approach to disability. These issues have also been highlighted in the alternative report submitted to the Committee on the Rights of Persons with Disabilities by a group of Bulgarian human rights organisations in 2018 (Alliance for Protection against Gender Based Violence *et al.*, 2018). I will revisit some of these forms of disablement in the following chapters.

3 These choices may seem trivial, but for many disabled people they are not: 'Although infringements on decision making can occur in almost any conceivable situation in the supported-living setting, there are some kinds of situations that recur in the material and that I want to mention here. The first one concerns what people with intellectual disabilities are allowed to eat. Interestingly, when asked open-ended questions about whether the interviewees know of situations in which restrictions are employed or can be justified, they often spontaneously give eating habits as an example. The efforts that go into achieving good eating habits are also stressed by the members of Grunden [the group home discussed by Altermark], which asked why healthy food should be such an overt concern for people with intellectual disabilities whilst the staffers are allowed to eat whatever they want' (Altermark, 2018: 102).

4 A similar argument has been put forward by UPIAS (1976a: 14): 'the impoverishment of physically impaired people arises out of the fact that, as a group, we are excluded from the mainstream of social activities'. When it is linked to advocacy for access to employment, such reasoning has productivist overtones – the document continues: 'In the final analysis the particular form of poverty principally associated with physical impairment is caused by our exclusion from the ability to earn an income on a par with our able-bodied peers, due to the way employment is organised' (UPIAS, 1976a: 14). In contrast, my reading of Independent Living is non-productivist – it suggests that disabled people's poverty is generated by inadequate support that restricts self-determination. The latter may or may not involve self-realisation on the labour market – as an alternative, it may involve self-realisation in the community and/or family, through assistance with parenting (see Morris, 2004: 433–434). In support of this reading, access to employment has been regarded as just one of the 'pillars' of Independent Living (Disability Rights UK, n.d.).

2

The European Network on Independent Living

This chapter substantiates the ideas discussed in Chapter 1 by introducing the European Network on Independent Living (ENIL) and its campaigning work. I argue that ENIL has advanced epistemic justice in the disability area by asserting the meanings elaborated within the Independent Living paradigm and the social model of disability in a context of continuing hermeneutical marginalisation perpetuated by disabling societies, service providers, and caring professionals. I discuss how ENIL's campaigning has challenged the conventional understanding of independence as self-sufficiency and how, in its stead, the organisation has promoted an alternative understanding, according to which independence means that one has choice and control in one's everyday life, including choice and control over one's support.

As argued in Chapter 1, this rendering of individual independence has challenged pivotal liberal-individualist assumptions inherited from the European Enlightenment and has been in line with relational or 'distributed' understandings of autonomy and agency, as well as with the feminist affirmation of *inter*dependence. The alternative understanding of independence promoted by ENIL has guided its campaigning for deinstitutionalisation reform and personal assistance schemes in Europe that will be discussed in detail in Chapter 6. Both campaigns can be described in terms of struggles for epistemic justice because both have been about asserting the meanings of the Independent Living paradigm in the face of hermeneutical marginalisation.

This chapter and Chapter 6 do not only analyse but also narrate and intervene. Thus, they self-consciously contribute to the ongoing work of creating an archive of disabled people's intellectual production and activism for social change. In addition, I have archived most of the sources, including all of ENIL's documents referred to in the book, by using the Wayback Machine (archive.org). As pointed out by Griffiths (2019), archiving makes the disabled people's movement stronger, more sustainable, and effective. The opportunity to create and consider an archive also enhances collective identification, self-awareness, and reflexivity: 'for the Movement, it is essential to utilise knowledge of its history and purpose in order to rethink current practice and to create or justify aspirations and a vision for disabled people's emancipation' (Griffiths, 2019: 65).

However, creating an archive from a position within British academia is not innocent. Academic production invites detachment, elitism, and a self-serving attitude, especially in the context of contemporary neoliberal academia with its quantification and performance management pressures (Cruickshank, 2016). But charges of 'intellectual masturbation' (Oliver, 1992b) targeted at theoretically heavy disability studies are equally suspect. With its witting or unwitting endorsement of dogmatism, anti-intellectual sentiment may be as pernicious as self-serving intellectualism. My response is to take the knowledge production of disability activists – as reflected in the work of ENIL – *seriously* and without compromising critical theorising. Another difficult question relates to the tendency of Western academics to produce a stereotypical, Eurocentric image of the disabled activist as a white, middle-class person with a physical impairment (see Griffiths, 2019: 67). I hope that by emphasising ENIL's intersectional turn, I'll be able to reinforce the efforts challenging this stereotype.

Introducing ENIL

As mentioned in the Introduction, ENIL is a membership organisation led and controlled by disabled people since its establishment in 1989 as 'a forum for all disabled people, Independent Living organizations and their non-disabled allies on the issues of Independent Living' (ENIL, n.d.-a). ENIL's vision is 'of Europe where all disabled people are able to exercise choice and control over their lives, on an equal level with others; where they are valued members of the community and can enjoy all of their human rights, as set out in the UN Convention on the Rights of Persons with Disabilities'; and its mission is 'to advocate and lobby for Independent Living values, principles and practices, namely for a barrier-free environment, provision of personal assistance support and adequate technical aids, together making full citizenship of disabled people possible' (ENIL, n.d.-a). Presently, the organisation is financially supported by the European Union and by ENIL's Nordic allies in Norway (ULOBA) and Sweden (GIL and STIL).

As of November 2023, ENIL has 83 full and 30 associated organisational members from over 40 countries (most of them in Europe), as well as 668 full and 216 associated individual members. Membership is free, which makes it accessible to grassroots disability activists and initiatives. The latter are often small and financially fragile, especially when campaigning for Independent Living, which still constitutes a radical and therefore marginalised and underfunded approach in disability policy, notwithstanding its prominent presence in the CRPD. ENIL upholds several criteria for membership, which are pivotal for ensuring self-determination at the collective level because full members elect ENIL's Board of Directors, the organisation's governing body. The membership criteria reflect geographical coverage, the primacy of the social model of disability, the Independent Living paradigm, and the 'nothing about us without us' principle.

More specifically, organisations can be full members of ENIL only if they are based in the Council of Europe area; support ENIL's vision and mission; adhere in their work to the social model of disability, the Independent Living philosophy, and the human rights approach; are controlled by disabled people (which means that at least 51 per cent of their board members are disabled people); and oppose institutional care (ENIL, n.d.-e). Full individual members should identify as disabled people (according to the tentative definition of disability included in the CRPD), live in the Council of Europe area, and adhere to the same principles as full organisational members (ENIL, n.d.-e). Associate organisational and individual members need to respect ENIL's principles but do not have to be controlled by disabled people or to identify as disabled people. However, associate members do not have the right to vote in the General Assembly.

ENIL is governed by a democratically elected Board of Directors (ENIL, n.d.-f). Nominations for Board membership are put forward by a Nominating Committee and the candidates are elected by a General Assembly, which also elects the members of the Nominating Committee. As already mentioned, only the full organisational and individual members of ENIL can vote in the General Assembly, in concert with the 'nothing about us without us' principle. The Board of Directors is comprised of nine disabled people. Its work is supported conceptually and ideologically by an Advisory Board whose members include Independent Living pioneers such as John Evans and Adolf Ratzka (ENIL, n.d.-f). In 2014, ENIL also established a Youth Network led by young disabled people, with its own organisational structure similar to the one underpinning ENIL's governance.

Operationally, ENIL is small but efficient, prolific, and impactful. This is achieved by harnessing the intrinsic motivation of staff and board members, volunteers, and supporters, as well as by utilising remote collaboration, peer support, and networking. The core team consists of between five and ten staff members (depending on funding), most of them located in ENIL's Brussels Office Secretariat, but some working remotely from other countries. The team is supported by volunteers (including myself) who are also working either on site or remotely (ENIL, n.d.-f). Recent projects have covered a wide range of issues including accessible transport, personal assistance (in partnership with a disabled people's organisation in Turkey), campaigning for deinstitutionalisation, sexual and reproductive rights (with a focus on disabled women and girls), and inclusive entrepreneurship (ENIL, n.d.-h). Some of this work reflects ENIL's intersectional turn, which will be discussed in detail in the last section of this chapter.

ENIL has also been active in the field of research and scholarship. The organisation has systematically collected data and produced reports, position papers, and evaluations of deinstitutionalisation and personal assistance in Europe (see Chapter 6). ENIL has hosted several research fellows (including myself). It has maintained an Independent Living Research Network that I have coordinated since 2017, which, as of November 2023, includes 38 researchers from 17 countries (most of them in Europe). In 2022–2023 the members of ENIL's Independent Living Research Network contributed research and 'current issues' papers to a special issue on Independent Living published in March 2023 in the *International Journal of Disability and Social Justice*. ENIL has also worked with the Centre for Disability Studies at the University of Leeds in the UK on developing and implementing postgraduate teaching in disability studies (ENIL, n.d.-h).

The organisation supports its organisational and individual members with information and advice. Through its website and monthly newsletter, ENIL enables the members to raise awareness about disability injustices in their countries and get in touch with fellow activists from other countries. There is also a monthly Members' Mailing distributed to members via email, which informs them about ENIL's current activities. Recently, these information bulletins have included a call for testimonies (including along intersectional lines) intended to amplify the voices of members and make ENIL more representative:

> We'd like to hear more about our members, have some discussion and interviews on some issues through our platforms. Whether it is on personal assistance, the situation of disabled people in Ukraine, intersectionality or a short story about disability you think is worth sharing – please let us know! Since we are from different countries, with different impairments and backgrounds, we think it is important to represent our diversity. Let's be proud, strong and visible! (ENIL, 2023b)

ENIL engages with other disability organisations from Europe and beyond. An example of a recent international collaboration is the COVID-19 Disability Rights Monitor (COVID-19 DRM), a global human rights monitoring initiative supported by ENIL and six other international disability rights organisations (Brennan *et al.*, 2020).[1] The COVID-19 DRM assessed the impact of national governments' responses to the pandemic on disabled people throughout the world. The initiative included collecting and analysing data, maintaining a dedicated website (www.covid-drm.org), publishing a report in October 2020 (Brennan *et al.*, 2020), and organising webinars and other events to disseminate the findings. Engagement with the COVID-19 DRM evidences ENIL's global reach, notwithstanding the organisation's European membership. This transnational dimension of the Independent Living advocacy will be discussed further in Chapter 7, in the context of de/colonial analysis.

ENIL's campaigning includes lobbying the governing structures of the European Union on Independent Living, the outcomes of which are periodically reported in ENIL's Members' Mailings. ENIL also engages in discussions and negotiations with service providers and their representative organisations such as the European Association of Service Providers for Persons with Disabilities (EASPD). Engagement with mainstream policy makers and service providers is necessary but risky because it may inadvertently legitimise practices that are contrary to the organisation's mission. Tokenistic involvement in advisory boards and working groups has always been a central concern for disabled activists:

> To get too close to the Government is to risk incorporation and end up carrying out their proposals rather than ours. To move too far away is to risk marginalisation and eventual demise. To collaborate too eagerly with the organisations for disabled people risks having our agendas taken over by them, and having them presented both to us and to politicians as theirs. To remain aloof risks appearing unrealistic and/or unreasonable, and denies possible access to much needed resources. (Barnes and Oliver, 1995: 115)

This dilemma can be regarded as the 'paradox of institutionalisation' (Stammers, 1999, 2009) – the more embedded one gets into mainstream assemblages of power, the more difficult it becomes to transform society. In his analysis of the process, Stammers (1999: 998) explains that 'the trajectory of institutionalization [of social movements] is always the same, from "change" to "order," from challenging the status quo to sustaining it'. ENIL has negotiated the treacherous waters of the paradox of institutionalisation by maintaining strong links with its membership base, as testified by its efforts at keeping in touch and hearing from the members. Being small and flexible by design has also helped the organisation avoid the 'Iron Law of Oligarchy'.[2]

Another way in which ENIL has endeavoured to preserve its transformational essence has been by organising the Freedom Drive, a biennial Independent Living advocacy event that celebrated its tenth occurrence in 2022. The Freedom Drive currently brings together several hundred disabled activists and allies from all over Europe. They gather in Brussels, the symbolic capital of the EU, for three days of discussions, lobbying, celebration, and protest. As the previous ones, the tenth Freedom Drive included workshops, an international conference, and a hearing in the European

Parliament. There was also a party. The culmination of the event, however, is a march past the EU institutions in the city in protest against the continuing violence and denial of self-determination experienced by disabled people throughout Europe.

Independent Living and ENIL's struggle for epistemic justice

As argued in Chapter 1, for disabled people and other oppressed groups, negotiation of meaning is often a power struggle against social hierarchies and for individual and collective emancipation. A central element of this struggle has been the contest over the meaning of independence. As part of the Enlightenment tradition discussed earlier, in the modern period independence has been understood predominantly as ability to cope on one's own, without external support. Medical and other caring professionals have reproduced this understanding in their treatment of disabled people. Professionals have put their efforts into fixing disabled people's bodies and minds so that disabled people become independent by becoming self-sufficient. Those who could not be fixed in this way have been confined to residential institutions or their homes (Oliver and Barnes, 2012).

In their analyses, ENIL's (2023d: 13) experts have similarly pointed out that Independent Living has been routinely 'misunderstood as referring to living without support, being self-sufficient, or even used to describe institutions (sometimes called "independent living centres")'. In Chapter 1, I argued that such misrepresentations have amounted to epistemic injustices. Here, I will develop this analysis further by suggesting that the specific form of epistemic injustice that ENIL has addressed could be productively conceptualised as *hermeneutical injustice*. The latter has been defined by the philosopher Miranda Fricker (2007: 158) as 'having some significant area of one's social experience obscured from collective understanding owing to hermeneutical marginalization'. The conventional understanding of independence as self-sufficiency has obscured the experiences of *inter*dependence that underpin self-sufficiency.

Historically dominant groups such as men and abled-bodied people have benefitted from this obscurity because the relations and structures of *inter*dependence have privileged them. For example, feminisation of care has privileged men while obscuring their dependence on women's caregiving (Fraser and Gordon, 1994); and ableist building conventions have privileged walkers while obscuring their dependence on environmental adaptations such as stairs (Oliver, 1993). Like women, disabled people have historically been prevented from challenging the one-sided interpretation of independence as self-sufficiency due to hermeneutical marginalisation – their oppression has prevented them from participating on equal terms in meaning-generating practices such as deliberation, research, and policy making (Oliver, 1992a).

Women have been able to overcome their hermeneutical marginalisation by engaging in collective action for individual and social change. A key instance of such collective mobilisation has been the activity of consciousness raising through peer support. The practice of group 'speak outs' has helped to awaken 'hitherto dormant resources for social meaning that brought clarity, cognitive confidence, and increased communicative facility' (Fricker, 2007: 148). As a result of these collective hermeneutical efforts, women have been able to overcome taken-for-granted interpretations of their experiences and 'to realize resources for meaning that were as yet only implicit in the social interpretive practices of the time' (Fricker, 2007: 148).

A similar increase of 'cognitive confidence' and 'communicative facility' leading to realisation of new 'resources for meaning' occurred among disabled people when they started speaking out among themselves about their experiences of institutional care and their desire to have more choice and control in their everyday lives. The Independent Living pioneer John Evans recounts:

> The Derbyshire and Hampshire disabled people involved in the development of [the first] CILs [in the UK] felt it was important meeting each other as regularly as they could arrange, so that they could keep the ideas and momentum going. This was as well as networking by telephone, correspondence and faxing, as at this point there were no e-mail communications as yet. This collaboration enabled both groups to prosper and develop a cross-fertilization of ideas. This helped them support each other strengthening their will and determination to secure a firm platform for their infrastructural development and to look at creating a national network and movement. (2002: 6–7)

Thus, consciousness raising through peer support underpinned the Independent Living movement.[3] The latter opposed the segregation of disabled people in institutions for social care and advocated for personal assistance and other forms of user-led, community-based support that enable disabled people's participation in social life. A central part of this activism has consisted in challenging the one-sided understanding of independence as self-sufficiency, imposed on disabled people by medical and other caring professionals, service providers, policy makers, public administrators, and the wider society. In this way, the Independent Living movement has initiated a process of rectifying a hermeneutical injustice suffered by disabled people.

ENIL's founding in 1989 and its work ever since can be understood as important milestones of this epistemic struggle. Other such milestones globally have been the drafting and subsequent ratifications of the CRPD – in its General Comment No. 5 on Article 19 of the CRPD, the Committee on the Rights of Persons with Disabilities (2017: para. 16) has emphasised that 'independent living is an essential part of the individual's autonomy and freedom and does not necessarily mean living alone. It should also not be interpreted solely as the ability to carry out daily activities by oneself'.

ENIL's definition of Independent Living

A key part of ENIL's struggle for epistemic justice has been the creation and promotion of definitions of Independent Living and kindred disability policy concepts such as personal assistance, deinstitutionalisation, and community-based services. These definitions have been based on ENIL's monitoring, research, and advocacy work and have incorporated the testimonies and lived experiences of ENIL's members. They were adopted by ENIL's Board in 2012 and since then have been actively disseminated by the organisation (for a recent example, see ENIL, 2023d: 13–17). ENIL's definitions have been aligned with Article 19 of CRPD and their aim has been to guide and enable the monitoring of disability policies on European and national levels. They have also been used to clarify misunderstandings and to prevent the 'hijacking' of the language of Independent Living advocates:

> The terms 'independent living' and 'personal assistance' have often been exploited and misused to profit organisations, charities and disability business which are not run and controlled by disabled people. These organisations do not appear to want to fully understand the concept of independent living as developed by the independent living movements across Europe and internationally. (Jolly, 2009: 4–5; see also Angelova-Mladenova, 2017: 11)

In addition to guiding and overseeing the deployment of the Independent Living discourse in Europe, ENIL has monitored the implementation of Article 19 of the CRPD by collecting and assessing country-specific information about the translation of Independent Living concepts into concrete policies and practices. The organisation has systematically gathered and analysed data on deinstitutionalisation reform and on development of personal assistance schemes as key areas of Article 19's implementation. I will now discuss ENIL's definition of Independent Living, while the organisation's work on deinstitutionalisation and personal assistance will be presented in Chapter 6. My analysis will be informed by the concept of epistemic injustice, and particularly of hermeneutical injustice and marginalisation, because the struggle over the meaning of independence has been a central concern of the Independent Living movement and, by extension, of ENIL's work.

At the heart of ENIL's advocacy is its understanding of Independent Living that has been captured in the definition already reproduced in the preceding chapter (ENIL, n.d.-d). To pay heed to the significance of this definition for the organisation's struggle for epistemic justice, I will discuss it here statement by statement. ENIL's definition begins by suggesting that Independent Living is about the implementation of rights-based policies, in concert with Article 19 of the CRPD that frames Independent Living as a human right: 'ENIL defines independent living as the daily demonstration of human rights-based disability policies' (ENIL, n.d.-d). In disability studies and activism, the rights-based approach has sometimes been opposed to the needs-based approach, and the shift from 'needs' to 'rights' has meant a transition from charity to entitlement, from passivity to activity, and from professional domination to self-determination of disabled people (Oliver, 1996: Ch. 5; for further analysis, see Ife *et al.*, 2022: Ch. 5).

As discussed in Chapter 2, in modernity the discourse of needs has been largely monopolised by the juridical–administrative–therapeutic state (Fraser, 1987) – hence the activists' preference for the alternative discourse of rights. Another reason for preferring rights over needs is that rights imply state obligations (Ife *et al.*, 2022: 121), whereas needs imply charitable involvement and passivity of the person being supported. This is not to say that the discourse of rights is unproblematic – obviously, it very much overlaps with the juridical–administrative dimensions of the state, as Fraser (1987) also makes clear. I will return to this point in Chapter 6, when I consider ENIL's advocacy for deinstitutionalisation.

The second statement of ENIL's definition of Independent Living makes the point that Independent Living policies pursue two strategies simultaneously: 'Independent living is possible through the combination of various environmental and individual factors that allow disabled people to have control over their own lives' (ENIL, n.d.-d). The first strategy is to design or modify mainstream environments – including buildings, housing, transportation, schools, and workplaces – to make them accessible and accommodating for disabled people. The creation of specialised services such as sheltered workshops or day-care centres, even when physically located within the community rather than on its margins, does not enable Independent Living but perpetuates segregation and exclusion (Angelova-Mladenova, 2017: 12). Instead of such services, Independent Living requires personalised support in the community that includes personal assistance, communication assistance, and assistive technologies, among others. These solutions comprise the 'individual factors', the second policy-making strategy that makes Independent Living possible. Only when applied in tandem can the two strategies effectively create the 'pillars' of Independent Living identified in the Introduction.

ENIL's definition then emphasises that disabled people should be enabled to make 'choices and decisions regarding where to live, with whom to live and how to live' (ENIL, n.d.-d). This point suggests that Independent Living excludes housing and servicing arrangements where disabled people are forced to live in designated buildings and groups, as well as to follow everyday routines determined by service providers or disabled people's carers. In policy terms, housing and support should be decoupled, otherwise, 'people who need support are forced to accept a "group home" type living arrangement, and vice versa – people who need a place to live are forced to accept the support provided there' (Angelova-Mladenova, 2017: 26). This is crucial when considering ENIL's fight over the meaning of deinstitutionalisation (Chapter 6).

Independent Living calls for redistribution of resources towards universally available and accessible services (positive measures), as well as for non-interference and respect of privacy (negative measures) – support should not be imposed through hard or soft power but freely chosen through informed consent: 'Services must be available, accessible to all and provided on the basis of equal opportunity, free and informed consent and allowing disabled people flexibility in our daily life' (ENIL, n.d.-d). Together with being universal and consensual, support should be flexible – its opposites are the rigid routines and one-size-fits-all solutions of residential institutions and other provider-led services. This point will be revisited in the discussion of ENIL's monitoring of personal assistance schemes in Chapter 6. Conceptually, the synthesis between positive and negative liberty presupposed by ENIL's definition could be understood in terms of 'freedom as non-domination' (Sépulchre, 2022), as already noted in Chapter 1.

The fifth statement of ENIL's definition of Independent Living revisits the environmental factors and the individual factors that make Independent Living possible: 'Independent living requires that the built environment, transport and information are accessible, that there is availability of technical aids, access to personal assistance and/or community-based services' (ENIL, n.d.-d). Finally, since Independent Living is conceptualised as a human right, support for it should be unconditional rather than restricted by identity categories or degrees of need: 'It is necessary to point out that independent living is for all disabled persons, regardless of the gender, age and the level of their support needs' (ENIL, n.d.-d). Here, we find an implicit response to the common critique that the Independent Living movement prioritises physically disabled people of working age (Westberg, 2010: 14–15) – rather, Independent Living is meant to be universally applicable, as also stated in Article 19 of the CRPD.

In sum, ENIL's definition suggests that Independent Living is a human right that requires both mainstream adaptations and personalised solutions in which housing and support are decoupled, and which are universal, consensual, flexible, and unconditional. From this perspective, to be independent means to have unrestricted access to mainstream environments and personalised support that is organised in such a way that one has maximum choice and control in one's everyday life. This understanding of independence excludes institutional care and rectifies the hermeneutical injustice suffered by disabled people when independence is one-sidedly interpreted as ability to cope alone, without external support, or to be self-sufficient. To overcome their hermeneutical marginalisation and to assert their own understanding of independence, disabled people have organised in a social movement and have set up organisations such as ENIL.

Intersectionality and ENIL's intersectional turn

In Chapter 1, I addressed the concern that the hegemonic concept of independence reproduces liberal-individualist exclusions, as argued by critical disability studies scholars such as Altermark (2018) , Ben-Moshe (2020), and Davis (2002). The charge that the Independent Living movement and analytic paradigm have tacitly or openly prioritised working-age, physically impaired, white, middle-class males from the Global North has been directed towards activists since the early days (Barnes, 2004: 8; Williams, 1983: 1003–1005). As we saw, in its definition of Independent Living ENIL (n.d.-d) has been careful to include 'all disabled persons, regardless of the gender, age and the level of their support needs'. This emphasis on inclusivity has also underpinned the organisation's more recent intersectional turn.

Intersectionality reveals the situation of people marginalised or oppressed on multiple grounds. Originally developed to explore 'the various ways in which race and gender intersect in shaping structural, and representational aspects of violence against women of color' (Crenshaw, 1991: 1244), intersectionality could help illuminate intra-group differences in experiences of injustice, but also internally generated oppression suffered by subgroups within the broader group of disabled people. Together with this, the intersectional perspective is capable of revealing experiences common to disabled and non-disabled people, considering that 'compulsory able-bodiedness' (McRuer, 2002) has an oppressive impact on everyone and not only on people with recognised impairments. Exemplary in this respect are the pressures to perform in specific (quantifiable) ways characteristic of present-day forms of neoliberal, techno-capitalist productivism (Mladenov, 2020a).

In disability studies, the intersectional analysis was pioneered by disabled feminists at the beginning of the 1990s (Begum, 1992; Morris, 1993a) and since then has become a prominent feature of the discipline (Berghs *et al.*, 2016). Disabled feminists were concerned that the disability movement has been dominated by men and has disregarded – or even actively suppressed – issues central to the lives of disabled women. Integrating the intersectional perspective in the critique of disablement has been a prominent element of recent reformulations of the social model of disability by critical disability studies scholars, who have argued that 'any analysis of disability should not preclude consideration of other forms of political activism. Increasingly, we are witnessing intersectional moments within new social movements and these crossovers and alliances should be attended to' (Goodley *et al.*, 2019: 977).

Indeed, intersectional analysis has gradually become part of global disability rights activism, including ENIL's advocacy. This trend has been reflected, for example, in the work on the COVID-19 DRM, where a key recommendation has been that

> emergency responses are disability-inclusive and take into account the diverse and individual needs of persons with disabilities, in particular those experiencing intersectional forms of discrimination and marginalisation such as women and girls with disabilities, persons living in rural or remote areas, deaf and hard of hearing persons, persons with deaf blindness, persons with intellectual or psychosocial disabilities, and persons with autism. (Brennan *et al.*, 2020: 13)

Notably, the intersectional analysis harbours its own contradictions. Most conspicuously, it may lead to the fragmentation of the collective subject, thus weakening political action. In her seminal paper on intersectionality, Crenshaw (1991: 1244) has mentioned the reluctance of some feminists to release statistics on police interventions in cases of domestic violence against specific minority groups for fear that this would present (and therefore undermine) the issue of domestic violence by framing it as a minority problem. Crenshaw (1991: 1244) has also identified the kindred reluctance of some anti-racists to release disaggregated statistics for fear of demonising racial minorities. Within disability studies, Goodley *et al.* (2019: 977) have discussed the risk that intersectional analysis may decentre or sideline disability by seeking to explore intersecting identities. Interestingly, four decades ago Esping-Andersen (1985: 31) made a similar point regarding advocacy for social democracy, whose successes have required 'displacing alternative community bases – religion, ethnicity, or localism; early "corporative" worker organizations, such as guild and fraternal associations; rival political identities, such as syndicalism or communism; and competitive individualism and market atomization'.

However, the intersectional perspective illuminates not only intra-group differences, but also inter-group commonalities, which might strengthen a social movement by enabling cross-movement alliances. Moreover, identities interact in co-constitutive rather than additive ways. For example, it is possible to argue that androcentrism and heterosexism have been as much underpinned and organised by ableism as the latter has been structured along the lines of the former – in the words of McRuer (2002: 94), 'the most successful heterosexual subject is the one whose sexuality is not compromised by disability (metaphorized as queerness); the most successful able-bodied subject is the one whose ability is not compromised by queerness (metaphorized as disability)'. Similar analyses have been done under the title of 'race-ability', which has highlighted the mutually constitutive (rather than merely additive) nature of racism and ableism (Ben-Moshe, 2020). Such intersections, complemented by classism and other injustices, have shaped actual oppression under conditions of modernity (Mladenov, 2021b). This 'mutually constitutive' understanding of intersectionality is reflected in compound terms such as race-ableism (Ben-Moshe, 2020), ablenationalism (Mitchell and Snyder, 2015), and neoliberal-ableism (Goodley *et al.*, 2014).

Moreover, the intersectional perspective has the potential to enhance Independent Living analyses of professional and parental power because they tend to restrict the self-determination of different subgroups of disabled people in different ways and to different degrees. For example, disabled women have been more likely than disabled men to be subjected to controlling and restrictive interventions (including abuse and violence) by the staff of residential institutions (Sumskiene and Orlova, 2015). The issue has also been highlighted by ENIL (2023c) in a recent position paper: 'Disabled people, and particularly disabled women and girls, are at a heightened risk of suffering violence, abuse, and neglect from carers and service providers, especially if they live in institutions. ... A gender perspective on support cannot exclude the experiences of disabled women.' At the level of practice, ENIL has recently been involved in a project on sexual and reproductive rights of women and girls, whose aim has been defined on ENIL's website as 'to shed light on perceived access barriers to and utilization of comprehensive family planning services by women living with HIV, women and girls living with disabilities, and survivors of intimate partner violence' (ENIL, n.d.-c).

Another consideration in support of the intersectional turn in Independent Living advocacy and analysis is that institutionalisation is racialised. For example, in postsocialist countries such as Bulgaria, Hungary, and the Czech Republic, 'disadvantaged children, especially children with disabilities and Roma children, are more likely to be institutionalised' (Woodin, 2017: 13). The region has been marked by a widespread practice of segregating Roma children in special schools and residential institutions based on presumed intellectual impairments (Woodin, 2017: 30). Similar analyses have been made regarding the overrepresentation of Black children in special education in the United States (Harry and Klingner, 2006). These are instances in which the mutually constitutive character of racism and ableism in restricting self-determination becomes conspicuous. Ben-Moshe (2020: 116) has argued that the disability rights movement needs to consider deinstitutionalisation as an anti-racist project, otherwise it would remain irrelevant to the experiences of many disabled people:

> The consequences of not engaging in abolition from an intersectional lens rooted in maroonage is that it becomes irrelevant to the majority of those it seeks to liberate, both demographically (as it is not based on the lived experience of people of color) but especially epistemologically and methodologically, by not underscoring race as a lens rooted in black radical tradition that critiques the state as violent and not the arena to seek remediation to injustice. (Ben-Moshe, 2020: 116)

As already mentioned, ENIL (2023d: 32) has emphasised that Independent Living is for all disabled people 'regardless of their race, ethnic origin, migrant or refugee status, socio-economic status, religion, political belief, age, gender, sexual orientation, language and other characteristics'. The organisation's recent proposal to the European Commission on creating guidance on Independent Living includes a separate section on 'Intersectional and intersectoral approaches' that states:

> The entrenched mind set which has been apparent in European countries around detaining and forcibly treating people under mental health and mental capacity law is having a still more negative effect on people who, for example, also belong to minority ethnic communities, including asylum seekers and refugees, experience particular socio-economic disadvantages, are deaf, or identify as lesbian, gay, bisexual or transgender. (ENIL, 2023d: 32)

ENIL's proposal to the European Commission also includes a call for 'an intersectional approach in any laws, policies, strategies or action plans relevant to disabled people', together with an insistence on paying particular attention to disabled people who are 'at a higher risk of multiple discrimination or of being left behind' (ENIL, 2023d: 33). ENIL's intersectional turn has also underpinned the organisation's work on promoting Independent Living for older people. These efforts have included a webinar on the topic of 'Age and Disability: A Blindspot in Policy Making?', conducted on 15 December 2022 with the participation of Adolf Ratzka (Sanden, 2022). Highlighting the relevance of Independent Living in older age constitutes an implicit critique of the pervasive productivism of mainstream disability policy that I will explore in Chapter 4. The entitlement of older people to Independent Living means that the right to self-determination should not be justified with reference to productivity.

Concluding remarks

In this chapter, I conceptualised ENIL's advocacy for Independent Living as a struggle for epistemic justice that has sought to overcome the hermeneutical marginalisation of disabled people in meaning-generating practices concerning disability policy. These practices have traditionally been dominated by caring professionals, service providers, politicians, and others occupying positions of power in areas such as disability-related research and policy making that have affected disabled people but have historically excluded their inputs, not to mention leadership. Powerful disability policy actors have perpetuated a liberal-individualist interpretation of independence as self-sufficiency – an interpretation whose reproduction has constituted a hermeneutical injustice inflicted on disabled people.

This hegemonic understanding of independence has been challenged by ENIL through an alternative interpretation that has rendered independence in terms of choice and control in one's everyday life, including choice and control over one's support – rather than ability to cope without support. To iterate, from the perspective of the Independent Living movement, to be independent does not mean to cope without support or to be self-sufficient but to have access to support that is organised in such a way so that the person who uses this support has maximum choice and control in their everyday life. ENIL's definition of Independent Living has affirmed this alternative understanding of independence.

The latter has also been incorporated in Article 19 of the CRPD, which represents a major – although not a decisive – achievement in disabled people's struggle for epistemic justice. The achievement of Article 19 has been consolidated by the Committee on the Rights of Persons with Disabilities (2017) in its General Comment No. 5, which has interpreted Article 19 along the lines of the Independent Living movement. However, it has not been a decisive achievement because there is still a lot of work to be done to translate the meanings implied in Article 19 into actual disability policies. The domination of caring professionals and service providers in defining disability issues continues to be strong and it takes an organised and consistent collective effort to articulate, maintain, and safeguard a truly transformative and emancipatory reading of the CRPD that is in line with the values and principles of the Independent Living movement.

In her analysis of epistemic injustice, Fricker (2007: 174) has pointed out that hermeneutical marginalisation results from unequal relations of power that exceed the domain of communication. The interpretation of independence as self-sufficiency is underpinned by material interests – most obviously, by the interests of the providers of traditional services, who have sought to preserve their dominant position in the arena of social support. The pivotal role of the material considerations for maintaining institutional forms of care has been identified in the early accounts of Independent Living: 'Provider groups tend to have a direct economic interest in issues of long-term care, and this interest is not well served by a participant-directed model of service delivery' (DeJong *et al.*, 1992: 91). The significance of material interests has also been emphasised by coining suggestive critical-theoretical concepts such as 'institutional–industrial complex' (Ben-Moshe, 2020).

It follows that hermeneutical marginalisation cannot be overcome by virtuous individual action alone – it is not enough that a decision maker is willing to listen to the ideas of those who use services and to be convinced by their arguments or by their reading of Article 19 of the CRPD. The very structure of decision making needs to change so that the members of the group whose interpretations have so far been marginalised become equal participants in meaning-generating practices. For this to happen, argues Fricker (2007: 174), collective political action is needed. The work of ENIL represents such an organised collective effort at becoming an equal participant in the negotiation of meaning that guides contemporary disability policy. As a user-led and user-controlled organisation, ENIL has developed and promoted a definition of Independent Living that draws on principles and values espoused by the Independent Living movement. In this way, ENIL has advanced epistemic justice in disability policy making in Europe and beyond.

ENIL's more recent intersectional turn has enhanced this work by attending to the specific forms of oppression experienced by subgroups of disabled people such as women, racialised people, people with intellectual impairments, and older people. Instead of weakening the organisation's advocacy and analyses, the intersectional approach has made them more nuanced, while also creating opportunities for building alliances with other progressive movements.

As we will see in Chapter 6, ENIL has used its interpretation of Independent Living to monitor actual deinstitutionalisation and personal assistance policies. On this basis, ENIL has been able to expose as flawed 'deinstitutionalisation' programmes that have amounted to renovating existing institutions or to moving residents to smaller institutions, as well as flawed 'personal assistance' schemes that have amounted to home care. Such policies have been exposed as flawed because they have pretended to maximise disabled people's choice and control, while effectively maintaining the status quo of professional and parental power. ENIL has advocated for their substitution with policies of deinstitutionalisation and personal assistance that reflect the meaning of independence elaborated by the activists of the Independent Living movement and incorporated in Article 19 of the CRPD.

Notes

1 The COVID-19 DRM was implemented by ENIL, Validity Foundation, International Disability Alliance, Disability Rights International, Disability Rights Unit at the Centre for Human Rights, University of Pretoria, International Disability and Development Consortium, and Disability Rights Fund/Disability Rights Advocacy Fund.

2 Theorising the paradox of institutionalisation has its roots in sociological analyses of social democracy such as the elite theory of Robert Michaels: 'Inspired by Max Weber's theory of bureaucracy, Roberto Michels ([1915] 1962) formulated his Iron Law of Oligarchy to account for the decay of German social democracy. According to Michels, the socialist party will contradict its own historical mission of democratic socialism. As it grows into a powerful political movement it will professionalize, bureaucratize, and lose sight of its real purpose as it becomes preoccupied with the demands of day-to-day administration. The party becomes an expression of antidemocratic rule, devoted to the task of its own self-perpetuation' (Esping-Andersen, 1985: 16).

3 Peer support has been key for other new social movements too due to its potential to disrupt existing hierarchies of professional power. For example, McCulloch (2021: 422) has highlighted the significance of peer support for former prisoners, as reflected in the 'desistance movement': 'the transformational value of peer support does not reside in its ability to replicate and reproduce existing social and public service systems and relationships, but in its ability to disrupt and transform them, including from the bottom up'. I will revisit peer support in Chapter 5.

3

Independent Living and the state

> I have a fantasy that in some future world people with disabilities will be able to insist on the right to interrogate doctors, rather than be interrogated by them. In this fantasy, a doctor is placed on a stage in front of a large audience of people with disabilities, in order that we may come to understand the stigma of a career in medicine, and the effect this may have on family and friends. Someone would then ask the doctor a series of searching questions, such as: 'When did your profession begin? Was it the result of an accident, or is it a deteriorating condition?' I suspect that we would learn very little about the individual beneath the white coat, but the feeling of power might prove too irresistible to be ignored. (Brisenden, 1986: 175)

The epistemic struggles of ENIL suggest that the Independent Living movement has consistently sought to challenge the power of caring professionals to define (and thus control) the lives of disabled people. From the perspectives of Fraser's (1987) politics of need interpretation and Fricker's (2007) epistemic injustice (both introduced in Chapter 1), the juridical–administrative–therapeutic apparatus of the contemporary state has imposed alienating interpretations on its subjects' situations and needs, while the subjects have resisted this alienation by seeking to overcome their hermeneutical marginalisation and create and promote definitions of their own.

ENIL's definition of Independent Living is an instance of this hermeneutical resistance, but this has characterised the movement since its earliest days. Simon Brisenden's (1986: 175) fantasy is a witty and subversive example. The recollections of Hale Zukas (1975) also testify that Independent Living pioneers had a clear intention of being recognised as experts on their own lives, seeking to reclaim this expertise from the professionals who cared for them. This struggle for reclaiming epistemic authority from professionals has animated pioneering Independent Living initiatives in Britain as well, as evidenced by UPIAS's *Policy Statement*: 'Our Union rejects entirely any idea of medical or other experts having the right to tell us how we should live, or withholding information from us, or take decisions behind our backs' (UPIAS, 1976b: n.p.).

In critical-theoretical terms, the power of caring professionals over disabled people's lives amounts to *biopower* – a concept imported into disability studies from the work of Michel Foucault (Tremain, 2005). According to Foucault (1978), biopower is power that works primarily by managing (regulating, transforming, enhancing, monitoring, partitioning, categorising) life, as opposed to 'sovereign power' that works primarily by restricting (taking, denying, impairing, seizing, suppressing) life. The concept illuminates 'what brought life and its mechanisms into the realm of explicit calculations and made knowledge-power an agent of transformation of human life' (Foucault, 1978: 143), which gets to the core of disabled people's experiences of different forms of professionalised care. In Foucault's (1978: 139) original account, biopower has two forms – disciplining individual bodies to enhance their vitality ('anatomo-politics of the human body') and regulating the vitality of whole populations ('bio-politics of the population'). Both forms of biopower are relevant when considering disability in the context of contemporary welfare states.

Besides Foucault's analyses of biopower, the critique of professional power voiced by the Independent Living activists since the 1960s can be contextualised with reference to other prominent critical positions of the time including anti-psychiatry (e.g., Szasz, 1991), critiques of medicalisation (e.g., Illich, 2013), sociologies of 'total institutions' (e.g., Goffman, 1974), and radical/critical social work (e.g., Kirkwood, 1970). These analyses and the associated mobilisations converged in targeting (more or less directly) the structures and agencies of the post-war welfare state in North America and Western Europe. For example, in a discussion of the historical development of child protection policies and practices in the UK, Steve Rogowski (2015: 100) refers to the 1970s as a time of manyfold discontents with mainstream social work:

> The left, including feminists and anti-racists, were concerned that Social Services Departments were ineffective, distant and oppressive, leaving the user powerless and without a voice. For some, social work was seen as an element of class control, preserving the status quo of capitalist societies by controlling and regulating the working class.

Thus, similar to other caring professions, professionalised social work has incorporated the contradictions of the welfare state, as analysed by the German critical theorist Claus Offe (1984). On the one hand, the welfare state has provided support to meet people's needs, thus decommodifying labour through need-based allocation. Yet on the other hand, the welfare state has sought to regulate individuals and families to facilitate capital accumulation, thus enhancing commodification through work-based allocation. The criticisms of mainstream social work voiced by the progressive social movements in the 1970s have been both a product of and a reaction to these contradictions. They have constituted resistances to the 'anatomo-politics of the human body' and the 'bio-politics of the population' made possible by biopower, since 'the welfare state has increased the "means of resistance" that are available to social groups in their attempts to minimize the exploitative effects of capital's control over the means of production' (Keane, 1984: 17).[1]

Rogowski (2015: 100) also points out that progressive criticisms of the welfare state inadvertently facilitated the neoliberal turn initiated in the UK by the British New Right, 'who were against public expenditure on welfare, instead wanting an increased emphasis on self-help, individual responsibility, "choice" and freedom, together with an extension of the commodification of social relations'. This implies a convergence between emancipatory social movements and neoliberalism; moreover, Rogowski's reference to 'choice' and 'freedom' strongly evokes the Independent Living paradigm. Such considerations have made some critical thinkers dismissive of critiques of professional power – Bernard Stiegler (2010: 119), for example, has regarded the progressives' discontent with the welfare state of the 1970s as an intellectual fad that, according to Stiegler, eventually turned out to be 'sadly, profoundly false'. But the alternative of heroising caring professionals that Stiegler seems to embrace is equally suspect, especially from a disability perspective.

Indeed, as an emancipatory critique of professional power, the Independent Living movement has resisted the interventions of the juridical–administrative–therapeutic state apparatus in the name of choice and freedom, as also suggested by the moniker of the biggest disability rights march in Europe, ENIL's Freedom Drive. However, reducing Independent Living to a neoliberal handmaiden or a 'profoundly false' activist fad would be grossly misleading. Conceptually, it would misrepresent key statements of the activists; in policy terms, it would strengthen the violence of institutionalisation; and politically, it would reproduce the hermeneutical marginalisation identified in Chapter 2.

Without disavowing the convergence between Independent Living and neoliberal marketisation (which will be explored in depth in Chapter 4), in this chapter I will consider Independent Living's interrogation of the welfare state as a legitimate strategy of emancipation deployed on the terrain of biopower. I will start by discussing the tensions between Independent Living and professionalised care. I will then explore the relations between Independent Living advocacy and the welfare state in several major welfare regimes. This will enable me to contextualise the analysis by paying attention to variations in national traditions, practices, cultures, and developmental trajectories. Care in the family (or 'informal care') will be discussed in Chapter 5. There is a significant overlap between professionalised care and family care, but there are also important differences. Historically, the family has been a primary source of caregiving, but the development of the welfare states and the emancipation of women has led to professionalisation of care – a trend which has amplified biopolitical forms of governance.

Independent Living and professionalised care

The Scottish Independent Living pioneer Jim Elder-Woodward (2001: 3, citing Oliver, 1994) has highlighted the branding of disabled activists as 'ungrateful bastards' due to their criticisms of ostensibly well-meaning professional interventions. Indeed, caring creates a situation where restrictions of freedom could easily be framed as exercised 'in the best interests' or 'for the good' of the cared for – consider, for example, discourses and practices of guardianship (Gooding, 2018). This entanglement between care and power has intensified with the professionalisation of caring in modernity, as the Foucaultian concept of biopower suggests: 'Biopower is a form of care, a historic form of the system of care charged to the State, as governmentality' (Stiegler, 2010: 114). According to Stiegler (2010: 173), rethinking care in terms of the theory of the modern state has been a major concern of Foucault's:

> The 'bourgeois State' is essentially biopower instituting a politics of governmental management of the future and of population growth, for example, as a politics of birth or public hygiene: biopolitics. Biopower as Foucault describes it is always a function of the State, specifically of the nation-state, resulting from the bourgeoisie's acquisition of power.

In the twentieth century, this process of 'careification' of the state culminated in the development of the welfare states in the countries of the Global North. Stiegler points out that Foucault used to see the power thus instituted as necessarily mutating into 'a constraining, even alienating, discipline, into norms, standards, and regulations in which individuals are embedded, dominated by a mass technocracy through which the State suffocates "society"' (Stiegler, 2010: 174). Unlike Foucault, Stiegler emphasises the positive side of the welfare state, as reflected in the institution of public education, whose ultimate telos, according to Stiegler (2010: 174), is to enlighten people, to enable them to use their reason autonomously (in the Kantian sense discussed in Chapter 1). However, disabled people's experiences of professionalised care resonate more strongly with Foucault's critique than with Stiegler's affirmation of biopower.

Without Foucaultian scepticism, it would be difficult to oppose control or violence that are (presented as) benevolent. This double bind of biopower has been a hallmark of disability policies in contemporary welfare states that have elevated care (in the form of 'social care') to a key organising principle in conceptualising, designing, and providing support to disabled people. In response, Independent Living activists have regarded the discourse of care as *itself* creating disablement. This discourse has been exposed by both campaigners and disability studies scholars as overwhelmingly paternalist, where 'paternalism' denotes 'policies and practices of authority figures that limit the right of self-determination of people with disabilities and increase further their dependency. Under paternalism, people with disabilities become subordinate to family members, health, and social service professionals' (Zaviršek and Fischbach, 2023: 97).

The paternalist discourse of care has reproduced biopower by allocating a docile role to disabled people, related to the expectation that the cared for should submit to the will of those who provide them with care – relatives, medical doctors, service providers, charities. 'For many disabled people the concept "care" is both patronising and oppressive', state Oliver and Barnes (2012: 66; for a discussion, see Hughes *et al.*, 2005; Watson *et al.*, 2004). Hegemonic understandings and practices of care have tended to subjugate their object and empower and heroise their subject:

> This representation, and the language that sustains it, has the effect of promoting patronizing attitudes towards the recipients of care. They become 'takers' and 'burdens'; men, women and children who live their lives vicariously and at the expense of others. For every self-sacrificing martyr, there is a parasite benefiting from the charitable nature of a heroic carer. (Watson *et al.*, 2004: 335–336)

Everyday language sustains these meanings. For example, a dictionary definition of the Bulgarian word for care, *грижа*, reads: 'Excitement of the soul, uneasiness [*притеснение*] associated with the thought of something; anxiety, worry [*безпокойство, тревога*]' (Institute for Bulgarian Language, n.d.). Care as uneasiness, anxiety, and worry strengthens the meaning of care as encumbrance, burden, and self-denial. The associated perception of disability as a personal tragedy (Oliver, 1996: 32) instead of social oppression reinforces the disparagement of the disabled people subjected to care. Accordingly, institutional confinement is often legitimised by the discourse of care as opposed to the discourse of punishment (Ben-Moshe, 2020: 65).

As a reaction, the advocates of Independent Living have substituted the discourse of care with a discourse of assistance – a term that presupposes horizontal relationships between equal partners and negotiations based on informed consent. The concept of 'personal assistance' has been an important part of this terminological and conceptual shift and will be discussed in detail in Chapter 6. Personal assistance is usually defined by Independent Living advocates in terms of relationships between employer and employee, which is in sharp contrast to the relationships between a caregiver and a care-receiver and implies a different configuration of biopower.

However, together with its paternalist and patronising connotations, the discourse of care has also made a positive contribution to the politics of disability. The critical and analytical potential of the concept of care has been emphasised by the 'ethics of care' developed and promoted by feminist philosophers such as Joan Tronto (1993) and Eva Kittay (1999; 2018). The ethics of care opposes liberal individualism, marketisation, and the work ethic, asserting the universal nature of the relations of *inter*dependence, as well as their intrinsic worth (Barnes *et al.*, 2015; Williams, 2002). This use of the notion of caring constitutes a strong counter-discourse to the 'instrumental reason' (Schecter, 2010) that has legitimised modern capitalist developments, producing disablement on a mass scale (Oliver and Barnes, 2012).

In this form, the idea of care is not necessarily in tension with the Independent Living paradigm. As already discussed, the Independent Living movement does not reject *inter*dependence but builds on it. The attendant critique of self-sufficiency is in concert with the analyses that emphasise the ethics of care. The latter can also help undermine productivism – a key mechanism for devaluing the lives of disabled people due to the strong association between disability and loss of productive capacity. The defining feature of productivist welfare systems is that they allocate support on the basis of work contribution. In contrast, caring societies allocate support on the basis of need. Need-based allocation eases the productivist pressure of the work-based allocation (Stone, 1984), which amounts to decommodification of labour (Esping-Andersen, 1990). The price is enhanced biopower and intensified struggles for need interpretation.

Due to its opposition to self-sufficiency, the ethics of care has attracted interest and (qualified) support from 'second wave' disability studies scholars such as Tom Shakespeare, Nick Watson, and Bill Hughes (e.g., Hughes *et al.*, 2005; Shakespeare, 2006, 2014; Watson *et al.*, 2004). A nuanced discussion of caring as both reinforcing coercion and enabling resistance to liberal-individualist exclusions has more recently been provided by Niklas Altermark (2018: Ch. 6). Such analyses have complemented the perspective of the caregiver with the perspective of the care-receiver and have emphasised their common interests in the struggle against oppression:

> The parties involved in the caring relationship are perpetually invalidated because the value of care is measured against the autonomous adult male who neither requires nor delivers care. To be a carer or cared for – male or female, disabled or non-disabled in either role – is to be found wanting, to be other

> in relation to the masculine subject of modernity, to be reduced to 'the other of the same'. Those who give and receive care are marginalized, 'used and wasted' bodies, existing, by and large, on the margins of what counts as the truly human community. (Hughes *et al.*, 2005: 265)

In my own work (Mladenov, 2021c), I have used the term 'egalitarian care' to distinguish an alternative understanding of caring (commensurate with the ethics of care) from the traditional approach of 'paternalist care'. Egalitarian care takes seriously the claim of the ethics of care that care 'is never a one-directional activity involving a caregiver and someone dependent on the care but an activity binding people together through our interdependencies' (Altermark, 2018: 118). This vision also entails universalisation of caring – everyone (potentially) receives and provides care. Indeed, for many Independent Living activists, egalitarian care would be a contradiction in terms, while the feminist 'ethics of care' discourse would seem to be overstating the benevolence of the welfare state, the allied professions, and the family. However, a radical rejection of the care discourse deprives activism of a key tool for resisting disabling rationalities centred on productivism and self-sufficiency – rationalities that underpin segregation, institutionalisation, and welfare-state retrenchment.

The distinction between paternalist care and egalitarian care reflects the distinction that Martin Heidegger (1962) – a major modern philosopher of care (in German: *Sorge*) – makes between two forms of 'solicitude' (*Fürsorge*). In the first form, which resembles paternalist care, *Fürsorge* amounts to standing in or serving as a deputy for the cared for: 'This kind of solicitude takes over for the Other [i.e., for the cared for] that with which he is to concern himself. ... In such solicitude the Other can become one who is dominated and dependent, even if this domination is a tacit one and remains hidden from him' (Heidegger, 1962: 158). The second form of *Fürsorge* resembles egalitarian care in that here the carer intervenes not to take control over care but to give it back to the cared for: 'This kind of solicitude pertains essentially to authentic care – that is, to the existence of the Other [i.e., the cared for], not to a "*what*" with which he is concerned; it helps the Other to become transparent to himself *in* his care and to become *free for* it' (Heidegger, 1962: 158, original emphases).

This Heideggerian perspective suggests that egalitarian care has not only practical and everyday ('ontic', in Heidegger's vocabulary), but also existential-ontological implications. It enables people receiving care to provide care themselves. Moreover, it makes it possible for the 'cared for' to attend to things and tasks (a 'what' of concern), but also to take charge of their own existence, thus caring for being itself. In other words, egalitarian care enables the people who receive care to realise themselves as world-disclosers (*Dasein*) instead of being reduced to objects ('present-at-hand' or *vorhanden* entities). This is what Heidegger (1962: 158, original emphases) means when he says that 'authentic care ... helps the Other to become transparent to himself *in* his care and to become *free for* it'. Becoming a world-discloser provides an opportunity to preserve and create meaning, including the meaning of one's own life and the meaning of being (which, for Heidegger, are inseparable). In essence, the egalitarian care made possible by the 'pillars' of Independent Living has enabled the members of the Independent Living movement to become fully human by avoiding the objectification effected by paternalist care.[2]

As we will see in Chapter 4, the perspective of egalitarian care also helps illuminate some relational aspects of one-to-one support such as personal assistance, thus potentially enriching the Independent Living paradigm that tends to regard personal assistance instrumentally. However, the idea of egalitarian care can be something more than a contradiction in terms only if it helps with the critical evaluation and problematisation of paternalist forms of care such as institutional care and kinship 'personal assistance' (discussed in Chapters 5 and 6). Moreover, due to the politics of need interpretation (Fraser, 1987), need-based allocation is itself saturated with relations of power. Understanding this type of allocation of public support in terms of 'anatomo-politics' and 'bio-politics' (Foucault, 1978) suggests that even egalitarian care is far from politically neutral. In the final analysis, 'care' must be handled with care: 'The discussion of care-less-ness and care, more than any other, is pharmacological: this discourse on evils and remedies could be the worst of all poisons' (Stiegler, 2010: 190).

The welfare state and welfare regimes

Historically, the power of the caring professionals grew significantly during the 'golden age' of the welfare state in the countries of the Global North. In Western Europe, this period lasted between the end of World War II and the end of the 1970s, facilitated by an intense regime competition with the socialist states in Central and Eastern Europe and the Soviet Union (Obinger and Schmitt, 2011; see also Esping-Andersen, 1999: 34). During this time, 'increase in state-sponsored welfare and the increased professionalisation of the services meant that the newly trained medical professionals and social workers, the so-called "experts", were increasingly making decisions about what a disabled person's needs were and what support was best for them' (Roulstone and Prideaux, 2012: 32).

As juridical–administrative–therapeutic assemblages, post-war welfare states had disabled people assessed, labelled, treated, and disciplined by caring professionals, in medical or medicalised settings, through medical–administrative categories. Some were left at home with little formal support, but many were confined in residential institutions for social care where they were subjected to segregation, paternalism, block treatment, rigid routines, deprivation of privacy, physical and medical restraint, neglect, and abuse. Thus, for many disabled people, professionalised care has amounted to restrictions, control, or outright violence generated by a toxic mixture of 'soft' biopower and 'hard' sovereign power (Oliver, 2009; Oliver and Barnes, 2012). This mixture has characterised all welfare states, but the proportions of its 'ingredients' and the specific identities, limitations, and injuries that it has produced have varied widely. To understand this variation, we need to consider differences between welfare regimes.

Towards the end of the 1980s, the Danish social policy analyst Gøsta Esping-Andersen (1990) famously identified three main welfare regimes under 'advanced' capitalism – liberal, social democratic, and conservative (also denoted as 'corporatist'). Esping-Andersen's main distinguishing feature was the degree to which welfare systems allowed people to live their lives independently from the market – that is, according to the degree of 'decommodification', a term borrowed from the work of Karl Polanyi (2001 [1944]). Other metrics originally used by Esping-Andersen (1990) were the degree of social stratification or in/equality created by the system, as well as the public–private mix or the predominance of public or private sources of social support.

Later, feminist scholars enriched Esping-Andersen's (1990) original analysis by considering the degree to which the state allows people to live lives independently from the family – that is, according to 'defamilialisation' (Lister, 1994). To provide a formal definition, defamilialisation identifies 'the degree to which policies redistribute the responsibility for and practice of care-related tasks and associated dependencies away from the family' (Daly, 2022: 317). The concept emerged as a critique of Esping-Andersen's strong emphasis on decommodification in his original classification of welfare regimes (Daly, 2022: 317; Mathieu, 2016: 578). As he himself recognised later, decommodification 'is not easily applicable to women considering that their economic role is often non-commodified or at least only partially commodified' (Esping-Andersen, 1999: 44). This meant that the original typology foregrounded the (male-centred) state–market nexus at the expense of (feminised) family relationships: 'the concept of decommodification is implicitly built on the situation of working *men*' (Mathieu, 2016: 578, original emphasis). Moreover, disregarding the non-commodified or pre-commodified status of women normalises their exclusion from paid labour outside the household.

These criticisms led to a revision of the original typology, which Esping-Andersen (1999) published in book form a decade later. There, he acknowledged that his earlier work had been 'too narrowly based on income-maintenance programmes, too focused on only the state–market nexus, and too one-dimensionally built around the standard male production worker' (Esping-Andersen, 1999: 73). In this revised work, the family has a prominent role as the third organising principle of social welfare, and policies of defamilialisation are extensively discussed. Notably, defamilialisation does not mean abolishing the family, but providing public support with the family's social-reproductive activities. Thus, instead of facilitating family breakdowns, defamilialisation may strengthen families (Mathieu, 2016: 578). Accordingly, 'active family policies are extraordinarily undeveloped in the most familialistic regimes' (Esping-Andersen, 1999: 51).[3]

A summary of the revised typology, with examples of states reflecting the overarching distinctions, is provided in Table 3.1. It is important to emphasise that the territory is much messier than this map – the three regimes identified by Esping-Andersen are ideal types, so no state embodies them fully.

Table 3.1 Welfare regimes (based on Esping-Andersen, 1999: 85–86)

	Market (support through the labour market)	State (support provided by the state)	Family (support provided by the family)
Liberal	**Little regulation** Australia, Canada, Denmark, New Zealand, Switzerland, the UK, and the United States	**Residual** Australia, Canada, New Zealand, the United States (and, to a degree, the UK)	**Non-familialist** Australia, Canada, Denmark, Finland, New Zealand, Norway, Sweden, the UK, and the United States
Social democratic	**Medium regulation** Finland, Ireland, Japan, the Netherlands, Norway, and Sweden	**Universalist** Denmark, Finland, Norway, Sweden, the Netherlands (and, to a degree, the UK)	
Conservative	**Strong regulation** Austria, Belgium, France, Germany, Italy, Portugal, and Spain	**Social insurance** Austria, Belgium, France, Germany, Italy, Japan, and Spain	**Familialist** Austria, Germany, Italy, Japan, the Netherlands, Portugal, Spain (and, less so, Belgium and France)

Esping-Andersen's typology has been subjected to extensive discussions, revisions, and critiques, including for its overwhelming focus on Western Europe. Critics have highlighted regime types presumably not fitting Esping-Andersen's typology: 'there is an ongoing debate in the literature over the number of "worlds" [of welfare] and the types of countries that might (or might not) cluster within them' (Deeming, 2017: 410). Moreover, some of the countries explored by Esping-Andersen (such as the UK or the Netherlands) constitute borderline cases that challenge the neat distinctions between the regimes. Federalism and processes of devolution further complicate whole-state generalisations. Historical change has also been an issue – for example, the UK, Australia, and New Zealand could be regarded as social democratic until the 1980s; and Esping-Andersen has not considered in sufficient depth the neoliberal reforms that gained pace at that time. There is also the question about internal non-homogeneity – within a single regime, some welfare policies may be liberal, while others may be social democratic. For example:

> Reality rarely conforms to the idealised pattern of the liberal model, and liberal principles rarely apply across all social programmes in market liberal societies. The British NHS provides another example of governmental intervention based on social democratic founding principles of universality and equity. Thus, in the field of healthcare, the UK, which belongs to the liberal welfare regime in *Three Worlds* [Esping-Andersen's 1990 book], is more similar to social democratic Sweden than it is to the US, another member of the liberal welfare regime. (Deeming, 2017: 409)

Some of these criticisms have been addressed by Esping-Andersen in his 1999 book, although discussions and debates about the number and features of welfare regimes, as well as about the sheer usefulness of the concept, continue. The history of the Independent Living movement suggests that Esping-Andersen's typology could help explain some of its successes or failures in different parts of the world. The next section attempts a preliminary account along these lines that would certainly benefit from further research and empirical refinements.

Independent Living and liberal, social democratic, and conservative states

Let me begin with the liberal welfare regime, in which decommodification is strategically undermined, while defamilialisation is weak. However, the overreliance on the market to provide social welfare stimulates the inclusion of women in paid labour, and the ensuing 'two-earner' model systemically undermines familialism. Moreover, the availability of affordable welfare services and flexible labour markets make it easier to purchase care on the market. The state provides minimal assistance which is means-tested, conditional, and targeted (through tight eligibility criteria) to those who are assessed as most needy – the rest are left to rely on informal support or buy the welfare services they need privately. Low levels of familialism, labour market flexibilisation, and critique of state intervention create favourable conditions for the adoption and implementation of Independent Living policies that enhance the self-determination of (some) disabled people, but commodification and welfare residualism undermine these achievements.

Historically, the Independent Living movement emerged in the United States in the 1960s. It is therefore reasonable to assume that (at least initially) there has been an affinity between the principles of liberal welfare and disabled people's struggle for self-determination. The suspicion towards the state, the emphasis on individual rights and freedoms, and the prioritisation of market forces characterising the liberal welfare regime resonate with the Independent Living paradigm and must have enhanced the policy salience of its pioneers. Indeed, as early as 1983, the British sociologist Gareth Williams (1983: 1004) described Independent Living activism as characterised by 'a basic commitment to the American capitalist system with its free-market pluralist ideology'. I will return to these points in Chapter 4, when discussing the links between Independent Living and the market.

In the social democratic regime, both decommodification and defamilialisation are strategically promoted. This means that the state provides services and support that are universally accessible, and that care work is also publicly supported. People are less dependent on paid labour for their welfare, while the markets of welfare services function as 'quasi-markets', in which state intervention and funding continue to be decisive but state monopolies in service provision are minimised. Defamilialisation and decommodification are favourable to Independent Living, but the movement has also encountered strong resistance from the powerful trade unions underpinning social democratic polity. The unions have opposed the labour market flexibilisation and the quasi-marketisation presupposed by direct payments and personal assistance schemes favoured by Independent Living advocates. In conceptual terms though, social democracy has been in agreement with Independent Living's promotion of independence, especially considering its grounding in specific relations of *inter*dependence: '*Homo socialdemocraticus* is … a believer in individual, personal empowerment. Collectivism is not pursued for its own sake, but in order to bring out the utmost in each and every individual soul' (Esping-Andersen, 1999: 171; see also Esping-Andersen, 1990: 47).[4]

As explained in Chapter 1, in the 1970s and the 1980s, the Independent Living ideas were introduced in Europe by disabled people who sought community-based alternatives to institutional care. Initially, they found fertile ground in Sweden and the UK – that is, in the context of a social democratic and a borderline-liberal welfare regime.[5] The combination of socialist and liberal elements characterising these regime types must have resonated with the Independent Living paradigm. By the 1980s, large residential institutions had already been closed in Sweden, although they had been substituted by group homes and cluster housing (Westberg, 2010: 18). Ratzka (1996) recounts the 'apparent paradox' that, on the one hand, disabled Swedes at the time had a relatively good standard of living due to being cared for by publicly funded structures and functions, but on the other hand, they lacked opportunities to make choices and be in control of their lives, and their social standing was poor. The paradox disappears when realising that widespread publicly supported measures such as clustered housing have been institutional in character – they may have kept people fed and warm, but they have also prevented the residents' self-determination:

> Among the shortcomings specific to the [clustered housing] solution, as cited by residents, is that services are based on the 'house arrest principle', i.e. they are not available outside the apartment, at work, about town or when travelling. … With time many residents have learned to assess the probabilities of receiving assistance for various tasks at a given time of the day and week and to adjust their needs to the staff's schedule. (Ratzka, 1996)

Clustered houses have been partially crowded out after the adoption of the Swedish Act Concerning Support and Services for Persons with Certain Functional Impairments (abbreviated in Swedish as LSS) of 1993 (Westberg, 2010: 18; an overview of LSS is also provided by Altermark, 2018: 91), which was pioneering legislation on direct payments for personal assistance – a key prerequisite for Independent Living, as will be explained in Chapter 6. Notably, LSS was adopted during a brief period of right-wing government in Sweden (1991–1994). Ratzka (1993; see also Brennan *et al.*, 2016: 6) recounts how in the preceding decade, right-wing Swedish politicians had been more sympathetic to disabled people's demands for direct payments than left-wing ones:

> The conservative parties who had been propagating 'freedom of choice under own responsibility' for decades embraced [our demands] wholeheartedly. The Social-democratic and Communist parties, both at that time in the government, reacted mainly negatively interpreting the demand for alternative solutions as a right-wing attack on the public sector.

In the UK, the disabled people's campaigning for deinstitutionalisation and direct payments for personal assistance contributed to the passing of the Community Care (Direct Payments) Act 1996. This legislation was supported by the then Conservative government because it advanced its efforts to minimise the 'nanny state' by developing public service markets – a strategy already codified in the NHS and Community Care Act 1990. Thus, the fight of the Independent Living activists against professional power in both the Swedish (social democratic) and the British (borderline-liberal) welfare regimes seems to have been enabled by its convergence with the (neo)liberal project of undermining state intervention through market mechanisms. Arguably, a right-wing political opening loosened the grip of the juridical–administrative–therapeutic state apparatus and enabled Independent Living advocacy to achieve a policy impact. Ironically, such an opening was co-created by the progressive social movements (including the Independent Living movement), themselves enabled by the embattled welfare state. However, as will be argued in Chapter 4, the convergence between Independent Living and neoliberalism has been only partial.

As far as the conservative welfare regime is concerned, in it decommodification is unevenly distributed because benefits are differentiated by occupation and family status, while defamilialisation is strategically undermined. The state provision is regulated by tripartite (corporatist) arrangements between the state, the trade unions, and the employers. Accordingly, public support is oriented towards preserving occupation-based, traditional status differentials and is based on social insurance, religious institutions are strong and influential, and the state uses various mechanisms to encourage traditional families in which women do the care work without compensation. Strong familialism and rigid labour market regulation undermine Independent Living policies, while social insurance-based welfare limits the access of many disabled people to formal supports. For their part, corporatist structures make it difficult for Independent Living reformers to have their voices heard in the policy-making arena. Notably, conservatism and corporatism are strongly affiliated:

> The unifying principles of corporatism are a fraternity based on status identity, obligatory and exclusive membership, mutualism, and monopoly of representation. Carried over into modern capitalism, corporatism was typically built around occupational groupings seeking to uphold traditionally recognized status distinctions and used these as the organizational nexus for society and economy. (Esping-Andersen, 1990: 60)

Indeed, family-based support has advantages over institutional care, but it also has gender implications impacting women and, moreover, tends to restrict the self-determination of disabled people through 'institutionalisation at home' (see Chapter 5). Therefore, both conservatism and corporatism have been hostile to the Independent Living paradigm due to their paternalism, support for traditional authority and hierarchies, and restrictive approach to political representation. Quasi-corporate decision making in disability policy has maintained the status quo of medicalisation, segregation, and institutional care by prioritising big, consensus-oriented, diagnosis-based disability organisations, while marginalising smaller, conflict-oriented organisations such as those supporting Independent Living policies and ideas (Mladenov, 2018: 94). The relationship between the Independent Living movement and the conservative welfare regime will be explored further in Chapter 5, where I will consider the role of the family, familialism, and paternalist care.

Social policy analysts have suggested other regime types such as the 'Mediterranean welfare state' (Gal, 2010), which resembles the conservative model but has a stronger emphasis on religion and the family as organising principles of social welfare; and the 'postsocialist welfare state' (Aidukaite, 2009), where the legacy of state socialism has combined with postsocialist neoliberalisation to create a unique set of features (Mladenov, 2018). I accept Esping-Andersen's (1999: 93–94) argument that it makes sense to consider the Mediterranean regime as a subtype of the more general conservative regime type, even if the former is more strongly familialistic. However, state socialism and postsocialism deserve separate treatment since they have not been discussed by Esping-Andersen, and because they reveal important aspects of state intervention and biopower.[6] During state socialism, the state played a very active role in shaping its subjects' welfare, and postsocialism has retained some of the worst elements of this approach, combining them with 'shock-therapeutic' neoliberalisation.

Independent Living and state socialist states

Postsocialist disability studies scholars have emphasised path dependency in their analyses by regarding state socialist legacies as a central (although certainly not the only) factor in developing disability policies in the countries of Central and Eastern Europe and the Former Soviet Union (Mladenov, 2018; Phillips, 2010; Rasell and Iarskaia-Smirnova, 2014). Therefore, understanding postsocialist disablement requires understanding state socialist approaches to disability. The analysis of state socialist welfare in the former Eastern Bloc countries could also help understand disablement in current socialist states such as China, as well as in some capitalist welfare regimes such as those in Eastern Asia (Holliday, 2000).

The form of the welfare state developed by the state socialist regime significantly suppressed disabled people's self-determination. Its medical–productivist systems for conceptualising, assessing, and treating disability monopolised the interpretation of disabled people's needs and elevated institutional care to a major instrument of disability policy (Mladenov, 2018). Medicalisation amounts to rendering human being in biomedical terms, while productivism denotes overvaluation of paid employment as a 'standard-bearer of moral meaning' (Giddens, 1994: 175). Indeed, state socialism partially decommodified and defamilialised its citizens' welfare through universal and comprehensive public provision resembling the provision in the Nordic social democratic countries. However, the state socialist regime also transformed paid work into a passport to citizenship, mimicking the insurance-based social policy approach of the conservative regimes. The creation of quasi-markets was ideologically blocked, and the state retained a virtual monopoly over service provision in the area of social care. Another difference with the social democratic mixture of liberalism and socialism that suppressed Independent Living ideas in state socialist countries was that individual independence was regarded with utmost suspicion and attempts at self-determination have been violently suppressed (Phillips, 2009).

Esping-Andersen (1990, 1999) limited the scope of his analysis to 'advanced' capitalist countries, but an older classification developed by Richard Titmuss (1974) provides some clues about identifying the general characteristics of social welfare under state socialism. Titmuss (1974: 31) conceptualised the socialist welfare state as following an 'industrial achievement-performance model' of social policy. In it, institutions of social support are regarded as 'adjuncts of the economy', the guiding principle being that 'social needs should be met on the basis of merit, work performance and productivity' (Titmuss, 1974: 31). Accordingly, social policy is summoned to enhance production by making and keeping people work-ready. Those deemed as lacking in productive capacity such as disabled people are entitled to support, but it is conditional on their inability to work rather than on substantive considerations such as social justice.[7]

I will note in passing that Titmuss's 'industrial achievement-performance model' matches the features identified by Ian Holliday (2000) in his analysis of East Asian welfare states, also regarded by Holliday as 'productivist'. According to Holliday (2000: 708), in Japan, Hong Kong, Singapore, South Korea, and Taiwan 'social policy is strictly subordinate to the overriding policy objective of economic growth. Everything else flows from this: minimal social rights with extensions linked to productive activity, reinforcement of the position of productive elements in society, and state–market–family relationships directed towards growth.'

Titmuss's (1974) classification suggests that (similar in part to their conservative capitalist rivals) state socialist countries developed 'workfare' rather than 'welfare' states, in which access to public support 'was a reward for work, not a right earned by citizenship' (Szelényi, 2009: 614).[8] Accordingly, the care that state socialist welfare systems provided to disabled people was strongly oriented towards re/insertion of disabled people into employment – the state socialist social policy was 'summoned to enhance production by making and keeping people work-ready' (Mladenov, 2018: 7). The productivism of this system was bolstered by enhanced medicalisation and by a strong emphasis on institutional care, seen as rational and efficient ways to manage support that 'frees' women for industrial labour:

> Soon there will be boarding houses for the aged, handicapped and chronically ill in every district; their capacity will depend on the character of the inhabited place. Every district will have effective welfare establishments with a great capacity, permitting a more rational use of investments and more effective servicing, the concentration of certain processes and the introduction of modern technology and apparatuses. (Golemanov and Popov, 1976: 33)

It should be noted that the *communist* ideal has been in tension with work-based distribution and its underpinning productivism. Communism requires the opposite – universalisation of need-based distribution, as suggested by Marx (1978: 531) in the formula 'from each according to his ability, to each according to his needs'. This ideal also presupposes a non-instrumental approach to work, in which 'labour has become not only a means of life but life's prime want' (Marx, 1978: 531). Theoretically, the contradiction between the socialist reality and the communist ideal was resolved by historicising it. Drawing on Marx, Lenin (1964: 472, original emphases; see also Negri, 2014: 234–245) presented working for a wage as an objective necessity and a transitory (socialist) phase of continuing duress in the progression towards communism:

> This [continuation of the 'bourgeois laws' by distributing resources according to labour contribution rather than according to need] is a 'defect', says Marx, but it is unavoidable in the first phase of communism; for if we are not to indulge in utopianism, we must not think that having overthrown capitalism people will at once learn to work for society *without any rules of law*. Besides, the abolition of capitalism *does not immediately create* the economic prerequisites for *such* a change.

Ideologically, the contradiction between the objective necessity of work-based distribution and the ideal of a need-based one was addressed by making recourse to productivist morality. Accordingly, labourers were summoned to adopt a 'socialist attitude to work' in which work was supposed to increasingly become a matter 'of honour, of glory and of heroism' (Antov, 1950: 85). An attempt was made to forge a version of the Protestant work ethic fit for the socialist reality. However, it would be neoliberal capitalism that would eventually make people internalise the value of work as 'honour, glory and heroism' to a much greater extent than state socialism, where these pronouncements remained little more than ideological clichés (see Popova, 2011). In Chapter 4, this mechanism will be discussed in terms of 'psychopower' (Han, 2017; Stiegler, 2010).

To return to state socialism, the enhanced public investment in institutional care cemented the power of caring professionals, who were 'trained to recommend residential care as the most appropriate form of support for disabled adults and children' (Rasell and Iarskaia-Smirnova, 2014: 6). This form of biopower ossified in institutionalisation mindsets and paternalist approaches to care that are still felt by disabled people and their families residing in the region, more than three decades after the fall of the state socialist regime: 'Even in the hospital, when they assigned this diagnosis, we were told: Leave her [in an institution], you will give birth to another child' (testimony of a Bulgarian mother, reported in Mladenov and Dimitrova, 2023: 1155).

As in the West, the cultures and practices in state socialist residential care facilities corresponded to Goffman's (1974) 'total institutions' by subjecting residents to surveillance, control, depersonalisation, block treatment, and rigid routines (Tobis, 2000: 11). However, due to widespread repression of civil society organising, coupled with state capture of disability organisations, Independent Living initiatives emerged in these countries only after the fall of state socialism: 'Rigid antiliberalism banned all forms of citizen's participation, grass-root movements, spontaneous associations as well as initiatives of individuals or of small groups' (Ferge, 1997: 163). As a result, grassroots forms of collective organising and protest became nearly impossible, as the violent suppression of the Hungarian Revolution of 1956 and the Prague Spring of 1968 testify. In particular, the strong socialist state prevented the emergence of transformative disability activism, although the institutional nature of its welfare provision required precisely the type of critique voiced by the Independent Living activists in the West.

Independent Living and postsocialist states

The first Centres for Independent Living emerged in the postsocialist regions of Central and Eastern Europe (CEE) in the 1990s. Prominent examples include the Centre for Independent Living–Sofia in Bulgaria (cil.bg), co-founded by Kapka Panayotova in 1995; the Centre for Independent Living Serbia (www.cilsrbija.org), co-founded by Gordana Rajkov in 1996; and the Slovenian organisation YHD–Association for the Theory and Culture of Handicap (yhd-drustvo.si), co-founded in 1996 by Elena Pečarič and Klaudija Poropat. Notably, these organisations are currently full members of ENIL, and their leaders and collaborators have regularly participated in

ENIL's Freedom Drive and supported the initiative (see Chapter 2). Gordana Rajkov and Kapka Panayotova (who both passed away recently – Kapka in 2021 and Gordana in 2022) have also been involved in ENIL's governance – Gordana was a member of ENIL's Advisory Board, and Kapka was a member of the Board of Directors and served as ENIL's president for a decade, until 2019. I have already discussed my links with the Centre for Independent Living–Sofia in the Introduction, and this book is dedicated to Kapka.

In the decades following the 1990s, the Independent Living activists consolidated their standing as the most critical voices of the disabled people's movement in the postsocialist region. In some cases, such as the Bulgarian one (Mladenov, 2018), this criticality eventually led to a chronic underfunding and isolation from mainstream disability policy making. Notwithstanding the partial successes with personal assistance programmes and other disability rights campaigns (Mladenov, 2017b; Ružičić-Novković, 2020; Zaviršek and Fischbach, 2023), the Independent Living movement has been largely unable to fully capitalise on postsocialist democratisation, liberalisation, and critique of the state (as it did in Western Europe). The substitution of paternalist with egalitarian care turned out to be extremely difficult and prone to frequent setbacks, as recent reports testify:

> In Slovenia, the progressive ideas of independent living and the rights of persons with disabilities are partially transformed into a repetition of the old-fashioned, family-based, patronising welfare system (with mostly parents becoming personal assistants), while in Serbia the ideas of independent living are still in their infancy and the implementation remains at the level of individual projects. (Zaviršek and Fischbach, 2023: 110)

In the early stages of the postsocialist transformations (1990s and 2000s), instead of being redirected from institutional care to community-based services, public funding was merely reduced, following the 'shock-therapeutic' manner of imposing liberal reforms in the postsocialist countries (Murrell, 1993). As a result, institutional care deteriorated, leaving residents in squalid conditions and without viable alternatives. Insider accounts of life in residential institutions during this period often amount to horror stories – consider, for example, this description taken from the landmark case of *Stanev v. Bulgaria* that depicts the conditions in a Bulgarian institution for people with intellectual and psychosocial impairments in the 2000s:

> The buildings did not have running water. The residents washed in cold water in the yard and were often unshaven and dirty. The bathroom, to which they had access once a week, was rudimentary and dilapidated. ... The toilets, likewise located in the yard, consisted of decrepit shelters with holes dug in the ground. They were in an execrable state and access to them

> was dangerous. Furthermore, basic toiletries were rarely available. (*Stanev v. Bulgaria*, no. 36760/06, §20, ECHR, 2012)

Rusi Stanev, the applicant in the case, was placed in this institution against his will, on the basis of unreformed guardianship legislation – another element of the state socialist legacy that has continued to shape disability policy under postsocialism, creating disablement. The institution where Stanev involuntarily spent many years of his life was located in an isolated mountainous region, 8 km from the nearest village and some 400 km from Stanev's hometown. In Chapter 4, I will discuss the ways in which neoliberalisation transformed biopower into psychopower, which included the transformation of state socialist biopower into postsocialist psychopower. However, the grim realities of institutional care in the CEE region are sometimes better captured by concepts referencing 'sovereign power' such as 'thanatopower'.

The strong link between the power of administering life (biopower) and the power of administering death (thanatopower) has been most prominently made in the work of Giorgio Agamben (1998), who has argued that Nazi concentration camps have revealed the true thanatopolitical face of biopolitics (for a discussion, see Tierney, 2016). This radical perspective suggests that every biopolitics is essentially thanatopolitics, not least because enhancing the life of some entails decisions about letting or making others die (Nasir, 2017). In times of emergency such as the one created by the recent COVID-19 pandemic, the biopolitical principle of enhancing life tends to shift towards the thanatopolitical principle of letting or making die in practices that concern the life and health of those disabled people considered particularly frail (Davis, 2021; Mladenov and Brennan, 2021). This process is conditioned by an ontological invalidation of disabled people (Hughes, 2007), whose expression in disability policies is the overwhelming focus on disabled people's individual vulnerability. This focus has disastrous effects when disabled people are subjected to utilitarian calculations, as productivist welfare regimes tend to do.

For many disabled people residing in CEE, postsocialist neoliberalisation created a state of emergency similar to the one created globally by the COVID-19 pandemic. Neoliberal reforms more or less gradually retrenched public support systems inherited from state socialism. Decommodification and defamilialisation declined, resulting in a retraditionalisation of CEE societies (discussed further in Chapter 5). People were left to cope on their own, and self-sufficiency became a cultural and political norm. Accordingly, there was no appetite for development of quasi-markets – instead, postsocialist reformers favoured radical marketisation (Ferge, 1997: 168). Independent Living initiatives, made possible by democratisation and the initial resurgence of civil society in the 1990s and 2000s, had to face the material and cultural barriers resulting from this toxic combination of state socialist legacies and postsocialist neoliberalisation. Biopower cast its thanatopolitical shadow over most disabled people, but those confined in residential institutions found themselves abandoned in its darkest corner:

> In one [postsocialist] European country, a recent investigation conducted by a non-governmental organisation with the Prosecutor's Office revealed that 238 children died in institutional care in a ten-year period. According to the report, 31 children died of starvation through systematic malnutrition, 84 from neglect, 13 due to poor hygiene, six in accidents such as hypothermia, drowning or suffocation, 36 died because they were bedridden and two deaths were caused by violence. It was also found that violence, binding and treatment with harmful drugs were widespread in institutions for children. (EEG, 2012: 43)

Indeed, since the late 2000s, deinstitutionalisation reforms have progressed in many postsocialist countries in Europe, supported by the EU through its Structural Funds. However, the results on the ground have been uneven and mostly reinstitutionalising, as will be argued in detail in Chapter 6. Countries such as the Czech Republic, Bulgaria, Hungary, Romania, Latvia, Lithuania, and Slovakia have used domestic and EU funds to maintain and renovate institutional settings or to build new, smaller institutions (Parker and Bulic Cojocariu, 2016).

As functions of paternalist care, institutional cultures and practices in the postsocialist region have been remarkably resistant to change. Both the old and the new institutions have been characterised by geographical isolation, prison-like confinement (including restrictions on freedom of movement), group treatment of the residents, deprivation of personal space and possessions, restrictions on everyday choices (e.g., regarding food, clothing, and relationships), lack of control over everyday routines, constant surveillance, restrictions on personal communication with the outside world, lack of control over medication and overmedication, medicalisation (e.g., people being deprived of liberty solely on the basis of their medical diagnosis as recorded on paper, without being spoken to or seen), confinement for indefinite periods of time (that may amount to years or even decades), and lack of alternative support in the community. There have also been reports of physical violence:

> On the male chronic ward, the delegation received allegations of orderlies slapping, punching and kicking patients; also, of orderlies carrying sticks and occasionally beating patients with them (a wooden stick matching the description given was found in the staff room on the ward). Furthermore, a patient complained that after being mechanically restrained with four-point fixation, he had been beaten by an orderly with a restraint belt. (Council of Europe, 2020: 12; for an analysis see Dimitrova and Mladenov, 2023)

In the final analysis, postsocialist Independent Living activists found themselves stuck on the opposite side of Simon Brisenden's fantasy of reversing professional power quoted at the beginning of this chapter. Paternalist care has been the norm, and the juridical–administrative–therapeutic state has effectively conspired with the market to control, devalue, neglect, and abuse disabled people. The successes of postsocialist Independent Living activists have been patchy and unsustainable. Their struggles for epistemic justice have been vocal and heroic, but frequently sabotaged by big disability organisations and undermined by service providers.

Concluding remarks

In this chapter, I discussed the relationships between Independent Living and the state. I conceptualised Independent Living as a critique of professional power that challenged the juridical–administrative–therapeutic state apparatus and associated epistemic injustices. As such, Independent Living has converged with other critical positions of the second half of the twentieth century, including critiques of biopower, anti-psychiatry, critiques of medicalisation, sociologies of 'total institutions', and radical/critical social work.

The concept and practices of care have been appropriated by the juridical–administrative–therapeutic state as part of the transformation of sovereign power into biopower. Independent Living activists and thinkers have criticised the discourse of care, yet without denying *inter*dependence or affirming self-sufficiency. This has created both tensions and affinities between the feminist ethics of care and the Independent Living paradigm. Affinities have also been facilitated by the potential of the ethics of care to challenge productivism and justify the substitution of the work-based allocation with a need-based one. Independent Living and the ethics of care could meet conceptually and practically on a terrain that I identified as egalitarian care (as opposed to paternalist care), but the politics of need interpretation would still remain a concern – egalitarian care cannot fully transcend biopower.

In the second part of the chapter, I discussed different welfare regimes and their interaction with the Independent Living paradigm. The Independent Living movement could usefully be contextualised by linking its successes and failures to the features of the dominant welfare regime in which advocacy is deployed. Historical analysis suggests that liberal, borderline-liberal, and social democratic regimes have been most hospitable to Independent Living, while conservative regimes have been more resistive to the ideas and policies promoted by the activists. Although the movement emerged in a liberal regime, it found a fertile ground in social democracy, aided by the latter's embrace of a mixture of liberal and socialist ideas and policies.

State socialist welfare was inimical to Independent Living due to its strong productivism, ubiquitous medicalisation of disability, resolute embrace of institutional care, and heavy suppression of civil society. Postsocialist welfare states inherited most of these mechanisms of disablement (sometimes with thanatopolitical consequences) and although Independent Living initiatives emerged in Eastern Europe in the 1990s, their room for manoeuvre has been limited. Such limitations have been imposed as much by state socialist legacies as by the radical undermining of the welfare state that characterised postsocialist neoliberalisation. At the beginning of this chapter, I made the point that the critiques of professional power voiced by the progressive social movements since the 1970s have been not only a reaction to, but also a product of biopower. Conversely, the market can be as averse to Independent Living as the welfare state. This argument will be developed in the next chapter.

Notes

1 A kindred contradiction associated with the welfare state is between de/commodification and profit-making – decommodification supresses profits, while extreme commodification makes capitalism unstable and, ultimately, may destroy it: 'In *The Great Transformation*, Polanyi (1944) identifies a fundamental contradiction in laissez-faire capitalism's drive to commodify labor power completely. While the system itself can only evolve by commodifying labor, by doing so it also sows the seeds of its own self-destruction: if labor power is nothing more than a commodity, it will likely destruct' (Esping-Andersen, 1990: 36). Decommodification is therefore necessary for the system's very survival. This contradiction is also thematised by Fraser (2022) in her analyses of the 'background conditions' of capitalism that shows that society cannot be fully commodified.

2 I have applied Heidegger's existential phenomenology to disablement in Mladenov (2015a). See also Abrams (2016).

3 Esping-Andersen (1999: 51) points out that defamilialisation policy 'seeks to unburden the household and diminish individuals' welfare dependence on kinship'. However, as Mathieu (2016: 580) notes, 'the concept of defamilialization is in practice used to document the degree of independence that mothers – more so than individuals or families – enjoy from the necessity of performing unpaid care work'. Therefore, the lack of gender reference in analyses of defamilialisation has been regarded by feminist scholars as problematic. It shifts attention away from what happens *within* families, as well as from the ways in which different policies promote different gender roles (or gender inequalities) (Daly, 2022: 318). This means that the focus on the family (and, by extension, defamilialisation) may distract from a more in-depth and comprehensive analysis of gender since 'the family is not the foundation of gender relations' (Walby,

2020: 426). In my analysis of the relationships between Independent Living and the family in Chapter 5, I take these criticisms into account by combining an analysis of defamilialisation with a discussion of gender equity.

4 Following this logic, Esping-Andersen (1990: 28, emphasis added) sometimes goes as far as defining social democracy as a mixture of liberalism and socialism: 'The social democratic regime's policy of emancipation addresses both the market and the traditional family. In contrast to the corporatist-subsidiarity model, the principle is not to wait until the family's capacity to aid is exhausted, but to preemptively socialize the costs of familyhood. The ideal is not to maximize dependence on the family, but capacities for individual independence. In this sense, the model is *a peculiar fusion of liberalism and socialism*. The result is a welfare state that grants transfers directly to children, and takes direct responsibility of caring for children, the aged, and the helpless [sic]. It is, accordingly, committed to a heavy social-service burden, not only to service family needs, but also to allow women to choose work rather than the household.'

5 Esping-Andersen (1990: 52) characterised the UK as constituting a liberal welfare regime in 1980, but he estimated Britain's decommodification score to be the highest among the six states in the liberal cluster. Moreover, 'Britain scored in the top de-commodification group in 1950: the universalist social citizenship of the Beveridge model that was launched after the war placed Britain as the highest scoring nation internationally. The system certainly was not undone by the 1980s, but it failed to progress further' (Esping-Andersen, 1990: 53–54). In Esping-Andersen's (1990: 74) analysis of stratification effects, the UK scores in the low-middle section in terms of its liberalism (measured by the degree of means testing and private welfare), which also evidences the UK's borderline standing in 1980. In the analysis of the public–private mix, the UK is regarded as a 'mixed case' between public and private provision (Esping-Andersen, 1990: 87). In his 1999 book, Esping-Andersen (1999: 75) characterised Britain and Australia as countries where 'the welfare state is more comprehensive and collectivist' that in the United States due to their stronger labour movements – a kind of a 'liberal-labour' model (the term is borrowed by Esping-Andersen from Francis Castles). Hence my characterisation of the UK welfare state as borderline-liberal during the 1970s and 1980s – in contrast, the US and Canada can be regarded as more straightforward examples of 'liberal hegemony' (Esping-Andersen, 1990: 54).

6 On state socialism, Esping-Anderson (1990: 14) points out that its different mode of production (in which the means of production are socialised) does not mean that it lacks a welfare state: 'Eastern Europe may perhaps not qualify as socialist, but neither is it capitalist. Yet there we find "welfare states", too.'

7 Titmuss (1974) identified two other models of social policy in his overview of actually existing welfare regimes at the time. His 'residual welfare model' overlaps with Esping-Andersen's (1990, 1999) liberal regime, and his 'institutional redistributive model' overlaps with Esping-Andersen's social democratic regime.

8 Conservative regimes have embraced productivist morality as a main vehicle for promoting social integration and for preserving traditional authority and hierarchy: 'When Bismarck and von Taaffe pioneered modern social insurance, they were in fact following the lead of Napoleon III in France. But Bismarck wanted to go further, and even contemplated legislating the right (or obligation, if you wish) to employment as part and parcel of his larger vision of *Sodaten der Arbeit*: workers as soldiers in an economy functioning like the army' (Esping-Andersen, 1990: 40).

4

Independent Living and the market

This chapter considers the convergences and divergences between market principles – choice, individualism, self-sufficiency, competition, deregulation, entrepreneurship – and the Independent Living paradigm. In the public policy of the last 50 years or so, the advocacy for marketisation has been most clearly and radically expressed in the political ideology of neoliberalism. Since this period coincides with the rise of the Independent Living movement and analytic paradigm, the main concern of this chapter will be to untangle the relationships between Independent Living and neoliberal marketisation. That said, neoliberalism has a longer history, which could be traced back to the work of the Austrian economist Ludwig von Mises in the 1920s, who criticised socialist planned economy and defended a return to classical liberalism. Eventually, Friedrich Hayek (2001), a close associate of von Mises, became the most influential proponent of this radicalised version of classical liberalism (Gamble, 1996).

Hayek's (2001) seminal book *The Road to Serfdom*, first published in 1944, became a key reference for neoliberal thought, but neoliberalism gained political traction only in the 1970s, with the establishment of Augusto Pinochet's regime in Chile. Neoliberal reforms spread to Western Europe and North America towards the end of the 1970s and the beginning of the 1980s, when the neoconservatives led by Margaret Thatcher in Britain and Ronald Reagan in the United States came to power, marking the end of the 'golden age' of the welfare state. Neoliberalisation was further bolstered in the 1990s by the disintegration of state socialism in CEE and the Soviet Union, followed by its 'shock-therapeutic' substitution by free-market capitalism (Dale, 2011). Since then, neoliberalism has become hegemonic throughout the world, promoted by international institutions such as the World Bank and the International Monetary Fund. In his seminal history of this ideology, David Harvey (2005: 2) has defined it as

> a theory of political economic practices that proposes that human well-being can best be advanced by liberating individual entrepreneurial freedoms and

> skills within an institutional framework characterized by strong private property rights, free markets, and free trade. The role of the state is to create and preserve an institutional framework appropriate to such practices. ... But beyond these tasks the state should not venture. State interventions in markets (once created) must be kept to a bare minimum.

This definition reflects a key difference between neoliberalism and classical liberalism – in the neoliberal approach, the state actively creates and maintains markets, whereas classical liberalism would abstain from such a radical promotion of marketisation: 'neoliberals deviate from laissez-faire economics in mobilizing law and policy to support the market and shape social goals' (Brown, 2006: 700). Accordingly, neoliberal marketisation tends to encompass areas that would be regarded by many liberals as separate from the market – including education, healthcare, social care, households, and public administration. As explained by Davies (2014), 'this may be so as to bring them inside the market, through acts of privatization; or to reinvent them in a "market-like" way; or simply to neutralize or disband them'. Part of this work of radical marketisation has been to minimise supportive social policy interventions (although not punitive ones), but neoliberal reforms have also transformed people's very selves by mobilising 'psychopower' (Stiegler, 2010) or making recourse to 'psychopolitical' mechanisms of control (Han, 2017).

As pointed out in Chapter 3, in his early critique of the Independent Living movement, Gareth Williams (1983: 1004) disapprovingly characterised it as reflecting a commitment to American-style capitalism and free-market ideology. Indeed, pioneering Independent Living legislation in Europe was adopted in the 1990s under right-wing governments that sought to restructure and/or retrench the welfare state. Accordingly, trade unions have, as a rule, been suspicious of the demands of Independent Living activists for direct payments instead of service in kind, perceiving them as a form of 'creeping marketisation': 'direct payments broke with public welfare traditions in two key ways: first, by offering cash payments in lieu of traditional services for those eligible to receive community care; second, by placing the recipient in control of the human and financial resources allocated for support' (Priestley *et al.*, 2010: 308).

Neoliberals were in agreement with Independent Living advocates that institutions for social care should be closed. Roulstone and Prideaux (2012: 46), for example, point out that neoliberal politicians in the UK perceived institutions as disabling, as providing poor value for money, as limiting people's freedom, and as state interference in private lives. Ben-Moshe (2020: 59) similarly notes that Ronald Reagan supported the closure of large institutions and psychiatric hospitals when he was governor of California and, later, president of the US. However, unlike disability activists, neoliberals favoured privatised and/or informal care, promoting the role of the open market and/or the family in supporting disabled people as cost-cutting alternatives to institutionalisation in large settings (Roulstone and Prideaux, 2012: 50). Thus, the neoliberal retrenchment of large institutions cannot be regarded as genuine deinstitutionalisation because it did not support public funding for the development of community-based alternatives.

This brief overview of neoliberalism already suggests that the deconstruction of the juridical–administrative–therapeutic state, realised by the critique of professional power of the Independent Living advocates and other emancipatory movements and analytical efforts since the 1960s and 1970s, converged only *partially* with the market-promoting and familialist neoliberal critique of the 'nanny state'. I will first discuss the impact of neoliberalisation on the welfare regimes outlined in Chapter 3. I will then contextualise these changes by positioning them within the broader historical transition from biopower to psychopower. The analysis of psychopower would help avoid a pitfall in the critique of professional power and the juridical–administrative–therapeutic state eloquently identified by Altermark (2018: 14): 'Although more or less all research on intellectual disability is very critical of state power, in its lyricism of the cold monster, it fails to detect government when it is no longer cold and monstrous but increasingly dispersed and embedded in promises of freedom.'

Against this background, I will highlight some of the convergences between Independent Living and neoliberalism. However, my main objective will be to identify the ways in which Independent Living has not only diverged, but also provided grounds for criticising neoliberal marketisation. This argument is particularly important from a social justice perspective – dependence on the market increases social risks such as unemployment and poverty 'because survival itself is at the mercy of conditions over which individuals have little say; markets cannot guarantee an income, nor a job' (Esping-Andersen, 1999: 37). Moreover, radical marketisation can be conceptualised as a form of institutional confinement akin to the confinement in asylums and in the family. This is precisely the way in which Esping-Andersen (1990: 36, emphasis added) describes the impact of commodification on propertyless people who do not have access to public support: 'With no recourse to property, and no state to which human needs can be directed, *the market becomes to the worker a prison* within which it is imperative to behave as a commodity in order to survive.'

Neoliberal marketisation, welfare regimes, and Independent Living

Although the ideas of neoliberal reformers were first tested in practice in the context of a military dictatorship (Chile in the 1970s), they became globally salient only after substituting Keynesian economic steering in liberal (US) and borderline-liberal (UK) welfare regimes in the 1980s. There, the rise of neoliberalism expanded the reach of the already established market forces. As explained in Chapter 3, the liberal model renders social policy as a minor, means-tested mechanism for last-resort and temporary relief provided to the neediest – all others are expected to cope with social issues and satisfy their social and care needs privately, on the open market (Esping-Andersen, 1990: 26–27; Titmuss, 1974: 121). Building on this anti-welfarist foundation, neoliberal restructuring sought to minimise further social protections by reinforcing the stigma around 'welfare dependency', retrenching welfare budgets, and tightening eligibility criteria. As a result, liberal welfare regimes have become 'highly commodifying in many respects, and the state now enforces work (not just for the poor population and lower classes but other groups in society)' (Deeming, 2017: 416).

Although they did not advocate retrenchment, progressive mobilisations targeting biopower – including the Independent Living movement – have been unwitting enablers of this process of neoliberalisation. The very emergence of the concept of 'biopower' and the associated critique of disciplinary institutions (hospitals, asylums, schools, prisons) has coincided with the decline of the welfare state's 'golden age' in the liberal West. Nancy Fraser (2003) has historicised Foucault's work along these lines, proposing to read Foucault as a critic of the post-war welfare state, although Foucault himself did not identify as such – rather, he perceived his project as a critique of modernity. Foucault, argues Fraser (2003: 160), 'mapped the contours of the disciplinary society just as the ground was being cut out from under it'. More specifically, Foucault's criticisms of the welfare state 'taught us to see the dark underside of even its most vaunted achievements. Viewed through his eyes, social services became disciplinary apparatuses, humanist reforms became panoptical surveillance regimes, public health measures became deployments of biopower, and therapeutic practices became vehicles of subjection' (Fraser, 2003: 160).

As already pointed out in the preceding chapter, Bernard Stiegler (2010) reads Foucault's critique of biopower in a way that resembles Fraser's reading.[1] With the benefit of hindsight, it is possible to similarly historicise the Independent Living paradigm. It emerged amidst the welfarism of the late 1960s, anticipating and facilitating the deconstruction of the post-war welfare state, which gained political traction with the onset of neoliberal marketisation in the late 1970s to early 1980s.

However, the agreement between Independent Living and neoliberalism has rarely extended beyond critique of traditional authority and the superficial promotion of 'choice'. I argue that differences between the two paradigms have been more important than similarities, although they have sometimes remained implied rather than explicitly stated within Independent Living advocacy. Moreover, differences have become increasingly salient with the mainstreaming and entrenchment of neoliberal marketisation. They boil down to the fundamental tension between the neoliberal (and classical-liberal) promotion of self-sufficiency, and Independent Living's relational understanding of freedom-as-independence. Recall that the independence promoted by the Independent Living movement presupposes a specific kind of *inter*dependence encompassing publicly provided support, collective organising, and peer support. This goes against the grain of neoliberal self-sufficiency.

Indeed, some prominent European Independent Living activists have embraced the consumerist ideas of the American pioneers and have sought to mobilise the market in the fight against the authority of the juridical–administrative–therapeutic state. For example, Adolf Ratzka (2012: 3) has criticised state monopolies in service provision and has argued for their substitution with 'demand-driven markets' where disabled people receive direct payments to choose and purchase support from a variety of competing providers. And yet, such arguments have sought redirection rather than retrenchment of public support, accompanied by a shift in the role of authorities from 'providers' to 'purchasers' of services (Deeming, 2017: 414) – that is, accompanied by the promotion of quasi-market solutions: 'as statutory authorities switch to become purchasers rather than sole providers of services, so users become more vociferous in their demands for a voice in shaping these services, whoever they are purchased or provided by' (Oliver and Zarb, 1992: 7).

It should also be noted that the attitude towards marketisation among Independent Living supporters has not been univocal. Some have been concerned about the negative impact of marketisation on social justice (e.g., Elder-Woodward, 2016). Others have highlighted the risk that the profit imperative may reduce the quality of social services while increasing the incentives to institutionalise support:

> Especially in Serbia, private service providers for long-term support for older people have mushroomed since the introduction of measures for welfare pluralism in 2011. A report published by the European Commission states that the number of providers of residential care for older people in Serbia more than tripled from 2015 to 2018 … Moreover, despite the fact that private 'long-term care' homes accommodate far fewer residents per facility – in 2018, 48% of private facilities had capacity for 30 or fewer residents and only 18% had capacity for 50 or more residents – the living conditions in nursing homes in Serbia are poor due to the providers' profit orientation. (Zaviršek and Fischbach, 2023: 103)

In a survey on personal assistance that I conducted in 2018, personal assistance users and Independent Living advocates were asked to assess statements describing various characteristics of a typical personal assistance scheme (Mladenov, 2020b). Their task was to assess whether a given characteristic was an enabler or barrier to 'choice and control'. The survey contained the statement 'The [personal assistance] scheme promotes the creation of markets of assistance services where service providers compete to attract customers' (Mladenov, 2020b: 14). Of the 54 personal assistance users and Independent Living advocates who responded to the survey, 27 assessed the creation of markets as enabling of choice and control, 17 assessed it as a barrier, and 10 remained neutral (Mladenov, 2020b: 16).

Internal divisions about marketisation notwithstanding, Independent Living advocates have resolutely defended public support. For example, the British activist and scholar Jenny Morris (2011: 16) has summoned disability rights campaigners to 'start from an explicit and vigorous promotion of the welfare state and of the concept of social security in its broadest sense'. ENIL's advocacy can be taken as exemplary in this respect – while consistently criticising state-sanctioned institutionalisation of disabled people, the organisation has been active in campaigning against austerity since cuts to public supports intensified in the aftermath of the financial crisis of 2007/8 (e.g., ENIL, 2014: 7; 2020: 8). The recognition of the need to simultaneously criticise and promote the welfare state has been a core feature of the Independent Living movement.

Neoliberalisation has affected all welfare regimes, although this has happened unevenly, at varying paces, and to different degrees. Arguably, the most radical reforms were implemented in the 1990s in the postsocialist societies in CEE and the countries of the former Soviet Union along the lines of the already mentioned 'shock-therapeutic' imposition of marketisation measures that included wide-ranging privatisation and deregulation programmes (Dale, 2011; Murrell, 1993). Market mechanisms intended to stimulate competition, self-sufficiency, profit seeking, and consumer sovereignty have been introduced in key areas of postsocialist life, including social security and public assistance (Ferge, 1997).

As explained in Chapter 3, the postsocialist version of neoliberal marketisation did not enable the social policy changes sought by the Independent Living movement. The latter emerged in the CEE region soon after the disintegration of state socialism. However, in the first three decades following 1989, Independent Living activists in the region encountered the worst of both worlds. On the one hand, Independent Living advocacy was hindered by the lingering legacies of state socialist paternalism in the organisation and provision of disability support. On the other hand, Independent Living activism was obstructed by welfare cuts and overvaluation of self-sufficiency.

State socialist legacies resisted marketisation by seeking to maintain state or local authority control over the provision of public support (in both traditional and new residential institutions – see Chapter 6). For their part, the advocates of 'shock therapy' preferred the full-blown marketisation that entailed complete welfare state withdrawal. At least initially, neither supported the creation of quasi-markets in which the state continues to fund and regulate social support while delegating its provision to non-state actors or individuals, which (partly) explains why personal assistance through direct payments has been so slow to emerge in CEE countries: 'It has to be emphasised that the "quasi-market" solution widespread in England … implying that the state retains its financing and regulatory role and abandons service delivery, is seen with less favour [by CEE reformers] than genuine marketisation' (Ferge, 1997: 168).

In contrast, the willingness to create quasi-markets, especially under right-wing governments, may be one reason why social democratic or borderline-liberal regimes such as the ones in Sweden and the UK provided the best conditions for the spread of the Independent Living movement in Europe. However, neoliberal restructuring became an increasing threat to the movement when the re-commodification elements of neoliberalisation intensified in the 2000s, reaching a peak during the period of austerity following the 2007/8 financial crisis. Post-2008 austerity was less strongly felt in postsocialist countries for the bleak reason that in this region, austerity has been normalised since the early 1990s (which for many disabled people – and especially for those confined in institutions – amounted to experiencing a permanent state of emergency). However, Western European countries experienced acute declines in publicly provided support, including cuts of disability programmes (Ryan, 2019). The neoliberal undermining of social welfare has affected even ideal-typical social democratic states such as Sweden, where in the 2010s Independent Living activists had to fight hard against cuts to retain the rights won merely two decades before:

> Sweden has been at the forefront of advocating for and developing wide ranging rights to personal assistance in Europe since the 1980s and has served as an inspiration to other countries. Due to this, in our study of the implementation of Article 19 in three Nordic countries, we assumed that Sweden would be the 'star' country. Instead we found that since Sweden ratified the CRPD in 2008 many disabled people have lost their personal assistance at a state-level or had their first application rejected. (Brennan *et al.*, 2016: 12)

The Swedish case also evidences the role of the politics of need interpretation and epistemic injustice in neoliberal retrenchment. Disabled people with high support needs in Sweden have been provided with funding for personal assistance after being assessed as requiring support for the satisfaction of their 'basic needs' by the Swedish Social Insurance Agency under the LSS act of 1993. However, in the wake of post-2008 austerity, the

Social Insurance Agency started reinterpreting the meaning of 'basic needs', making the definition increasingly restrictive. These reinterpretations were grounded in decisions made by the Swedish courts, instead of being subjected to political decision making and/or co-produced with organisations of disabled people (Brennan *et al.*, 2016: 7–8; Norberg, 2022: 659). In other words, they have been monologically imposed on disabled people, generating epistemic injustices with clear material effects. As a result, many lost access to personal assistance for activities exceeding un/dressing, feeding, and personal hygiene, which severely restricted their opportunities to live independently (Brennan *et al.*, 2016).

Although in conservative regimes the established tripartite arrangements between the state, the trade unions, and the employers may have initially slowed down the neoliberal reforms (Buğra and Keyder, 2006), social partners have eventually been widely co-opted into promoting neoliberalisation (Kay, 2003). As will be argued in more detail in the next chapter, the conservative approach of keeping care unpaid, informal, feminised, and family-based has been in concert with the neoliberal version of familialism and has complemented neoliberal (re)commodification (Cooper, 2017). Both have hindered Independent Living advocacy.

The marketisation of subjectivity and productivism

A distinctive feature of neoliberalisation has been its targeting of the psyche, as opposed to the targeting of the body characteristic of biopower. In the apt formulation of Margaret Thatcher (1981: n.p.), 'economics are the method; the object is to change the heart and soul'. Put slightly differently, neoliberal rationality has sought to create an equivalence 'between a responsible and moral individual and an economic-rational individual' (Lemke, 2002: 59). Thus, under the banner of 'freedom', people have been nudged towards (but sometimes also coerced into, for example by way of workfare) internalising the injunctions to enhance themselves individually, self-sufficiently, and self-reliantly – that is, against all structural odds – by studying, working, self-caring, and consuming.

This entailed the proliferation of responsibilising discourses and practices. They have covered up or disregarded not only the foundational structures of *inter*dependence that enable individuals to act and be, but also the structural mechanisms oppressing people or hindering their self-determination. As pointed out by Nikolas Rose (1999: xxiii), neoliberal governmentality 'entails a twin process of autonomization plus responsibilization – opening free space for the choices of individual actors whilst enwrapping these autonomized actors within new forms of control'. This reflects a key contradiction of the neoliberal doctrine that simultaneously advocates freedom and promotes subjugation (Hall, 2011: 710). Below, I will discuss this contradiction as one of surface-level convergence but deep-level divergence between neoliberal marketisation and the Independent Living paradigm.

Of note here is that state socialism attempted its own version of 'governing the soul'. In concert with its productivism, the regime sought to create a new type of person, 'the Soviet man', modelled after the ideological cliché of the hyper-able and intrinsically motivated labourer (Mladenov, 2021a). Arguably, the failure to transform these injunctions into effective psychopolitics contributed to the disintegration of state socialism in Eastern Europe and the former Soviet Union at the end of the 1980s: 'the obsolete steel-per-head philosophy proved no match for the lure of the narcissistic culture of self-enhancement, self-enjoyment, instant gratification' (Outhwaite and Ray, 2005: 101, drawing on Bauman, 1992). In comparison to their increasingly neoliberal rivals in the West, state socialist societies became increasingly unsustainable and uncompetitive because they were unable, among other things, to soften coercion with consent (Verdery, 1995: 30). In a nutshell, state socialism failed to transform biopower into psychopower – a transformation that will be fully explained in the next section.

Since the 1990s, the consolidation of neoliberal psychopower across all welfare regimes has been aided by the new information and communication technologies, including the internet and proliferating mobile devices. On the everyday level, this meant enticing individuals to continuously externalise, quantify, compare, and self-monitor their lives, experiences, and relationships (Mladenov, 2020a; Moore and Robinson, 2016). Thus, neoliberal marketisation conspired with new technologies to construct subjects who have internalised market-based morality and rationality – in other words, subjects embracing their own economic subjugation:

> This aspect of neoliberalism also entails a host of policies that figure and produce citizens as individual entrepreneurs and consumers whose moral autonomy is measured by their capacity for 'self-care' – their ability to provide for their own needs and service their own ambitions, whether as welfare recipients, medical patients, consumers of pharmaceuticals, university students, or workers in ephemeral occupations. (Brown, 2006: 694)

The work of self-caring has resonated with the critiques of professional power discussed in Chapter 3 by further undermining the dominance of the caring professionals. When people take up the tasks of caring for themselves amidst a radically marketised society, they also tend to internalise self-regulating and self-exploiting. For their part, caring professionals have imperceptibly transmogrified into auditors – as explained by Fraser (2003: 168), 'substantive welfare policy gives way to formal technologies of economic accountability as auditors replace service professionals as the frontline disciplinarians'.

The marketisation of subjectivity has also entailed a transformation of productivism (Mladenov, 2017a). Esping-Andersen makes a suggestive distinction between the non-coercive productivism of social democracy and the overtly coercive productivism of liberal workfare:

> Scandinavian welfare and employment policy has always been couched in terms of 'productivism', that is of maximizing the productive potential of the citizenry. Superficially this seems like an echo of what Americans call 'workfare'. In reality the two are different. Workfare in America implies that social benefits are conditional on accepting work whereas Nordic 'productivism' implies that the welfare *state* must guarantee that all people have the necessary resources and motivation to work (and that work is available). (Esping-Andersen, 1999: 80, original emphasis; a similar distinction is made by Deeming, 2017: 413)

However, from a critical-theoretical perspective such a distinction is unconvincing – both forms of productivism create a pressure to engage in paid work, although with the non-coercive (social democratic) form this pressure may be more subtle. Still, work remains the 'standard-bearer of moral meaning' (Giddens, 1994: 175), as the gendered analysis of welfare suggests. This will be further explored in the discussion of the 'caregiver parity' model of gender equity in Chapter 5 – both the coercive and the non-coercive forms of productivism overvalue paid work and self-sufficiency while devaluing unpaid care, together with the diversity associated with impairments that diminish labour capacity.

Social democratic 'activation' has also been subjected to strong criticism by disability studies scholars. In his analysis of the exclusionary and disempowering effects of the policy of 'inclusion' on people with intellectual impairments in Sweden, Altermark (2018: 79) has argued that 'power may not only take the form of the brute clenching of freedom that dominated the history of institutionalisation; it can also operate by promoting a certain kind of freedom, in this case as "activation" and "independence"'. My analysis of the state socialist experience also suggests that productivity-oriented disability policies tend to cross the thin line separating enablement from coercion even when they are explicitly framed as supportive and benevolent. Thus, under the banner of labour (re)integration, state socialist disability assessment systems have coerced disabled people into employment (Mladenov, 2021a).

Neoliberalisation generated a comparable coercion by extending conditionality and enhancing sanctions for publicly supported people who fail to seek or find paid work. In this, ironically, neoliberal workfare reproduced some of the features of state socialist workfare (Chapter 3). At the same time, neoliberalism's targeting of the psyche also heralded the transition from 'societies of discipline' to 'societies of control' and from biopower to psychopower. Neoliberal reforms achieved this by building on the more subtle or non-coercive forms of productivism attributed by Esping-Andersen to the Scandinavian model and exposed by Altermark in his critique of the Swedish policy of 'inclusion'. As will be explained in detail in the next section, whereas the productivism of disciplinary societies was externally imposed, enclosed in the factory, centrally administered (most clearly in its state socialist variety), and rigid (characterised by full and secure employment), the productivism of societies of control has been internally imposed, let loose by way of networking and peer-to-peer communication, market-based or decentralised, and flexible (characterised by precarious, insecure employment) (Han, 2017).

Indeed, some early Independent Living activists have been strongly productivist, albeit in the non-coercive, social-democratic way. This is unsurprising, considering that for groups that have traditionally been excluded from the labour market – such as disabled people, women, and racialised people – access to paid work and the attendant 'commodification' can be profoundly emancipatory (Mathieu, 2016: 578). Productivism underpins universalisation of breadwinning that enables excluded people to work for a wage, thus making them less dependent on the family and the state for their welfare (Chapter 5). For example, UPIAS – the British disabled people's organisation that engendered the social model of disability – considered the most important form of support for disabled people to be support for (re)insertion into the labour market:

> Financial and other help is placed here in relation to the achievement of independence and integration into ordinary employment. This is the fundamental principle by which schemes for meeting the financial and other needs of disabled people can be judged. This means that for people of working age financial and other forms of help must above all be geared to the retention or achievement of integrated employment: dependence on the State must increasingly give way to the provision of help so that a living can be earned through employment. (UPIAS, 1976a: 15)

On this reading, genuine independence is achieved by way of earning a wage. It follows that public support should be oriented towards helping disabled adults with 'retention or achievement of integrated employment', and disabled children with 'their progressive integration into ordinary employment' (UPIAS, 1976a: 15). Subsequent disability scholarship has criticised this 'fundamental principle'. For example, Abberley (1998: 89) has pointed out that 'just because a main mechanism of [disabled people's] oppression is our exclusion from social production, we should be wary of drawing the conclusion that overcoming this oppression should involve our wholesale inclusion in it'. In their critique of the disability rights movement's 'masculinist ethic and idealiz[ation of] masculinist notions of autonomy', Hughes *et al.* (2005: 263–264) have been even more emphatic by stating that the 'transition from feudalism to capitalism may be a distant historical memory but it should not be forgotten that many disabled people are still fighting for the right to be wage slaves'.

Notably, non-coercive productivism has been a prominent feature of Marxism, as implied in the first part of the slogan 'from each according to his ability, to each according to his needs' (Marx, 1978: 531). Arguably, Marx considered the activity of labouring as constituting the very essence of human being (Abberley, 1998) – accordingly, the meaning of free time was reduced by Marx to enhancement of productivity (Han, 2017: 51). Similarly, the members of UPIAS considered exclusion from education, transportation, and housing as significant to the extent to which it leads to exclusion from the labour market:

> In the final analysis the particular form of poverty principally associated with physical impairment is caused by our exclusion from the ability to earn an income on a par with our able-bodied peers, due to the way employment is organised. This exclusion is linked with our exclusion from participating in the social activities and provisions that make general employment possible. For example, physically impaired school children are characteristically excluded from normal education preparatory to work, we are unable to achieve the same flexibility in using transport and finding suitable housing so as to live conveniently to our possible employment, and so on. (UPIAS, 1976a: 14)

In concert with its name and mission, UPIAS advanced a radical critique of the segregation of disabled people that, according to Finkelstein (2005), stemmed from his own struggle in the 1960s against apartheid in South Africa. It may seem that the critique of segregation strikes at the heart of disciplinary power, which is a power that isolates and confines – in disciplinary societies, 'the individual never ceases passing from one closed environment to another' (Deleuze, 1992: 3). However, by promoting mainstream factories as alternatives to segregated ones (UPIAS, 1976a: 19) – or to confinement of disabled people to residential institutions for social care – UPIAS substituted one form of enclosure with another. The factory has prison-like qualities shared with other disciplinary spaces of enclosure such as the hospital and the residential institution: 'at the sight of some laborers, the heroine of Rossellini's *Europa '51* could exclaim, "I thought I was seeing convicts"' (Deleuze, 1992: 3).

UPIAS (1976a: 15) also argued that support in the form of benefits 'which are not carefully related to the struggle for integrated employment and active social participation' engenders 'dependence on the State [that] must increasingly give way to the provision of help so that a living can be earned through employment'. This critique of 'welfare dependency' was iterated by other disability rights activists and scholars (see, for example, Oliver, 1996: 54). Such criticisms would eventually open up a space for the neoliberal retrenchment of the welfare state (Roulstone and Prideaux, 2012: 80–81). To promote work as the alternative to 'dependence on the state' of disabled people is a form of 'cruel optimism' (Dimitrova, 2019, drawing on Berlant, 2011). There may be people who are not able to work, but more importantly, work is a cruel vehicle of emancipation. This issue becomes central in the advocacy for Independent Living of people with intellectual impairments and older people. Conceptually, Independent Living is also at odds with productivism since it grounds independence in specific relations of *inter*dependence and criticises self-sufficiency.

From biopower to psychopower

Neoliberal 'self-caring' partly overlaps with, but also differs from, the 'caring of the self' and the attendant 'technologies of the self' conceptualised by Foucault (1988) in the final years of his life. I will return to this point later, when discussing the technologies of the self that have been mobilised within the Independent Living movement. Understood in the neoliberal sense of people's 'ability to provide for their own needs and service their own ambitions' (Brown, 2006: 694), 'self-caring' is part of the historical transformation of discipline into control (Deleuze, 1992), biopower into psychopower (Stiegler, 2010), and biopolitics into psychopolitics (Han, 2017).

Disciplinary societies and biopower have been analysed in considerable depth by Foucault (1978; 1991), but societies of control have received only marginal attention in his work. Han (2017: 23) points out that Foucault started exploring neoliberalisation in the late 1970s, but continued to frame the issues he observed in terms of biopolitics – a framing that, according to Han, was not appropriate for analysing the newly emerging societies of control that increasingly relied on psychopolitical mechanisms for governing their subjects. This leads to Han's (2017: 23, original emphasis) conclusion that Foucault 'failed to do what the circumstances actually called for: to make the turn to *psychopolitics*'. But such a 'failure' is understandable, considering the thinker's premature death in 1984, at the dawn of the transformation of discipline into cybernetic control. Societies of control, psychopower, and psychopolitics have been theorised in subsequent analyses influenced by Foucault such as those developed by Deleuze (1992), Stiegler (2010), and Han (2017). Below, I summarise their key arguments to help position Independent Living within this important historical transformation.

Disciplinary societies reached their heyday when the post-war welfare systems were consolidated in capitalist and state socialist countries. They enclosed their subjects in residential institutions, hospitals, schools, prisons, and factories (Deleuze, 1992: 3). Disciplining works by way of segregation, isolation, confinement, asceticism, and physical training. The main form of power in a disciplinary society is biopower, which is discontinuous and somatic, in the sense that it targets the body within closed systems of governance (Stiegler, 2010: 116). Biopower is orchestrated by publicly owned, managed, or regulated institutions – as discussed in Chapter 3, biopower is a function of the caring state. Its telos is to organise production by administering life – 'to compose a productive force within the dimension of space–time whose effect will be greater than the sum of its component forces' (Deleuze, 1992: 3). Accordingly, biopower renders labour as an essential human activity. Underpinned by industrial production, biopower is characterised by rigidity, long-term planning, and externally imposed exploitation or 'allo-exploitation' (Han, 2017: 5–6). In technological terms, this form of power is analogous and mechanical – it is associated with (and enabled by) engines and walls.

In contrast, societies of control have emerged with the rise of post-1970s neoliberal capitalism. They entangle their subjects in networks that transcend closed systems. Societies of control work by way of connection, free-floating stimulation, motivation, activation, self-disclosure, and psychological compulsion: 'the man of control is undulatory, in orbit, in a continuous network' (Deleuze, 1992: 6). The main form of power in a society of control is psychopower, which is continuous and cognitive, in the sense that it targets the psychic system (Stiegler, 2010: 13). Psychopower is orchestrated by deregulated industries and deterritorialised corporations – it is a function of the market. Its telos is to organise consumption by controlling the mind through marketing, which becomes 'the center or the "soul" of the corporation' (Deleuze, 1992: 6). This entrapment of the mind by marketing leads to people's attention being captured and, ultimately, destroyed in the service of consumption (Stiegler, 2010: 94). Accordingly, consumption and entrepreneurship displace labour as the essential human activity. Reflecting the demands of post-industrial, service-oriented financial capitalism, psychopower is characterised by flexibility, short-termism, and internally imposed exploitation or 'auto-exploitation', which is worse than 'allo-exploitation': 'Although the achievement-subject deems itself free, in reality it is a slave. In so far as it willingly exploits itself without a master, it is an *absolute slave*' (Han, 2017: 2, original emphasis). Technologically speaking, psychopower is digital – it is associated with (and enabled by) multimedia and networked computers (see Table 4.1).[2]

Table 4.1 Biopower and psychopower

Type of power	**Biopower**	**Psychopower**
'Foucault's biopower ... is no longer the force behind *our* age: without significant modifications it cannot account for the specifics of *psychotechnological* psychopower, nor of the new situation of biopower that results from it – nor of a "biopolitics" that has become a psychopolitics no longer emerging from the nation-state (and its programming institutions) but from deterritorialized economic forces (and their programming industries)' (Stiegler, 2010: 126).		
Type of society	**Disciplinary society**	**Society of control**
'We are in a generalized crisis in relation to all the environments of enclosure – prison, hospital, factory, school, family. ... It's only a matter of administering their last rites and of keeping people employed until the installation of the new forces knocking at the door. These are the *societies of control*, which are in the process of replacing the disciplinary societies' (Deleuze, 1992: 3–4).		
Period and politico-economic system	**Post-war state-managed capitalism and state socialism**	**Post-1970s neoliberal capitalism**
The transformation of state-based biopower into market-based psychopower 'began in the early 1970s, shortly after 1968 and at the same time as the gasoline crisis and shocks to the welfare state' (Stiegler, 2010: 128).		
Mechanisms of power	**Discipline** – enclosure, isolation, segregation, confinement, asceticism, physical training	**Control** – networking, connection, 'free' movement, stimulation, motivation, activation, compulsion, self-disclosure, attention-capture (or attention-destruction), marketing
'Here [in societies of control] there is no torture – just tweets and posts. Nor is there a mysterious 'Ministry of Truth'. Transparency and information have taken the place of truth. The new conception of power does not involve controlling the past, but steering the future psychopolitically' (Han, 2017: 38).		
Sites of power	**Regulated institutions** – residential institutions, hospitals, schools, factories, prisons	**Deregulated industries** – deterritorialised corporations
'Just as the corporation replaces the factory, *perpetual training* tends to replace the *school*, and continuous control to replace the examination' (Deleuze, 1992: 5).		

(*continued*)

Table 4.1 (Cont.)

<table>
<tr><th>Target of power</th><th>(Docile) body</th><th>(Docile) mind</th></tr>
<tr><td colspan="3">In societies of control, ‘physical discipline has given way to mental optimization’ (Han, 2017: 25). Although biopower affects the mind as well, it is not its primary target: ‘Disciplinary technology also reaches beyond the physical realm, into the mental sphere. After all, industry means “hard work”. “Industrial school” was another term for “reform school”. Bentham observed that his panopticon assures inmates’ moral improvement too. That said, disciplinary power does not focus on the psyche. The orthopaedic technology of disciplinary power is too crude to penetrate into the deeper layers of the soul – with its hidden wishes, needs and desires – and take it over’ (Han, 2017: 20).</td></tr>
<tr><td>Organising principle</td><td>State</td><td>Market</td></tr>
<tr><td colspan="3">‘The State’s biopower is transformed into market psychopower’ (Stiegler, 2010: 128).</td></tr>
<tr><td>Telos</td><td>Production</td><td>Consumption and entrepreneurship</td></tr>
<tr><td colspan="3">The ‘goal is no longer to form and exploit producers (of things) but to control the behavior of consumers (as such)’ (Stiegler, 2010: 131). ‘The subject of today’s world is an entrepreneur of the self practising self-exploitation – and, by the same token, self-surveillance’ (Han, 2017: 61).</td></tr>
<tr><td>Temporal horizon</td><td>Long term</td><td>Short term</td></tr>
<tr><td colspan="3">‘Control is short-term and of rapid rates of turnover, but also continuous and without limit, while discipline was of long duration, infinite and discontinuous’ (Deleuze, 1992: 6).</td></tr>
<tr><td>Prominent characteristic</td><td>Rigidity</td><td>Flexibility</td></tr>
<tr><td colspan="3">‘Enclosures are molds, distinct castings, but controls are a modulation, like a self-deforming cast that will continuously change from one moment to the other, or like a sieve whose mesh will transmute from point to point’ (Deleuze, 1992: 4).</td></tr>
<tr><td>Form of exploitation</td><td>Allo-exploitation</td><td>Auto-exploitation</td></tr>
<tr><td colspan="3">‘Today, everyone is an auto-exploiting labourer in his or her own enterprise. People are now master and slave in one’ (Han, 2017: 5).</td></tr>
<tr><td>Associated technology</td><td>Analogous, mechanical (e.g., engines and walls)</td><td>Digital (e.g., multimedia, networked computers)</td></tr>
<tr><td colspan="3">‘At the beginning of the twenty-first century, cell phones, networked computers, and the many other devices ... work through cognitive numerization and cultural technologies whose linking psychotechnological connections compound their effects on intergenerational relations’ (Stiegler, 2010: 176).</td></tr>
</table>

As was the case with the analysis of neoliberalism in the preceding section, this discussion of the transition to societies of control suggests a convergence between Independent Living and psychopower. Indeed, such an argument has taken centre stage in analyses of deinstitutionalisation developed by contemporary critical disability studies scholars, where the enemy is not (only) institutional confinement but (also and above all) 'inclusion' and 'independence' (Altermark, 2018; Ben-Moshe, 2020). For example, Altermark (2018: 80) has argued that these notions presuppose a specific type of subjectivity that reasserts the primacy of rationality and liberal individualism – values that have produced the exclusion of people with intellectual impairments in the first place. He even explains the continuation of segregation and exclusion that characterise reinstitutionalising deinstitutionalisation (Chapter 6) with the attempts to promote inclusion and independence, or 'the universalism of citizenship as full participation in all areas of society' (Altermark, 2018: 82). From such a perspective, the concept of independence is inherently exclusive because it requires specific intellectual abilities.

Mental capacity, then, becomes the ultimate litmus test for the emancipatory potential of the Independent Living movement in times of psychopower. Altermark is sceptical. For him, the concept of independence creates a double-bind: 'when we are called upon and follow the challenge to "be free" or to be "independent", we are simultaneously adhering to an exterior power which either sets the terms of our freedom or incites our independence' (Altermark, 2018: 84). In practical terms, mechanisms intended to enable people with intellectual impairments to live independently in the community – such as *supported* decision making – can only soften the paternalism of *substitute* decision making, without effectively affirming the possibility of exercising capacity with assistance: 'supported decision making itself is an expression of a lack of legal capacity' (Altermark, 2018: 86). This suggests that for people with intellectual impairments, there is no escape from paternalist care, and all efforts to create systems for egalitarian care are doomed to merely reassert liberal-individualist oppression.

In this book, I avoid such a conclusion by emphasising that the Independent Living movement has embraced an alternative understanding of independence. I also argue that this alternative understanding has been in constant struggle with the hegemonic liberal-individualist meaning of independence. The same applies to the tension between supported decision making, embraced by Independent Living activists with intellectual impairments, and substitute decision making, asserted by most caring professionals. As argued in Chapter 2, the advocacy of the Independent Living movement for self-determination, reflected in ENIL's work, has illuminated the contexts of *inter*dependence that the discourse of self-sufficiency has obscured – including in the psychopolitical context of cognitive functioning or 'mental capacity'. Accordingly, whereas neoliberals have insisted on cutting public support to promote self-sufficiency (or individual enterprise), Independent Living activists have argued for redirecting public resources towards support that enhances self-determination – such as personal assistance funded through direct payments, or mechanisms for supported decision making (further discussed in Chapter 7).

Moreover, Independent Living has an irreducible collective dimension that undermines the psychopolitical emphasis on self-enhancement. From its very inception, the Independent Living movement has been characterised by a strong reliance on peer support and mutual empowerment (DeJong, 1979). In his otherwise scathing critique of Independent Living, Williams (1983: 1004) has recognised that what he identified as the individualist, free-market ideology underpinning the movement has been counterbalanced by 'mutual aid, community action and support, a focus on environmental pathology as opposed to victim-blaming and the development of coalitions with other vulnerable groups'. For Independent Living activists, peer support has been a cornerstone of their resistance to professional and parental power. Thus, CIL–Berkely became possible because its founders

> were in close, continuing contact with other people having similar problems and concerns. A sense of unity and self-confidence gradually developed, largely as a result of the free flow of communication and sharing of experience. The residents' political consciousness grew as they became aware of the degree to which control over their lives had been taken over by medical and rehabilitation professionals. (Zukas, 1975: n.p.)

In the next section, I substantiate these arguments by using the concept of psychopower to analyse a prominent model for the provision of personal assistance according to Independent Living principles (I have explored this scheme before, but from the perspective of existential phenomenology – see Mladenov, 2012). The model was developed in 2004 by Independent Living organisations from nine European countries (CIL Mainz, Germany; ILI, Sweden; CIL Helsinki, Finland; ULOBA, Norway; CIL Dublin, Ireland; Vienna Assistance Cooperative, Austria; ENIL Italia, Italy; CIL Thessaloniki, Greece; and CIL Zurich, Switzerland), in the framework of the project 'European Center for Excellence in Personal Assistance'. It has been described in a document written by Adolf Ratzka (2004) and since then has been regarded as foundational for contemporary developments of Independent Living policy (Jolly, 2009), including by ENIL – the organisation has stated that it 'supports our members, other disabled people's organisations and the authorities, when requested, by providing technical assistance on personal assistance. The model national personal assistance policy, developed by Adolf Ratzka in 2004, is one of the key documents explaining how a personal assistance scheme should work' (ENIL, n.d.-g).

Independent Living, personal assistance, and psychopower

In the following analysis of the model of personal assistance described by Ratzka (2004), my aim is to outline both the (surface-level) convergences and the (deep-level) divergences between this policy and psychopower. To begin with, whereas psychopower promotes self-exploitation achieved by way of radical marketisation, Ratzka's (2004) model promotes self-determination enabled by quasi-marketisation – the policy should provide 'assistance users with purchasing power which, in turn, creates a market for assistance services with a multitude of service providers with different service delivery solutions' (Ratzka, 2004: 3). Accordingly, the policy is geared towards 'eliminating monopolies, public or private, in the provision of assistance services' (Ratzka, 2004: 2). As already pointed out, quasi-marketisation retains the role of the state as funder (purchaser) and regulator, as opposed to genuine marketisation that promotes complete state withdrawal once markets are established.

From a different angle, advocacy for personal assistance has sometimes been criticised for its productivism: 'give us rights [i.e., personal assistance] and we will become happy workers' (Griffiths, 2019: 66). However, Ratzka's (2004) model shifts the emphasis from production to consumption and entrepreneurship – in it, Independent Living is enabled when the disabled person assumes the role of 'customer or boss' (Ratzka, 2004: 3). In other words, it is not by becoming a worker that the person gets emancipated but by becoming a customer of support and employer of the supporters. As customer, the person chooses from a variety of services provided on the quasi-market; as boss, the person directly employs and manages their own assistants. Notably, the suggested mechanism of needs assessment considers 'the whole life situation', including 'the culturally customary division of work within the family, care of small children, aging parents, household and property', as well as the 'need of assistance at the work place, while attending educational institutions from kindergarten through university, during leisure time, outside the home, on travel and abroad' (Ratzka, 2004: 4).

Like the role of worker, the roles of customer and employer presuppose training – the users of personal assistance need 'to develop the skills required to take on more control over their services' (Ratzka, 2004: 3, n. 3). The additional pedagogical support needed for the development of these skills must be covered by the general funding for personal assistance and is ideally provided by peers: 'Peer support has proven to be effective in informing, training, supporting and advocating for assistance users' (Ratzka, 2004: 7, n. 18). With peer support, informal training displaces professionalised training as the primary driver of emancipation, challenging professional power in concert with the deconstruction of the juridical–administrative–therapeutic state discussed in Chapter 3. This is different from the psychopolitical training that enhances self-exploitation through 'self-management workshops, motivational retreats and seminars on personality or mental training [which] promise boundless self-optimization and heightened efficiency' (Han, 2017: 29). Although peer training includes self-management, motivational, and personality elements, they are oriented towards self-determination rather than self-exploitation.

Completing the needs assessment process and managing personal assistance presuppose work on the self. Reflecting key features of psychopower, these tasks require considerable self-knowledge and self-control. The latter are achieved through self-observation and self-analysis that make transparent the minute details of one's everyday life. The translation of one's needs into assistance hours is achieved by way of self-exposure meant to identify and disaggregate one's needs for support in various areas of life, including 'personal hygiene, eating, dressing, doing household work, assistance outside the home, about town or when traveling, at school, work and during leisure time, and, if applicable, in communicating, structuring the day or with similar cognitive or psychosocial support' (Ratzka, 2004: 3). In existing personal assistance programmes, such identification and disaggregation of needs is often the essence of the application process:

> Reflecting on the process of helping a friend apply, Marleigh described the application [for direct funding for personal assistance] as a 'dramatic' process of questioning: 'asking how many hours do you need in the morning? For what? Break it down, break it down, break it down. What are you going to do with that 15 minutes? You're gonna brush your teeth and this and this and this and this? How many hours do you need for lunch? What are you going to do with that time?' (Katzman and Kinsella, 2018: 1444)

This process is different from the monologically imposed interpretation of needs characteristic of state-based biopower, where one is being *told* what to do and for how long to do it, instead of being *asked*. Less conspicuously, the process also differs from the interpretation of needs characterising market-based psychopower. Granted, the work on the self that personal assistance users engage with includes learning to be an employer – as another respondent in Katzman and Kinsella's (2018: 1441) study points out, 'I run two businesses: my job and my direct funding business'. This learning is enabled by peer support, but part of it happens through trials and errors in recruiting, hiring, training, managing, and firing personal assistants.

It also entails managing one's emotions and *presenting* oneself as 'autonomous, self-sufficient, enterprising and managerial' (Katzman and Kinsella, 2018: 1450).

However, what neoliberal subjects do to their selves under the sway of psychopolitical control, personal assistance users do to their selves for the sake of self-determination. Psychopolitics 'is constantly calling on us to confide, share and participate: to communicate our opinions, needs, wishes and preferences – to tell all about our lives' (Han, 2017: 15). But with personal assistance according to the model described by Ratzka (2004), such self-disclosure is not a neoliberal con. It opens up a space of self-determination that may or may not be occupied by neoliberal psychopolitics. In this sense, it corresponds to Foucault's (1988) original conception of 'technologies of the self',

> those practices whereby individuals, by their own means or with the help of others, acted on their own bodies, souls, thoughts, conduct, and way of being in order to transform themselves and attain a certain state of perfection or happiness, or to become a sage or immortal, and so on. (Martin *et al.*, 1988: 4)

According to Han (2017: 27), Foucault imagined the 'technologies of the self' as actions on one's self that are free from power and domination. Han (2017: 27–28, original emphasis) criticises this vision as remaining oblivious to neoliberal psychopower: 'Foucault did not see that *the neoliberal regime utterly claims the technology of the self for its own purposes*'. However, when considered as part of the policy of personal assistance described by Ratzka (2004), the technologies of the self that personal assistance users engage with do not reveal themselves as insidious instances of auto-exploitation. On the contrary, by being oriented towards self-determination, such uses of the technologies of the self affirm what was originally intimated by Foucault – that one's work on one's self can be genuinely emancipatory.

The care for the self that Ratzka's (2004) model promotes could also be understood in terms of 'noopolitics'. Stiegler (2010: 113) defines noopolitics as psychopower harnessed by the public towards enabling self-determination or human 'maturity'. In this rendering of noopolitics, Stiegler (2010: 129) affirms the Kantian framing of the human being as essentially 'noetic, endowed with consciousness, capable of passing from minority to maturity, a maturity without which no politics worthy of the name is truly possible'. However, against the grain of Stiegler's argument, his concept of noopolitics presupposed a distributed understanding of agency that goes beyond Kant, because in noopolitics people are able to reach maturity only by using psychotechnological supplements – the '*hypomnemata* operating as supports for techniques of the self (i.e., the writing of the self) are the technical condition for this dialogic life as *self-attention*, as care' (Stiegler,

2010: 172, original emphasis). This comes very close to the idea of relational autonomy mentioned in Chapter 1, or to the Heideggerian *Dasein* mentioned in Chapter 3, as opposed to Kant's liberal autonomy.

Stiegler also points out that societies of control appropriate the techniques of the self for their own purposes – contemporary techno-cultural industries 'instrumentalize psychotechnologies derived from psychotechniques, practically implementing the technics of self Foucault describes' (Stiegler, 2010: 112). The same point is made by Han (2017: 27–28), but unlike Stiegler, Han is sceptical of the possibility of reclaiming psychotechnologies for the purposes of emancipation (a scepticism that resembles Altermark's attitude towards independence). Indeed, care for the self requires disciplining one's body and mind through psychotechnical supplements such as writing (Stiegler, 2010: 136). In the case of the personal assistance model discussed here, such supplements would amount to training and peer support intended to help assistance users to manage their own support systems. There is an irreducible element of self-care in Independent Living, but it should be understood in the noopolitical sense of taking charge of one's existence via egalitarian care provided by others, rather than in the psychopolitical sense of coping without support. Moreover, the model described by Ratzka (2004) embraces decision-making relationality (or the relationality of supported decision making) to accommodate people with intellectual and psychosocial impairments:

> Citizens who, despite appropriate information, counseling and other support, are unable to select and evaluate services or to employ their assistants themselves can also benefit from the policy provided that they receive the support from third persons such as a legal representative, family member or other person close to them. The costs of such support need to be covered by the policy, if necessary, by higher payments for the average assistance hour. (Ratzka, 2004: 3, n. 4)

Indeed, the distributed understanding of agency that underpins supported decision making is alien to disciplinary societies that isolate, segregate, and enclose individuals, but commensurate with societies of control that promote networking and peer-to-peer connectivity (Deleuze, 1992). The reach of psychopower extends towards the soul, but as with the work on the self of Ratzka's (2004) model, this is not a neoliberal con. Instead, the psychopolitical management of the soul by way of supported decision making (potentially) enables genuine emancipation and could be regarded as another deployment of the technologies of the self that undermines paternalist care.

However, besides being in relation with oneself, the personal assistance user is also in relation with their assistant(s). In their entrepreneurial role – the role of employer – the users may reduce their assistants to instruments for achievement of self-determination. This instrumentalisation of one's support workers – regarded in Independent Living literature as reducing assistants to 'extensions of the self' (Shakespeare *et al.*, 2017: 13) – may suggest that the assistance user embraces neoliberal subjectivity: 'As the entrepreneur of its own self, the neoliberal subject has no capacity for relationships with others that might be *free of purpose*' (Han, 2017: 2, original emphasis).

Ratzka (2004) does not advocate for such instrumentalisation, but it is not uncommon among Independent Living advocates (Shakespeare *et al.*, 2017) – consider, for example, this statement by DeJong *et al.* (1992: 90): 'The personal assistant who provides services to the disabled person acts, in a sense, as an extension of the disabled person and follows the individual's directions as to how to meet his or her needs.' My own work has revealed a mixed picture. In the survey on personal assistance that I already mentioned, there was no consensus on the statement 'Assistants are regarded by the users in instrumental terms, for example as "arms and legs" or "staff"', with 22 respondents seeing such instrumentalisation as enabling, 16 regarding it as a barrier to choice and control, and 16 remaining neutral (Mladenov, 2020b: 16–17).

The support envisioned by Ratzka (2004) is not restricted by enclosures of any kind. Personal assistance is decoupled from housing: 'The term "personal assistance" cannot be used for service delivery solutions where housing and assistance with the activities of daily living are provided in one inseparable package' (Ratzka, 2004: 3). Accordingly, personal assistance is not available to people in residential care: 'Persons who live in residential institutions or equivalent solutions are not eligible under the policy' (Ratzka, 2004: 4). As an exception, those who would like to leave the institutional enclosure where they currently reside are entitled to six months of personal assistance, intended to enable their move to the community (Ratzka, 2004: 4). Support is also unrestricted by the enclosure of the nation state by making payments 'exportable to countries where users cannot receive equivalent payments' (Ratzka, 2004: 4), while the enclosure of local authority is avoided by centralisation of funding that 'promotes users' geographical and social mobility and liberates them from local governments' finances and priorities' (Ratzka, 2004: 6, n. 15). In addition, personal assistance is not wedded to employment: 'Eligibility is granted … regardless of … employment or insurance situation' (Ratzka, 2004: 3). Finally, personal assistance is not restricted by the provider – users receive cash benefits rather than services in kind because the latter 'reduce users' choices, in particular, if they are provided by monopolistic service providers which often tie users to certain buildings and other limited geographical areas' (Ratzka, 2004: 5, n. 12).

In a nutshell, flexibility is key for personal assistance, in concert with the shift from the disciplinary enclosures of biopower to the free-floating control of psychopower (see Deleuze, 1992: 4). In the model described by Ratzka (2004), flexibility is achieved by providing personal assistance users with purchasing power, training them to be customers and employers, creating a quasi-market of competing service providers, and building an infrastructure of peer support. Flexibility also requires a supply of flexible workers employable as assistants: 'Many assistance users prefer workers to get paid by the hour' (Ratzka, 2004: 5, n. 10). The more control over the assistant the user has, the more flexible the service the user receives. The situation of personal assistants as precarious workers corresponds to the mode of work in the neoliberal, highly marketised society. As argued in Chapter 3, a main concern of the ethics of care has been to protect the caregivers (the majority of whom are women) from the arbitrariness and violence of the free market (Barnes *et al.*, 2015).

Ratzka (2004: 6–7) addresses this concern by requiring funding for personal assistance that allows paying 'competitive wages', to cover 'all indirect labor costs', and maintaining a 'safe and healthy working environment'. Notably, personal assistance users tend to consider the good working conditions of their assistants as enablers of the users' choice and control (Mladenov, 2020b: 11). For their part, the assistants report higher levels of job satisfaction than the staff employed in traditional services such as institutional care or home care (Leece, 2006; Woolham *et al.*, 2019). Thus, the interests of the two groups are not necessarily at odds. Taking care of the working conditions of the assistants enables the users to receive better support, while avoiding neoliberal precarity. This has been recognised by the trade unions as well:

> In later years, Kommunal [the Swedish Municipal Workers' Union] had changed its position and now agrees that members working as personal assistants enjoy better working conditions than workers in municipal home care services do, the reason being that personal assistants work longer contiguous shifts with one person only compared with many short interventions for home care service clients. Also, personal assistants can choose whom they work for, unlike their colleagues in home care services or cluster housing facilities. In 2009, the union voiced their opposition against a Parliamentary Committee proposal that would replace personal assistance for many users with services similar to home care services. The union argued that the change would worsen the working situation of its members and the quality of life of their users. (Westberg, 2010: 18)

The rights and working conditions of the most precarious workers – migrants – are of special concern for analyses of Independent Living in the rich countries of the Global North. Migrant women's care work has been widespread in Continental and Southern Europe, where it has 'emerged as an important solution to the challenges of dependents in need of care' (Mathieu, 2016: 580–581). For example, Turkey has been a major destination for carers from Eastern Europe, the Caucasus, and Central Asia. These workers have been mostly undocumented and have worked without contracts; they have also frequently moved back to their home countries. As a result, care relationships in Turkey have been unstable, unreliable, and unpredictable, with blurred boundaries between the employer and the worker (Bezmez and Porter, 2022: 56). From the supply side, the postsocialist countries of CEE have been a key source of care labour for Southern and Western Europe: 'in countries like Serbia where there are few employment opportunities in the health and social services sector, women seek paid employment in the care sector abroad' (Zaviršek and Fischbach, 2023:109). To avoid achieving Independent Living and gender equity in the Global North at the price of impoverishment and exploitation of Southern and Eastern European women, Independent Living advocates have sought to strengthen the rights of migrant workers (e.g., ENIL, 2023a).

Finally, the relationship between the personal assistance users and their assistants contains an irreducible element of emotional attachment and even friendship (Shakespeare *et al.*, 2017: 6). The concept of egalitarian care highlights these emotional and relational aspects of personal assistance that sometimes remain in the periphery of Independent Living advocacy because of its emphasis on rational bargaining and informed consent. As suggested by the example of the change in the attitude of the Swedish trade union Kommunal, as well as by considering the case of migrant carers, there is a great potential for coalition building along these lines, which would strengthen the advocacy for Independent Living. A similar point is made by Ben-Moshe (2020: 226) in a practical recommendation intended to enable deinstitutionalisation:

> What labor unions could be doing, for example – and some have already begun this transition – is advocating for better wages and opportunities for their employees to work in community noncarceral settings, for example, advocating for legislation that ensures good pay for personal care attendants outside of institutions and using the experience of such devoted institutional employees to work with (and sometimes for) disabled people in the homes in which they reside. This will require more than a policy shift, though; it will require an epistemic one. Such employees, and all of us, will need to understand disability not as devalued and deficit driven and people with even complex disabilities as agents of their own lives. (Ben-Moshe, 2020: 226)

Concluding remarks

This chapter looked at the relationships between Independent Living and the market, focusing on neoliberalisation as the currently dominant form of marketisation. My main argument was that there has been a surface-level convergence between Independent Living and neoliberal marketisation, counterbalanced by deeper-level divergences. I started by exploring the ways in which neoliberal marketisation has affected the different types of welfare regimes outlined in Chapter 3. Independent Living emerged in a liberal welfare context (US) but subsequently spread to Europe by finding favourable conditions in social democratic and borderline-liberal regimes (Sweden, the UK). The fact that landmark personal assistance legislation was adopted in these countries in the 1990s under right-wing governments may suggest that neoliberalisation has been a key enabler of Independent Living reforms in Europe.

However, neoliberal retrenchment in the 2000s and 2010s eventually eroded the early gains of the Independent Living movement in the West. Moreover, the most radical neoliberal reforms – the ones implemented in the postsocialist countries of CEE – did not provide a fertile ground for Independent Living advocacy and policy making. Both the lingering statism of the socialist regimes and the minimisation of the welfare state sought by the postsocialist 'shock therapists' proved hostile to the Independent Living paradigm. The form of productivism embraced by neoliberal reforms has reproduced state socialist workfare, together with its invalidating consequences for disabled people. In the final analysis, neoliberalisation has done more harm than good to Independent Living advocacy.

In the second part of the chapter, I contextualised further this analysis by looking at the wider historical transformation of biopower into psychopower. The substitution of body-targeting industrial discipline with psyche-targeting post-industrial control has been a key feature of neoliberal marketisation. To explore how Independent Living has related to this process, I analysed the model for the provision of personal assistance described by Ratzka (2004). This enabled me to outline the following divergences between Independent Living and neoliberal marketisation.

First, while neoliberal restructuring has favoured genuine marketisation, Independent Living advocates have promoted quasi-marketisation. In contrast to genuine marketisation that undermines socio-economic redistribution, quasi-marketisation depends on strong redistribution. Hence the peculiar duality of Independent Living advocacy that simultaneously criticises and defends the welfare state. Second, whereas neoliberal psychopolitics has appropriated the work on the self to enable self-exploitation, Independent Living advocacy has promoted the work on the self to enable self-determination and emancipation. Third, neoliberal individualism has been countered by the Independent Living movement's foundational collectivism. This collectivism has been egalitarian, as opposed to the professionalised collectivism of institutional care.

In sum, the reduction of Independent Living to a neoliberal assault on the welfare state misrepresents the movement. This misrepresentation has been enabled by other misconceptions, such as the rendering of Independent Living in terms of self-sufficiency that has sometimes been used to legitimise cuts to social support amidst creeping austerity (Elder-Woodward, 2016; Manji, 2018). This analysis is very much in line with analyses developed by the Independent Living activists themselves. On the one hand,

> the language of independent living has been appropriated by Government and public bodies to justify the cuts they are making. ... It is common practice for essential support to be removed from Disabled people through social care assessments under the justification of 'helping' them to 'improve their independence'. (Reclaiming Our Futures Alliance, 2018)

Yet on the other hand,

> if new campaigners come into the movement who are only aware of the appropriation of the language of independent living rather than the proud history of the independent living movement, then it is our job to share our history and learning. We must also remember that the politics of the independent living movement, based as it is on collectivisation and grassroots struggle, will not appeal to all. (Reclaiming Our Futures Alliance, 2018)[3]

As already argued, Independent Living activists have actively campaigned against austerity measures. Independent Living is about *inter*dependence, although unqualified praise of *inter*dependence can also be counterproductive and end up bolstering professional power, institutionalisation, paternalism, and familialism. Independent Living is about a particular kind of *inter*dependence, one that enhances self-determination.

Elder-Woodward (2016: 254) has argued that the movement and paradigm of Independent Living have incorporated several political philosophies – the classical liberal one, associated with individual choice and control; the communitarian one, associated with peer-support and peer-advocacy; and the civic-pluralist one, associated with the ideas of co-production or the 'nothing about us without us' principle. In a previous analysis (Mladenov, 2015b: 445), I have argued that in the age of austerity and radical marketisation, disability activists need 'to defend self-determination while criticising market-based individualism, and to defend the welfare state while criticising expert-based paternalism'. Both Elder-Woodward's insight about the political-philosophical grounds of Independent Living and my suggestion about the need to adopt a double-edged activist strategy in neoliberal times correspond to the complexity of Independent Living's relationships with the state and the market explored in Chapters 3 and 4. The next chapter complicates the analysis even further by adding the family to the picture.

Notes

1 Stiegler seeks to defend modern schooling by mobilising Kant's conception of education against Foucault's, and by highlighting the dual (or 'pharmacological') essence of writing as both constraining and enabling: 'Foucault's analysis of the school as a disciplinary establishment, in which the discipline is that of the army, not of knowledge, and where normalization and individualization are produced through what Foucault calls "the apparatus of writing" – this analysis completely ignores the fact that writing, as a technology, and more precisely as a psychotechnology of attention, is also pharmacological and can just as easily construct an apparatus of disindividuation through individualization as the process of individuation in service to a self, as "the writing of the self," one of Foucault's last subjects shortly after his study of the techniques of self' (Stiegler, 2010: 115–116). I discuss the potentially emancipatory function of the 'technologies of the self' later in the chapter.

2 Esping-Andersen's typology of welfare regimes would add context-sensitive nuance to the sweeping 'transition to psychopolitics' thesis. For example, in terms of employment, the transformation of biopower into psychopower has meant substitution of industrial jobs with service jobs (e.g., in social care, leisure, or entertainment). However, such changes have been regime-type specific: 'Germany represents stagnation and sluggish service-evolution; Sweden is overwhelmingly biased towards highly professionalized social-welfare employment; and, in the United States, several trends compete: one is the sustained dynamism in the conventional industrial economy; another is a powerful thrust towards professionalism, especially in business-related services; and a third is an explosion of unqualified jobs with an accent on "fun" services' (Esping-Andersen, 1990: 200). This uneven development of services has implications for the uneven spread of the ideas and practices of Independent Living, but its analysis goes beyond the scope of the present discussion.

3 The Reclaiming Our Futures Alliance includes the British disability rights organisations Sisters of Frida, People First, ALFIE, DPAC, and Inclusion London.

5

Independent Living and the family

This chapter explores the relationships between the Independent Living paradigm and the family, considering the latter as the third organising principle of social welfare, together with the state and the market. The family is an institutionally differentiated domain that requires a separate analysis, although it interacts with both the state and the market, as the boundaries between the private and the public are socially negotiated and contested. Thus, feminist scholars have insisted that familial support should be considered as a political rather than a personal matter due to, among other issues, the gendered division of labour (Orloff, 2009). Indeed, comparative analyses of welfare regimes are incomprehensible or partial without considering the role of the family, as also recognised by Esping-Andersen (1999: 35) in his update of the 'three worlds' typology:

> The family, then, cannot be dismissed as a haven of [private] intimacy and consumption. It is an all-important [public] actor whose decisions and behaviour directly influence, and are influenced by, the welfare state and the labour market. Welfare regimes must be identified much more systematically in terms of the inter-causal triad of state, market, and family.

As argued in Chapter 3, Independent Living activists and thinkers have interrogated state-provided support by voicing a strong critique of professional power that has resonated with analyses of biopower. Chapter 4 explored how the Independent Living paradigm has partly affirmed but essentially challenged marketisation of support and the attendant instances of psychopower. In this chapter I consider criticisms of parental power voiced by Independent Living advocates to question the positioning of disabled people as 'eternal children' within their families.[1] In social policy terms, such criticisms have targeted familialism in disability policy, defined as arrangements in which families assume full responsibility for supporting their disabled members. Familialism is usually underpinned by patriarchal values, but also by the political aim of reducing government spending on social care (Zaviršek and Fischbach, 2023).

In terms of welfare state theory, the Independent Living critique explored in Chapter 3 has sought qualified deétatisation of support (associated with challenging the authority of the state), the one outlined in Chapter 4 has promoted qualified decommodification of support (associated with challenging the authority of the market), and the critical approach discussed here advocates for qualified defamilialisation of support (associated with challenging parental authority). These three critiques are strongly interrelated. Calls for defamilialisation of support usually entail advocacy for its commodification and/or étatisation. For its part, decommodification may enhance étatisation and/or familialisation, and deétatisation may also lead to familialisation. In its neoliberal form, deétatisation may entail demonising the state and idealising the private sphere of the family, thus engendering 'neoliberal neopatriarchy' (Campbell, 2014). Esping-Andersen (1999: 36) has discussed these complex interactions between (de)étatisation, (de)commodification, and (de)familialisation in the following way:

> At the macro-level, the welfare production of either of the three components is obviously related to what happens in the other two. And at the micro-level, individuals' welfare depends on how they manage to 'package' inputs from the three. To exemplify, a traditional male bread-winner family will have less demand for private or public social services than a two-career household. But, when families service themselves, the market is directly affected because there will be less labour supply and fewer service outlets. In turn, if the state provides cheap daycare, both families and the market will change: there will be fewer housewives, more labour force participation, and a new demand multiplier caused by double-earner households' greater propensity to purchase services.

Disability studies scholars have also explored the role of the family in relation to other sources of welfare. As an example, consider Kateřina Kolářová's (2011) crip-theoretical analysis of the American movie *I Am Sam*, in which, according to Kolářová,

> the state is figured as the non-inclusive patrolling force, incapable of assessing and accommodating the individual(ized) potential of each and every particular subject/person. Instead, it is the private space and specifically the family space – embodied by the two mothers – that holds the promise of a more inclusive society capable of appreciation and accommodation of diversity. (Kolářová, 2011: 139)

Kolářová (2011: 139) concludes that *I Am Sam* affirms diversity and inclusion by idealising the heteronormative family 'as not only the best solution for the child of the future but as the best solution for the future itself'. Indeed, while familial support has been crucial for the survival and thriving of many disabled people, the family has also been a site of norming, ableist oppression, and restrictions to self-determination. The family provides protection and caring, but it also institutionalises hierarchies such as those between parents and children, breadwinners and home-makers, young and older, abled and disabled. Unsurprisingly, Deleuze (1992: 3–4) identifies the family as an 'environment of enclosure' on a par with the school, the factory, the hospital, and the prison – thus, as a key site of the exercise of biopower. For disabled people, paternalism (inherently linked to infantilisation) has routinely underpinned disciplining interventions or outright restrictions of freedom. This insight parallels feminist criticisms of the family as a site of gender-based violence and exploitation, as well as the queer/crip analyses of the family as a site of heteronormative/ableist socialisation (Lewis, 2022; McRuer, 2006). It also reflects the mutually constitutive intersections between ableism, androcentrism, and heterosexism (Mladenov, 2021b).

Indeed, informal care in the family may be more benign and inherently more egalitarian than professionalised care – Esping-Andersen (1999: 35–36) identifies the family as a space of reciprocal allocation, in contrast to the market (a space of instrumental allocation) and the state (a space of authoritative allocation). However, this should not prevent critical analyses of parental power, nor suppress attempts at identifying paternalist care (or, indeed, violence, neglect, and abuse) amidst – or in the stead of – familial warmth, concern, and safety. Such a critical approach is all the more important given that care in the family – unlike professionalised care – is treated as a private (rather than public) matter, which prevents its public scrutiny (as child protection social work professionals know all too well).

Disabled people's parents have been vocal advocates of institutional care and, accordingly, have stood out as opponents of deinstitutionalisation (Ben-Moshe, 2020: Ch. 6). But even at home, over-protective and norm-conforming parenting has been a major barrier to Independent Living, including by preventing disabled people from becoming parents themselves. It is therefore hardly surprising that the struggle for Independent Living has also been a struggle for parental rights (Ratzka, 2019). However, in strongly familialist and neoliberal-neopatriarchal contexts, this fight has risked re-affirming heteronormativity and gendered division of labour. The corollary is that, similar to campaigning in relation to (de)étatisation and (de)commodification, knowing the context is crucial for understanding advocacy strategies and their outcomes in terms of (de)familialisation. The first part of this chapter therefore revisits welfare regimes by discussing the role of the family in each of them, as well as the specific responses of the Independent Living movement.

I then consider briefly parental advocacy for Independent Living. As the disability studies scholars Sara Ryan and Katherine Runswick-Cole (2008: 201–202) have argued, the parents of disabled people – overwhelmingly the mothers, who tend to remain caregivers during disabled people's adult life – may be regarded as both 'oppressors' and 'allies'. As oppressors, parents restrict self-determination and transmit ableism (often in the name of protection); as allies, they experience and fight disablement as they are subjected 'directly and by proxy' to the ableist oppression faced by their young or adult children.

In the second part of the chapter, I explore these contradictions by looking at recent parental mobilisations in postsocialist CEE, with special attention to parental campaigning in Bulgaria and Slovenia (Dimitrova, 2020; Mladenov and Petri, 2019; Zaviršek and Fischbach, 2023). These mobilisations have included protests, lobbying, and peer support that have criticised professional power, opposed neoliberal retrenchment, and demanded reforms in public support for disabled people, including increase in disability benefits, funding for personal assistance, and changes to legal capacity legislation. Still, the outcomes of these initiatives have often amounted to strengthening of familialism. The latter has a negative impact on the self-determination of both the parents (mothers) and their disabled children – on a placard carried by a disabled person during one of ENIL's Freedom Drives we read: 'I need more personal assistance budget so my mother could help more in the refugee camp' (ENIL, 2022b: 24). Moreover, familialism is bad for the family, considered as a major provider of welfare.[2]

The analysis in this chapter is gendered. I consider three different models of gender equity – analysed by Nancy Fraser (1997) under the titles of 'universal breadwinner', 'caregiver parity', and 'universal caregiver' models – to clarify the significance of gender in the analysis of welfare, as well as the intersections between gender and disability. By applying the Independent Living perspective to this typology, I suggest that to realise a gender equity regime that promotes self-determination *for all* and avoids paternalist care, one needs to complement the 'universal caregiver' model (the most promising, according to Fraser) with a vision of 'universal care-receiving'.

Drawing together these different threads, I conclude by identifying the attitude of Independent Living advocacy towards the family as ambivalent. It is important to emphasise that although the Independent Living movement has challenged parental power, it has also recognised the significance of familial support, as well as the value of enabling disabled people to be parents. As explained in Chapter 2, Independent Living is not about living on one's own, in isolation, and self-sufficiently. Independent Living is also not about 'abolishing the family' (Lewis, 2022) but about living in families of self-determining equals, in concert with the concept of egalitarian care (Chapter 3). This goal overlaps with the goal of those feminists who seek to increase the independence of women both within and outside families (Orloff, 2009). As Ratzka (2019: 4) explains:

> My wife was familiar with my system of personal assistance. We both wanted to live together but also needed to feel free in a relationship where we, independently from each other, could develop and grow as human beings. We knew this was possible with personal assistance. With the help of my assistants I would continue to take care of myself, with the help of my assistants, I would do my part of the household chores.

Independent Living and the family in Esping-Andersen's welfare regimes

Historically, the denial of disabled people's self-determination has overlapped with the denial of women's self-determination. However, the intersections between ableism and androcentrism have assumed different forms in different welfare regimes, soliciting different responses from Independent Living activists and feminists. To begin with, liberal regimes have been reliant on a traditional, 'male breadwinner' family (Esping-Andersen, 1999: 50–51; see also Daly, 2022: 313) to offset the problems generated by keeping public support minimal, means-tested, and conditional. In fact, one of the reasons for the success of neoliberal marketisation since the 1980s has been the alliance between the social-conservative defence of 'family values' and the economic-conservative advocacy for welfare state retrenchment (Brown, 2006; Cooper, 2017).

True to their mission of preserving the status quo of established mores and hierarchies (that facilitate intergenerational transmission of capital), socially conservative politicians in the US and the UK have been interested in maintaining patriarchal families and the attendant gendered division of labour. This has amounted to keeping reproductive work unrecognised, unremunerated, and feminised. Neoliberals have also supported the male breadwinner model, but for a different reason – traditional families maintain social stability by protecting individuals against the precarity, poverty, and inequality engendered by neoliberal marketisation. In other words, neoliberals needed the family to fill in the gaps in social reproduction opened by welfare state retrenchment (Cooper, 2017).

The male breadwinner model has also characterised conservative welfare regimes, although there, the gendered division of labour has been maintained by tripartite agreements and status-differentiated benefits for formally employed workers (mostly men). Accordingly, the care for disabled people, children, and older people has been provided by women (mostly mothers), with minimal or no public support. In his analysis of absenteeism from work in the conservative regimes, Esping-Andersen (1990: 156) mentions Germany, where low absenteeism rates of women are related to their low levels of participation in the labour market. Another example is Turkey – a country representing (to some extent) the Mediterranean variety of the more general conservative welfare regime – where 'the image of the mother as the carer of her impaired adult "child" is almost a cultural norm' (Bezmez and Porter, 2022: 57). Similar patterns characterise other Southern European states such as Greece, Italy, Portugal, and Spain. In these countries, the strong emphasis on traditional family structures has been complemented by adherence to religious norms and religiously motivated charity (Buğra and Keyder, 2006).

The over-reliance on women/mothers to provide care in familialist contexts has contributed to the 'institutionalisation at home' of disabled people, exacerbated by the lack of adequate formal supports in the community. As explained by the activists from ENIL (2023d: 15):

> If someone is 'forced' to live under specific conditions which are limiting their personal choices and they lack control over their life, they can be institutionalized in their own home. If a family does not consider the needs and wishes of the disabled member, they can act as an institution.

To explore institutionalisation at home is to consider the family in terms of biopower, which is consistent with Deleuze's (1992) treatment of the family as a disciplinary environment of enclosure. Dependence on informal family care and charity tends to limit self-determination and produce institution-like confinement for the people on both sides of the caring relationship. These home-institutionalisation pressures become increasingly acute with the ageing of the parents. Moreover, institutionalisation at home cements the gendered division of labour. Within the parental couple, it is usually the mother who experiences restrictions of independence due to informal caring obligations: 'The functional equivalent of market dependency for many women is family dependency. In other words, female independence necessitates "de-familializing" welfare obligations' (Esping-Andersen, 1999: 45). Defamilialisation here means provision of public support with caring tasks. Esping-Andersen does not consider disabled people, but they are equally affected by 'family dependency' in familialist contexts, as the concept of institutionalisation at home makes clear.

Neoliberal restructuring in conservative welfare regimes has intensified the gendering of care work along patriarchal lines. Revisiting the Turkish example, since the 1980s, Turkey has been experiencing neoliberalisation approximating the one unfolding in the liberal regimes. The coming to power of the Justice and Development Party in 2002 marked a resurgence of social conservatism, but neoliberal reforms continued – a policy trend described by Buğra and Keyder (2006: 213) as reflecting 'a liberal residualism, flavoured with social conservative values, that are premised upon the centrality of the family and the significance of communal solidarity'. Women continued to be the main pillars of support provided to disabled people, children, and older people. As in the US and the UK, familialism has not only been conducive to, but also necessary, for effective neoliberalisation:

> Neither the current Turkish government's notions of subsidiarity, according to which the state has little business in the realm of poverty alleviation that should be left to the family and the community, nor the meeting of minds of neo-liberal advocates of unregulated markets and market-oriented Islamists, would be foreign to the type of conservative liberalism advocated by von Hayek and de Tocqueville. The latter would fully agree with the view that the free functioning of the market mechanism requires the supporting presence of traditional institutions such as the family and religion. (Buğra and Keyder, 2006: 224–225)

So far, the analysis in this section suggests that Independent Living advocacy in both liberal and conservative welfare regimes has been confronted with the task of defamilialising support – a task that has become increasingly pressing with the rise of neoliberalisation since the 1980s. Where the welfare state has been retrenched (as in the US and the UK, especially during the period of austerity following the 2007/8 financial crash) or formal support has been withheld due to conservative expectations of family-based provision (as in Turkey and other Southern European states), Independent Living advocacy has also voiced (qualified) support for étatisation and decommodification.

As far as social democratic welfare regimes are concerned, they have been characterised by generous public support for care-related tasks. The result has been high participation of women in the labour market, coupled with high fertility rates:

> Next to paid holidays, by far the greatest non-sickness progam [in Scandinavia] is maternity and parental leave – a program which in effect permits women to reconcile working life with fertility. ... In Sweden, maximum female labor-force participation is a principle of social policy. It has found practical expression in the world's highest participation rates, more than 80 percent. But the associated cost is obviously high rates of absenteeism. (Esping-Andersen, 1990: 155)

This approach to welfare has been associated with the 'caregiver parity' model of gender equity (Fraser, 1997: 55–59). It is a major alternative to the male breadwinner approach characterising liberal and conservative regimes. Caregiver parity is achieved by providing allowances to women as a compensation for their caring responsibilities and is commensurate with the feminist ethics of care (Chapter 3). In theory, this would enable women to gain economic independence and social recognition through a revaluation of feminine life-patterns, intending to make gender difference costless. However, supporting women's care work in the family has also entrenched disparities in income between men and women, while reinforcing the feminisation of care work (Fraser, 1997: 58) – a conclusion also supported by recent studies on familialism in European social policy (Daly, 2022).

In essence, caregiver parity has amounted to 'motherisation' of support amidst broader efforts at defamilialisation (Mathieu, 2016). Although qualitatively different from the motherisation generated by liberal, conservative, and neoliberal welfare, social-democratic motherisation has nevertheless restricted the self-determination of both women and disabled people. Mathieu identifies this as 'implicit maternalism' – it 'occurs when mothers – sometimes in gender-neutral terms as "caregivers" – are offered time or money to look after dependents' (Mathieu, 2016: 582). The implicit maternalism of the caregiver parity model undermines gender equality 'because women are not encouraged to participate in the labor market to the same extent as their husbands, assuming a heterosexual marriage' (Mathieu, 2016: 584). In response, Mathieu (2016) has called for 'demotherisation' of care work – a call that (partially) resonates with Independent Living advocacy against institutionalisation at home.

Demotherisation can lead to universalisation of breadwinning (discussed in the next section) when it is achieved by transferring the family's care work to non-familial, state-funded institutions like day-care centres for children or residential institutions for disabled or older people (Mathieu, 2016: 578). An alternative approach to demotherisation is to support men to assume caring responsibilities through fathers' quotas and paternity leaves (Mathieu, 2016: 584) – this would in theory lead to 'universalisation of caregiving', identified by Fraser (1997: 59–62) as the most promising model of gender equity. Yet without taking into account the perspective of the people who are 'cared for', both these alternatives could reproduce paternalist (as opposed to egalitarian) care.

Some of these points will become clearer when I consider the tensions between defamilialisation and the Independent Living paradigm through exploring two prominent campaigns for personal assistance and their outcomes in Bulgaria and Slovenia. However, let me first prepare the ground by saying a few words about the family in post/socialism.

Independent Living and the family in state socialist and postsocialist countries

State socialist welfare sought to promote women's employment on a par with men's – an approach identified by Fraser (1997: 51–55) as adhering to a 'universal breadwinner' model of gender equity. The associated policies – such as provision of publicly funded, professionalised, and institutionalised care for children, disabled people, and older people – contributed to a partial equalisation of the opportunities and status of men and women. However, this approach also resulted in overvaluing productive labour and devaluing reproductive care work. The latter was rendered by socialist policy experts in terms of 'los[ing] a work force unit that could be put to more appropriate use' (Golemanov and Popov, 1976: 32). Moreover, reproductive labour remained 'women's work' (Ferge, 1997: 163), burdening women with 'double shifts'. As explained by Phillips *et al.* (2023: 2) in a recent article on disabled people in Ukraine:

> The older generation of women dealt with the socialist state's expectation of full-time employment for all able-bodied citizens, but without adequate structures to alleviate the burden of childcare, domestic chores, and community work, which largely fell to women. After the collapse of the socialist state, the social safety net shrunk even further, and it was women who took up much of the state's slack caring for vulnerable citizens, such as children with disabilities, the elderly and infirm, people living with HIV/AIDS and other chronic conditions, and others.

In state socialist countries, the application of this productivist approach to gender equity led to the creation of a massive infrastructure of educational and care facilities, including institutions for disabled people, whose bleak legacy has already been outlined in Chapter 3. The aim was to free women's labour for the demands of socialist industrialisation by placing children, disabled people, and older people in state care. However, the latter remained largely inadequate, as Phillips and her co-authors also note, but more importantly, it was designed and realised in a markedly top-down, expert-centred, paternalist, institutional, and disciplinary manner.[3]

The Independent Living movement that emerged in the postsocialist region of Central and Eastern Europe (CEE) only after the fall of state socialism (Chapter 3) has been fighting against this inheritance since its inception. As explained in Chapter 4, postsocialist neoliberalisation did not make things easier for the activists because it resulted in the erosion of public support rather than its quasi-market deétatisation. In the 1990s, the living conditions in residential institutions in CEE 'drastically deteriorated' (World Bank, 2003: 24), while the number of children and adults in need of state care increased significantly due to rising poverty and lack of adequate social protections for families (Tobis, 2000: 23). At the same time, the institutions' embeddedness in local economies increased. Postsocialist villages and small towns have been heavily affected by neoliberal restructuring, including deindustrialisation. Consequently, in remote areas where most institutions have been located, the latter have provided the means for economic survival to impoverished postsocialist citizens with few remaining opportunities for gainful employment. In sum:

> Economic vulnerability has implications for the disability rights field, particularly for deinstitutionalisation. Many people facing resource scarcity are moved into large semi-closed institutions as a 'last resort' and the only option for housing and basic daily and long-term support. The large facilities have also been integral parts of survival economies for the local population, staff, and outsourced local food suppliers and tradespeople (e.g. plumbers, electricians). (Zaviršek and Fischbach, 2023: 97)[4]

Against this socioeconomic background, it is hardly surprising that the deinstitutionalisation reforms in the postsocialist region, which gained traction towards the end of the 2000s (supported by EU funds), have generated reinstitutionalising outcomes by moving disabled people from big to small institutions instead of creating community-based alternatives, as will be explained in more detail in Chapter 6.

Women experienced postsocialist neoliberalisation as retraditionalisation, in which they 'have been ushered back into hearth and home, while men play the dominant roles in the new market economies and new political structures' (Phillips, 2010: 178). This exclusion of women from productive labour and their redirection towards (inadequately supported or unsupported) reproductive work in the family effectively reinstated the male breadwinner model. Retraditionalisation included a rise of nationalist sentiments and pro-natalist policies that can also be linked to neoliberal restructuring: 'Traditionalist discourses use growing unemployment to argue that women should indeed return to their primary caregiving roles in families and stay at home' (Zaviršek and Fischbach, 2023: 108).

The concept of 'neoliberal neopatriarchy' (Campbell, 2014) neatly captures the essence of these reactionary developments from a feminist perspective. For Independent Living activists, it meant fighting on several fronts – the campaigners needed to criticise the continuing institutionalisation of support (underpinned by the state socialist legacy), its deterioration due to retrenchment (underpinned by postsocialist neoliberalisation), and its familialisation due to the reactionary trends outlined above (underpinned by postsocialist retraditionalisation, itself an aspect of neoliberalisation). I analyse these processes in more depth in my book *Disability and Postsocialism* (Mladenov, 2018).

Postsocialist retraditionalisation also entailed the resurgence of religious institutions, discourses, and practices, especially in countries with strong Catholic traditions such as Hungary and Poland (Ferge, 1997; Szarota, 2023), but also in countries with Eastern Orthodox traditions such as Serbia

(Zaviršek and Fischbach, 2023) and Bulgaria (Mladenov, 2015a). To iterate, neoliberal retrenchment of the welfare state is bound to enhance alternative sources of welfare: 'A removal of the welfare safety net would also force benefit recipients to rely on resources given by family, church and the charitable sector' (Deeming, 2017: 411–412). In postsocialist Europe, religious institutions gradually recovered from their state socialist suppression and/or co-option, eventually regaining public support, economic independence, and political and social influence comparable to their counterparts in conservative regimes. Thus, the aforementioned alliance between religious institutions and neoliberalisation in conservative Southern Europe (Buğra and Keyder, 2006) reoccurred in postsocialist CEE:

> In the field of social policy, over and above the encouragement of interpersonal charity, the main practical principle advocated by the Catholic Church is subsidiarity, a shift of responsibility for help or social action in general from the center or higher levels to the lowest practically possible level. ... The consequences of this principle coincide with those of the neo-liberal efforts to cut back the state. From the present perspective they both imply a growing role of the caring functions of the family, which means first and foremost increasing the tasks and responsibilities of women for the care of children, the elderly, and the sick. (Ferge, 1997: 164)[5]

Gender equity and Independent Living

As a reaction against the postsocialist retraditionalisation and the creeping familialism described above, parental advocacy seeking state funding for informal care work was on the rise in CEE countries in the second half of the 2010s. For example, parents of disabled children in Serbia campaigned for legislation that would formally support their caregiving activities: 'Such a law, they claim, would give a parent the right to stay home with the disabled child with financial compensation for the care work and lost income' (Zaviršek and Fischbach, 2023: 99). Similar campaigns were organised in other postsocialist countries such as Bulgaria, Hungary, and Poland (Dimitrova, 2020; Mladenov and Petri, 2019). I will now consider a mobilisation that took place in Bulgaria in 2018 by drawing on Mladenov and Petri (2019), where parallel Hungarian initiatives have also been analysed. I will then draw parallels with a Slovenian initiative. These case studies will help understand how the motherisation of support under the caregiver parity approach to defamilialisation may hinder both women's and disabled people's self-determination.

In 2018, parents of disabled children took to the streets in the Bulgarian capital Sofia and other cities around the country with demands for adopting legislation that guarantees the provision of state funding for the assistance of their children (Marinova, 2018). This campaign included several months of protest camping in front of the Bulgarian Parliament under the slogan 'The system kills us', public demonstrations, and heated discussions on Facebook. The media presence of the protesting parents was very strong and initiated a nationwide debate on the need to reform disability support in the country (Stoyanova and Stoynova, 2018).

The parents (mostly mothers) were aided by the then Bulgarian Ombudsman Maya Manolova, who collaborated with the activists in drafting a new Personal Assistance Bill. Eventually, the bill was adopted by the Bulgarian Parliament and entered into force on 1 January 2019 as the Personal Assistance Act (PAA; in Bulgarian: *Закон за личната помощ*).[6] One of the aims of this legislation is to provide disabled people with opportunities for 'independent living' (Article 2 of the PAA), with the term being defined in the Additional Provisions of the Act as 'the opportunity for a person with disability to make autonomous decisions about their life and to implement them, receiving the necessary support'.

However, the assistance provided under the PAA could be assessed as restricting the self-determination of the people who use it for a number of reasons. Eligibility remains tied to the medical expert assessment of the ability to work (Article 8 of the PAA), which is strictly focused on individual impairment. This does not help identify the real needs of the applicants. The grouping of applicants by degree of 'dependence' (Article 12 of the PAA) has a homogenising effect, reproducing the main problem with the outcome of the medical expert assessment – the neglect of individual needs. As of November 2023, the maximum number of assistance hours is still limited to 168 hours per month or 8 hours per day (excluding the weekends). People who need more support are forced to use additional services, which are often unavailable, especially in small towns and villages. There is also a requirement to waive the monthly allowances for raising a disabled child, as well as the allowance for attendant services (Article 13 of the PAA), which deprives the people who use assistance under the PAA of funds to purchase additional support. The employment contract that is concluded with the assistant nominally protects the assistant's rights but limits the possibilities for flexible support arrangements. The pay, which currently amounts to 140 per cent of the minimum wage, is often not sufficient to attract appropriate candidates for assistants, especially in big cities.

All these restrictions resonate with the continuing dominance of paternalist and medicalised approaches to disability in Bulgaria (Mladenov, 2018). Inadequately funded personal assistance leads to 'disabled people not having enough PA hours and to reliance on family members for support, or to disabled people having restricted lives' (ENIL, 2023d: 22).

Formal limitations on personal assistance also (indirectly) reinforce postsocialist retraditionalisation by pressurising families to continue the work of care – in nearly all cases, it is family members who are hired as assistants. Moreover, anecdotal evidence suggests that families seek the funding available for personal assistance under PAA as a way to offset neoliberal impoverishment and the impacts of deindustrialisation, especially in remote regions of the country. In effect, personal assistance is reduced to a cash benefit for the mother, contrary to the aims of the legislation. Progress towards egalitarian care is blocked, and both parents/mothers and disabled people get trapped in the institutionalising *inter*dependence of paternalist care. Unsurprisingly, the act has been criticised by Bulgarian Independent Living activists precisely because it pressurises disabled people and their families to employ family members as assistants – CIL–Sofia has argued that providing support in this way reduces it to social assistance for families (CIL, 2018).

An uncannily similar fate befell kindred initiatives in other postsocialist countries. As an example, the Slovenian Personal Assistance Act of 2019 was adopted after a prolonged campaign for legislating personal assistance in the country, spearheaded by the Slovenian Independent Living organisation YHD. In some respects, the Slovenian act has been less restrictive than its Bulgarian counterpart, although it has excluded disabled children from the group of eligible recipients of personal assistance. However, like the implementation of the Bulgarian PPA, the implementation of the Slovenian act resulted in widespread hiring of family members as personal assistants.

According to a recent analysis of this policy (Zaviršek and Fischbach, 2023), the Slovenian act had failed to envisage that family members of disabled people, and particularly mothers who have been disproportionately affected by postsocialist impoverishment and unemployment, 'would be the first to want to provide personal assistance to their disabled relatives' (Zaviršek and Fischbach, 2023: 105). The benefitting families were helped financially, but the ensuing institutionalisation at home created new restrictions of freedom and new forms of coercion, as happened in Bulgaria. This situation prompted YHD and other disability rights organisations to demand the imposition of limitations on the number of family members who could be hired as assistants to a person. Zaviršek and Fischbach (2023: 106) conclude:

> The paternalistic attitude, dating back to the [state socialist] time when the family was the only 'security haven' and the state was considered dangerous and unreliable, continued. In the neoliberal era of post-socialism, the state uses family members, mostly women, for paid care work in families to reduce welfare costs and unemployment.

The cases of the Bulgarian and the Slovenian personal assistance acts illustrate how defamilialisation reforms seeking caregiver parity are not particularly conducive to either women's or disabled people's self-determination. Using Fraser's (1996) distinction between 'affirmative' and 'transformative' redistribution, Mladenov and Petri (2019) have argued that paying mothers to care for their disabled (adult) children exemplifies affirmative measures that amount to surface reallocation of resources, without changing the underlying mechanisms maintaining disabled people's ableist subjugation and women's patriarchal oppression. Indeed, caregiver parity policies promoting defamilialisation – such as maternity leaves and family allowances – 'do not challenge the gendered division of care work within families and can even aggravate gender inequalities' (Mathieu, 2016: 581). Such policies also do not challenge the reduction of disabled people to objects of care and the attendant denial of their self-determination. In contrast, developing community services such as (non-parental and adequately funded) personal assistance could have transformative effects, making disabled people more equal to non-disabled people, and women freer to explore life outside home. As Fraser (1996) has suggested, it is not enough to advocate for social and economic rights, what is needed is to advocate for *transformative* measures for the achievement of these rights.

Notably, caregiver parity is one side of the 'Wollstonecraft dilemma' – the dilemma between universalist policies that fight 'othering' by universalising breadwinning, and differentialist policies that fight 'saming' through valorising caregiving on a par with breadwinning:

> On the one hand, women have demanded that the ideal of citizenship be extended to them, with the liberal-feminist agenda of a gender-neutral social world being the logical conclusion of this demand. In other words, if women are to achieve citizenship rights, they must become like men. On the other hand, women have also insisted, often simultaneously, that their particular social and bodily situations be taken into account and that the expression of their citizenship be differentiated from that of men. (Mathieu, 2016: 583; see also Fraser, 1996: 63)

From a disability perspective, the value of living with an impairment as a form of bodily/mental diversity (a value strongly asserted by critical disability studies scholars) is undermined when asserting universal breadwinning policies that tend to be strongly productivist. For their part, caregiver parity policies, by emphasising women's care work at home, risk objectifying and infantilising disabled people. The importance of including the perspective of the care-receiver in discussions of defamilialisation has been emphasised by Leitner and Lessenich (2007). Although the analysis of these authors focuses exclusively on children as care-receivers, many of the points they make apply to disabled people as well, so it is worth exploring their arguments in some detail.

From the perspective of the caregiver, the defamilialisation of universal breadwinning (e.g., by providing day-care services) may realise 'the right not to care' of the people providing care (mostly women) but does not necessarily lead to women's economic independence (Leitner and Lessenich, 2007: 256). The reason is that, on top of caregiving, there are numerous other attitudinal and structural barriers that prevent women's equal and effective participation in the labour market. From the perspective of the care-receiver, a universal breadwinner approach to defamilialisation realises 'the right not to be cared for by the (i.e. one) parent exclusively' (Leitner and Lessenich, 2007: 251). As far as disabled adults are concerned, this is a crucial right, but it may end up in institutionalisation in a care home. And if, instead of institutionalisation, it encourages economic independence through labour market participation, it may end up entrapping disabled people into poverty and substandard work. Thus, defamilialisation through universal breadwinning is suspect from both perspectives. Productivist defamilialisation may generate more misery than welfare for both the caregivers and the care-receivers, as discussed earlier with regard to state socialist productivism.

However, care-oriented defamilialisation does not fare better. In the case of caring for children or disabled adults, caregiver parity is achieved through parental leaves and childcare or family-based assistance allowances. As already pointed out, caregiver parity policies tend to increase women's entrapment in the caring role (see also Leitner and Lessenich, 2007: 257). From the perspective of the care-receiver, defamilialisation towards caregiver parity erodes the opportunities to choose and control care, whereas 'just like in the case of a women-friendly welfare state, a "children-friendly welfare state" would, above all, enable choices – and take children seriously as an essential and equitable part of the care relationship' (Leitner and Lessenich, 2007: 258). The same applies to disabled adults. Only adequate financial support – for example, in the form of appropriately personalised direct payments or extra-cost disability benefits – enables real choice and control, or egalitarian care. Leitner and Lessenich (2007: 259, original emphasis) conclude that '*economic* de-familization is always in the child's interest as care receiver' and, we may add, in the disabled person's interest as well.

Independent Living and universal caregiving/care-receiving

The alternative to both universal breadwinning and caregiver parity is the 'universal caregiver' model of gender equity (Fraser, 1997: 59–62). It includes policies targeted at creating caregiver-friendly employment (e.g., shorter workweek, employment-enabling services), deinstitutionalisation of public support for caregiving (e.g., provision of public support for informal care work), and empowerment of caregivers through self-management and peer networks (e.g., state-funded local carers' organisations, self-help activities). A combined 'universal caregiver/care-receiver' model of gender and disability equity, informed by the Independent Living paradigm, would engender very similar policies, while helping to counter the paternalism inherent in universal caregiving.

First, concerning labour, Fraser's caregiver-friendly employment corresponds to Independent Living advocacy for disability-friendly employment. Care-receivers share with caregivers a precarious position in the job market that is rectified by a combined 'universal caregiver/care-receiver' model. Thus, Fraser's (1997: 61) provision that the 'employment sector would not be divided into two different tracks; all jobs would be designed for workers who are caregivers, too' corresponds to making all jobs accessible for workers who are also care-receivers. Similar policies serve both groups, including employment mainstreaming (as opposed to employment segregation), a shorter working week, generous parental and sick leaves, flexible employment opportunities, and employment-enabling supports (including personal assistance). Such policies would guarantee that disabled people are not confined to sheltered workshops or relegated to low-skilled, precarious jobs in the mainstream job market.

Second, concerning support in the community, Fraser's vision of deinstitutionalised, community-based caregiving corresponds to Independent Living's deinstitutionalised, community-based vision of care-receiving. Institutionalisation has a negative impact on both caregiving and care-receiving and is therefore negated in a combined 'universal caregiver/care-receiver' model. Thus, Fraser's (1997: 61) provision that 'employees would not be assumed to shift all carework to social services. Some informal carework would be publicly supported' corresponds to Independent Living advocacy for community-based support (another term for deinstitutionalisation). People would not be forced to seek care in institutions but would be enabled to receive publicly provided support in their communities; disabled children would be enabled to stay with their families. Some disabled people would have their relatives as (publicly funded) personal assistants, but the choice of familial support would not be forced on people by lack of non-familial alternatives or by familialist expectations.

Third, concerning self-organising and peer support, Fraser's advocacy for democratic self-organising of carers and peer-supported caregiving corresponds to Independent Living's emphasis on self-organising and peer-supported care-receiving. Self-organising and peer support empower both caregivers and care-receivers and are therefore promoted by a universal caregiver/care-receiver model. Thus, Fraser's (1997: 61) advocacy for 'state-funded but locally organized institutions, childless adults, older people and others without kin-based responsibilities [to] join parents and carers in democratic, self-managed carework activities' overlaps with Independent Living advocacy for the creation of local user-led organisations (modelled after CILs) and peer support groups.

In the final analysis, a universal caregiver/care-receiver model represents an intersectional synthesis between defamilialisation (its primary strategy), decommodification, and deétatisation. Such a synthesis would be incomplete without a discussion of universal basic income. Fraser does not explicitly mention this policy in relation to her universal caregiver approach, but other analysts have included a consideration of basic income in their analysis of the familial dimension of welfare. For example, Leitner and Lessenich (2007: 259) promote basic income as a substitute for policies stemming from productivist ('universal breadwinning') or parentalist ('caregiver parity') defamilialisation. A good example of a productivist strategy grounded in the universalising of breadwinning are Esping-Andersen's (1999: 178–180) proposals for organising welfare in 'postindustrial' society, including dual-earner families, employment flexibilisation, activation, and publicly provided care services that enable caregivers to work. Examples of a parentalist strategy grounded in seeking parity for caregivers are the Bulgarian and Slovenian personal assistance schemes analysed in the preceding section.

Universal basic income is dismissed by Esping-Andersen (1999: 180) as 'impossibly expensive', yet without any analysis or evidence. Indeed, basic income is compatible with the combined universal caregiver/care-receiver model presented here and, moreover, promises to bring about a recognition of the universality of human *inter*dependence. In the case of disabled people, a universal basic income policy needs to be complemented by various top-ups such as an extra-cost top-up and additional funding for personal assistance. An adequate universal basic income, topped up with disability-specific funding, would enable a women-friendly defamilialisation, decommodification, and deétatisation of disability support. As Fraser (Fraser and Honneth, 2003: 78) has also pointed out, universal basic income is a form of 'non-reformist reform' (Gorz, 1967) that has the potential to bring about deep-level social transformation through surface-level resource reallocation.

Last but far from least, the binary of caregiver versus care-receiver needs deconstructing – disabled people also care (for other disabled people, households, carers), and many carers are disabled themselves (Ben-Moshe, 2020: 212). A combined universal caregiver/care-receiver model of gender and disability equity is a step towards such a deconstruction, although an alternative terminology may help convey the message better. Egalitarian care is a two-way street.

Independent Living's ambivalence towards the family

Notwithstanding the strong critique of paternalism voiced by the Independent Living advocates, their attitude towards the family has been characterised by a certain ambivalence that also needs to be recognised. On the one hand, informal support within the family has been targeted by the activists as restricting the self-determination of disabled people, and even as leading to institutionalisation at home, as the Bulgarian and Slovenian cases analysed earlier suggest. Since the early days of activism in the US, the pioneers of the Independent Living movement have argued that 'the "nonpolicy" of reliance on the informal support model has placed an unfair burden on disabled persons and their families' (DeJong *et al.*, 1992: 90). Yet on the other hand, familial support has been regarded by disability rights campaigners as preferable to a placement in a residential institution, especially when such support can be combined with formal personal assistance and other enablers of living independently in the community.

The benefits of familial support highlighted by disability studies scholars include decommodification by avoiding the financial costs of care, as well as the 'intimacy and trust common to positive filial relationships' (Bezmez and Porter, 2022: 61). These benefits have made some Independent Living advocates regard support provided by relatives as a (qualified) enabler of self-determination (Angelova-Mladenova, 2017: 21). The survey on personal assistance mentioned in Chapter 4 included the statement 'The [personal assistance] scheme does not allow for family members to be recruited as personal assistants' (Mladenov, 2020b: 14). Of the 54 personal assistance users and Independent Living advocates who responded, 26 assessed the restriction on recruiting family members as a barrier to 'choice and control', 18 assessed it as an enabler, and 10 remained neutral. Considering the dispersal of individual scores, this statement emerged as representing one of the least consensual characteristics of a personal assistance scheme, indicating an ambivalent stance on the role of the family in support.

In contrast, the survey statement 'The [personal assistance] scheme is provided irrespective of family (including marital) situation' was almost unanimously assessed as among the greatest facilitators of self-determination, ranking fourth in a long list of 100 enablers (Mladenov, 2020b: 9). Independent Living requires that disabled people have access to public support even when their families can support them. Importantly, this requirement also facilitates the self-determination of those family members who are in a position to provide the support – 44 of the 54 respondents of the survey assessed positively the statement 'The scheme "frees" family members from "caring" obligations, enabling them to undertake other activities'. As already argued, there is an overlap between the interests of disabled people and women, especially in familialist contexts, where the availability of close relatives excludes disabled people from qualifying for formal support, while entrapping women into reproductive labour (Buğra and Keyder, 2006: 222).

Another expression of Independent Living's ambivalence towards the family concerns the right to parenting. Independent Living requires that disabled people are enabled to become parents and exercise parental rights (Ratzka, 2019). However, ableist understandings of parenting, coupled with the pervasive desexualisation of disabled people (Shakespeare *et al.*, 1996), have made parental rights unattainable to many disabled people. A person regarded and supported as if they are an eternal child cannot be a parent.

In postsocialist societies, a disabled person's attempt at parenting has amounted to a 'subversive act' (Phillips, 2010: 207) – not only due to ableist attitudes, but also due to lack of support for self-determination that would enable the disabled person to fulfil their parental duties (Iarskaia-Smirnova, 2011). In strongly familialist contexts, the consequences of this type of disablement have disproportionately affected women. Thus, in the conservative welfare regimes, the gendered expectation that female members of the household should provide formally unsupported care has made womanhood unattainable for disabled women: 'Leyla said that she felt unable to be "an ideal wife" because she did not feel "in a position to give care"' (Bezmez and Porter, 2022: 62). This example clearly evidences the mutually constitutive intersection between androcentrism and ableism – patriarchal motherhood and homemaking impose able-normative requirements upon women's bodies, aptitudes, and minds, making it difficult if not impossible for disabled women to become mothers. Yet even in less patriarchal, socially liberal contexts where support for Independent Living has been available for decades, such as in the UK, a major issue for disabled parents has been 'whether they can access assistance without their parenting capabilities being called into question, or their children being considered to be at risk' (Morris, 2004: 433).

As an aspect of Independent Living advocacy, the fight for disabled people's parental rights has entailed challenging norm-conforming parenting, and particularly the paternalist attitudes, policies, and practices explored in this chapter. For many disabled people, access to the family has meant questioning familialism. At the same time, the desire for normality (that striving for a family often implies) makes it difficult not to affirm, in a 'cruelly optimistic' (Berlant, 2011) way, the gendered, ableist, and heteronormative expectations that keep access to the family foreclosed in the first place. In the final analysis, the relationship between Independent Living and the family has been as contradictory as the relationship between the movement, the state, and the market. In parallel with the double-edged task of criticising and supporting the welfare state, and the equally double-edged task of rejecting and affirming marketisation, Independent Living advocates have faced the necessity of both challenging and affirming the family.

Concluding remarks

This chapter considered the family as the third organising principle of social welfare, on a par with the state and the market. In the first part of the chapter, I explored the context-specific relationships between Independent Living and the family in liberal, conservative, social democratic, and post/socialist welfare regimes. Each of these regimes was associated with a specific model of organising the relationships between productive labour ('breadwinning') and reproductive labour ('caregiving'). Drawing on Fraser's (1997) seminal work, I then considered the ways in which different approaches to gender equity, intended to substitute the gender-unequal 'male breadwinner' model, have enhanced or undermined familialism in different welfare state regimes. This enabled me to develop a context-sensitive critique of the family as an organising principle of social welfare that combines welfare state theory, feminist analysis, and analysis from the perspective of Independent Living.

I highlighted the impact of neoliberalisation on various welfare regimes, paying particular attention to the tensions between breadwinning and caregiving. Adding neoliberalisation to the picture reveals a tendency of convergence between the different welfare regimes. The homogenising effects of the neoliberal hegemony have been well explored (Harvey, 2005). In the area of the family, neoliberalisation has enhanced the reliance on informal, family-based support in all main welfare regimes. This has contributed to retraditionalisation, most conspicuous in postsocialist states (due to the contrast with their state socialist past), but also identifiable in other regime types as well. The consequences for both women and disabled people have been increasing restrictions on self-determination (as evidenced recently in limitations imposed on abortion rights in the US).

The convergence thesis clashes with the regime-specificity thesis. The analysis conducted by Esping-Andersen in the late 1990s suggested that neoliberalisation has different effects in different welfare regimes. The 'path dependencies' of the prevailing regime logic determine to what extent deregulation, decentralisation, and welfare-state retrenchment would be adopted and what will be the regime-specific effects of these reforms: 'In the analytical framework that I prefer, the gist of resilient logics is to be found in institutional path dependencies. These derive from the prevailing nexus between households, welfare state, and labour markets' (Esping-Andersen, 1999: 140). However, a quarter of a century later, the global spread of neoliberalisation (enabled by modern technologies) engenders scepticism towards this belief in the resilience of different regimes to neoliberalisation's homogenising tendencies. It may well be the case that most of us are now living in societies of control and are subjected to psychopower, no matter whether we are inhabiting the Global North or the Global South.[7]

Another key concern of this chapter was to highlight the intersections between ableism and androcentrism (and, to a lesser extent, heteronormativity). This argument was most clearly developed in the second part of the chapter, where I discussed two prominent postsocialist mobilisations in support of personal assistance, as well as their familialist outcomes. These case studies helped me to show that ableism and androcentrism are not only mutually reinforcing, but also mutually constitutive mechanisms of oppression (see also Mladenov, 2021b). In other words, most instances of androcentrism are underpinned by ableism and vice versa. It is therefore difficult to challenge androcentrism without challenging ableism. This is a key corollary of the analysis of the relationship between Independent Living and the family developed in this chapter. It also explains some of the contradictions encountered by Independent Living advocacy in its defence of the family, as discussed just before the chapter's conclusion.

Nancy Fraser (1997) has identified a promising approach to resolving the tension between productive and reproductive labour that she termed 'universal caregiving' (see also Leitner and Lessenich, 2007). In this model of gender equity, men are enabled to be more like women by being incentivised and supported to share reproductive work. Accordingly, universal caregiving is commensurate with the strategy of 'demotherisation' of welfare proposed by Matthieu (2016). My contribution to this discussion in this chapter (as in my previous work – see Mladenov, 2016) was to argue that the universal caregiver model risks reproducing paternalist oppression of disabled people, and that this could be avoided by complementing universal caregiving with universal care-receiving – an approach to disability policy that would consider all humans as recipients of support. I now see this as yet another attempt to articulate the background conditions for making care egalitarian.

In the same way in which universal caregiving enables differently gendered humans to become equal in providing care, universal care-receiving enables differently abled humans to become equal in receiving care. Further, in the same way in which universal caregiving is meant to deconstruct the (hierarchically organised) binary opposition between productive and reproductive labour, universal care-receiving is meant to deconstruct the (hierarchically organised) binary opposition between giving and receiving care (or the opposition between independence and dependence). Consequently, the perspective of Independent Living is commensurate with universal care-receiving due to its affirmation of the universality of *inter*dependence.

However, to enable Independent Living, universal care-receiving needs to enable care-receivers to have choice and control in their everyday lives, including over their support.

Notes

1 Notably, people with intellectual impairments have been among those most strongly affected by such infantilisation: 'In essence, the person with intellectual disabilities is seen as an eternal child having "special needs." In terms of social treatment, this leads to paternal and infantilizing attitudes as well as the denial of agency. This could result in loss of reproductive rights, voting rights, freedom, and legitimation of segregation and incarceration in the name of treatment; the innocent is only dangerous to himself or herself and therefore requires care' (Ben-Moshe, 2020: 65).

2 'The great paradox of our times is that familialistic policy appears counterproductive to family formation. At the heart of Catholicism's subsidiarity principle lies the ideal of large, well-integrated, stable, and responsible families. Yet, as things stand today, two Catholic countries – Italy and Spain – boast the world's lowest fertility levels while the most defamilialized welfare regimes in Scandinavia rank among the highest in Europe' (Esping-Andersen, 1999: 67). Recent data suggests that this trend has continued. However, Esping-Andersen's arguments against familialism are couched in the productivist terms of 'waste of human capital' (Esping-Andersen, 1999: 70). The universalisation of breadwinning stemming from such a productivist critique of familialism has a negative impact on the self-determination of both women and disabled people, as I argue in my analysis of Independent Living and the family under state socialism.

3 Notably, since the mid-1960s, the approach changed and familialism in state socialist CEE intensified due to pro-natalist concerns, preparing the ground for the rise of neoliberal neopatriarchy in the aftermath of 1989. At the policy level, the changes included 'the provision of welfare incentives for the home-making woman; more or less serious limitations of human rights in the case of abortion and divorce; the condemnation of "illegal", out of marriage relationships; taboos placed on sexuality, especially on homosexual relationships, on wife and child abuse, and such like. The "communist" morality relating to women and the family varied from country to country, but in quite a few cases it became similar to the most orthodox Catholic morality' (Ferge, 1997: 163).

4 This embeddedness is also highlighted by Ben-Moshe (2020: 226) in her analysis of incarceration in the US context: 'In many hearings regarding the potential closures of institutions or prisons, one of the most pervasive arguments to keep them open (second only to "safety") is about the facilities being major economic engines for their surrounding areas and the loss of jobs their closures will entail.' Ben-Moshe (2020: 226) emphatically criticises this political-economic

rationale for institutionalisation/incarceration: 'Employment cannot triumph over people's freedom. One cannot and should not profit from oppression.'

5 Notably, the Catholic Church has been a major advocate of familialism in social policy: 'The Catholic principle of subsidiarity in its present-day form means strong welfare guarantees to the male bread-winner so as to cement familialism' (Esping-Andersen, 1999: 44).

6 The Act is available in Bulgarian on the legislation page of the website of the Bulgarian Ministry of Labour and Social Policy: www.mlsp.government.bg/zakoni (accessed 9 November 2023).

7 Esping-Andersen (1999) identifies the following regime-specific 'postindustrial' trends. Liberal regimes champion neoliberal deregulation and flexibilisation of the labour market that multiply low-skilled, low-paid, and insecure service sector jobs. The welfare state gets retrenched and transformed into a workfare state. The result is increased inequality, low-wage, and poverty 'traps', but also high economic activity for both men and women (two-earner families) (Esping-Andersen, 1999: 154). Social democratic regimes retain secure and well-paid jobs, including in the public sector, which results in high employment of both men and women (the latter overwhelmingly in the public sector), but the cost of maintaining massive public sectors is constantly increasing. Flexibilisation is offset by generous public support (income maintenance) and activation programmes – as a result, 'there are no major groups that show any significant degree of entrapment, be it in social exclusion or poverty' (Esping-Andersen, 1999: 155). Conservative regimes maintain well-paid, highly skilled, and secure jobs for men at the expense of early retirement (to absorb excess labour), high youth unemployment, and women's ongoing exclusion from the labour market. Deregulation and flexibilisation are mostly targeted at young people, while welfare continues to be delegated to women in male-breadwinner families (that absorb the risks of youth unemployment) (Esping-Andersen, 1999: 153).

6

Independent Living, deinstitutionalisation, and personal assistance

To better ground the ideas discussed so far into policy and practice, this chapter revisits ENIL's advocacy. I begin with a brief overview of deinstitutionalisation reforms in Europe. This provides the context for understanding ENIL's campaigning for deinstitutionalisation as a prominent expression of the organisation's struggle for epistemic justice, complemented by a strong critique of biopower. The specific activities I highlight are ENIL's management of the European Coalition for Community Living, the organisation's participation in the European Expert Group on the Transition from Institutional to Community-based Care, ENIL's monitoring of national deinstitutionalisation reforms supported by European Structural and Investment Funds, and its involvement in the Global Coalition on Deinstitutionalisation.

The overview of ENIL's advocacy for deinstitutionalisation suggests that the overcoming of disabled people's confinement has required a profound social and policy transformation that has not yet been realised in Europe. To understand the depth of the change implied by deinstitutionalisation reform (in other words, to understand its non-reformist essence), one may consider its convergence with prison abolition (Davis, 2003). As Ben-Moshe (2020: 1) has pointed out, disability and incarceration overlap in multiple ways but are seldom seen as interrelated. Most conspicuously, imprisonment (be it therapeutic or punitive) creates impairments, while disabled people are routinely locked up in prison-like facilities such as institutions for social care. Moreover, the different forms of confinement – including in prisons, psychiatric hospitals, and residential institutions – have common histories and rationalities. Highlighting such overlaps between deinstitutionalisation and prison abolition allows Ben-Moshe to frame deinstitutionalisation as part of a paradigm shift in public policy and mentality: 'there are vast connections between disability, deinstitutionalization, and prison abolition as epistemologies of abolition (critique of corrections, maroon knowledges) and dis-epistemologies (refuse certainty, embrace the unfinished, prefigure)' (Ben-Moshe, 2020: 133). Notably, understanding the common grounds of deinstitutionalisation and prison abolition makes it possible to seek intersectional alliances between Independent Living and racial justice movements, given the racialised nature of confinement in its different forms.

The paradigm shift implied in genuine deinstitutionalisation reflects the liberatory aspects of Deleuze's (1992) transition from disciplinary societies to societies of control. Thus, the analysis of ENIL's work in this chapter will support a point already made in Chapter 4 – that Independent Living advocacy does not necessarily substitute biopower with psychopower but can also enable emancipation. In line with theorising on epistemic injustice (Chapter 2), I identify the hermeneutical marginalisation of disabled people maintained by the structures and agencies of the juridical–administrative–therapeutic state as a key barrier to genuine deinstitutionalisation. Thus, instead of substituting residential care with community-based support, European states have been misusing the term 'deinstitutionalisation' to justify investment of national and EU funds in renovating existing institutions or in building smaller settings that nevertheless reproduce institutional approaches, cultures, and practices. Consequently, biopower has assumed more benign manifestations while continuing to enclose, segregate, separate, pathologise, make docile, and surveil. ENIL's monitoring of deinstitutionalisation programmes suggests that this *re*institutionalising form of deinstitutionalisation is most conspicuous in the postsocialist countries of CEE but is characteristic of Western Europe as well. It transcends welfare regimes, which reflects the profundity of the change required by genuine deinstitutionalisation.

Later in the chapter, I also discuss ENIL's advocacy for personal assistance (PA) that complements the organisation's campaigning for deinstitutionalisation. The advocacy for PA has included the development and promotion of a definition of PA underpinned by the Independent Living paradigm, which I consider as yet another instance of ENIL's struggle for epistemic justice. The organisation has used its definition of PA to guide its monitoring of PA services in Europe. The outcomes of these watchdog activities have been presented in several reports. I outline their key findings, making links to some of the critical concepts introduced in the preceding chapters. In particular, I discuss ENIL's criticisms of institutionalisation at home engendered by inadequately resourced, poorly organised, and/or familialist PA programmes. As with reinstitutionalising deinstitutionalisation, institutionalisation at home is most conspicuous in CEE (also evidenced by the Bulgarian and Slovenian case studies developed in Chapter 5), although certainly not limited to this part of Europe.

The geographical scope of ENIL's work makes this chapter Eurocentric. However, many of the struggles described here have analogues in other socioeconomic and cultural contexts, as ENIL's recent experience in the Global Coalition on Deinstitutionalisation suggests (ENIL, 2023f).[1] Moreover, where public programmes for supporting disabled people are currently emerging or undergoing significant reform (such as in some African and Asian countries), institutional care is often considered by policy makers as a preferred model for organising the new schemes. The result is the emergence of institutions for social care in contexts with no traditions in formal institutionalisation. As an example, in March 2023, 14 Korean civil society organisations and 5 European and international disability organisations issued a joint statement to condemn the attempts by Korean policy makers to present institutionalisation in Europe as compliant with the CRPD and as a model to follow: 'The Korean and European disability communities are gravely concerned by the recent claims in Korea that institutions for disabled people in Europe are in line with the UN Convention on the Rights of Persons with Disabilities (UN CRPD) and should be considered as models of good practice' (ENIL, 2023e).

The signatories of the joint statement conclude by calling on countries around the globe to 'refrain from importing bad practices from elsewhere, under the guise of innovation' (ENIL, 2023e). Such policy transfers, they argue, often replicate European practices of institutionalisation due to their sheer entrenchment. The latter explains the ability of institutional care to absorb funding targeted at deinstitutionalisation. This suggests that in non-European contexts, disability policies may need to be decolonised by challenging the hegemony of the European model of institutional care and the attendant medicalisation of disability (Musengi, 2023). Within Europe, the parallel work of decolonising amounts to challenging the hegemony of caring professionals and service providers in framing disability policy (Elder-Woodward, 2023). The analysis in this chapter suggests that it is the hermeneutical marginalisation of the Independent Living activists that makes it possible to present institutional confinement as a form of community-based support in Europe and beyond, thus feigning compliance with the international disability rights legislation (with or without reference to European 'good practices'). Still, the persistence of the confinement paradigm in disability policy is astonishing and reflects the resilience of biopower in the disability area. I revisit this point in the concluding section of the chapter.

Independent Living and deinstitutionalisation in Europe

Since the 1950s, first in North America and Europe and later in other parts of the world, various conceptual and policy responses to the injustices and horrors of institutional care have crystallised. In the late 1960s, the Independent Living movement itself emerged as a reaction to disabled people's institutional confinement. Independent Living activists and their allies have criticised institutions for systematically depriving their residents of self-determination and dignity. A prominent legislative expression of this struggle is Article 19 of the CRPD, widely recognised by Independent Living advocates as an important achievement of the movement. Article 19 is oriented towards challenging and preventing institutionalisation by asserting the right of disabled people 'to live in the community, with choices equal to others'. Subparagraph (a) of Article 19 clarifies that this right presupposes 'the opportunity to choose their place of residence and where and with whom they live on an equal basis with others'.

At the level of critical theorising, the responses to institutional care voiced by the members of the Independent Living movement and incorporated in the CRPD have overlapped with the critiques of the juridical–administrative–therapeutic state and biopower outlined in Chapter 3. At the policy level, these responses have underpinned deinstitutionalisation reforms that, when commensurate with the Independent Living paradigm, have included the provision of publicly funded community-based supports such as PA, housing adaptations, assistive technologies, peer support, supported living arrangements, person-centred planning, and supported decision making, among others (EEG, 2012). Such supports have enabled (some) disabled people in (some) European countries 'to live in the community, with choices equal to others', as advocated by Article 19 of the CRPD. Pioneering policies along these lines have been implemented in social democratic and borderline-liberal welfare regimes in Europe such as Sweden and the UK (Chapter 3).

And yet, in 2007, a major European report estimated that 1.2 million people, including children and adults with psychosocial impairments, were living in residential institutions in 25 European states (Mansell *et al.* 2007: 25). Ten of the 15 top-ranked countries from this sample, as arranged according to the rate of institutionalisation in large institutions (with over 30 places), were former socialist states. Since then, the situation has remained relatively unchanged, despite widespread reforms ostensibly promoting deinstitutionalisation and supported by the EU through its Structural and Investment Funds. In 2020, 1.4 million people still lived in residential institutions in the 27 EU member states (Šiška and Beadle-Brown, 2020). How is this possible, considering the history of Independent Living advocacy in Europe, EU's ratification of the CRPD in 2010, and EU's explicit commitment to deinstitutionalisation (European Commission, 2021, 2010)?

The persistence of institutional care could be explained with the entrenchment of biopower that underpins it at the national and local levels. Financially and organisationally, the European Independent Living movement has been tiny and weak when compared with the publicly supported service provider industry, its academic partners, and the associated provider-led civil society organisations. Parental organisations have also been a strong opponent to deinstitutionalisation, as was discussed in Chapter 5. The same applies to trade unions. Consider, for example, the following apt observation by Ben-Moshe. It was made in the US context but could easily be applied to Europe, adjusting for diversity in welfare regimes, with conservative countries being most likely to match the description due to their strong corporatist arrangements and familialist traditions:

> To keep their jobs secure in economically insecure times, unions had historically and contemporarily resisted closures of prisons and disability institutions. Despite the opportunity for coalition building between progressive social movements such as labor/workers' rights, disability rights, and prison abolition, it is most often the case that unions represent the fiercest opposition to the abolition and closure of prisons and institutions. (Ben-Moshe, 2020: 202–203)

The stakeholders mentioned in the preceding paragraph continue to reproduce the (still) dominant discourse of paternalist care (Chapter 3), itself underpinned by the embeddedness of institutionalisation in local economies (Chapter 5). Institutions have provided livelihoods to the residents of remote areas, while the local elites have exploited the opportunities to accumulate financial and political capital through refurbishment and (re)construction projects: 'Every time a new facility was built or renovated, the cameras of national television showed the proud-looking mayor and his team in front of a newly built residential home, a rebuilt sheltered workshop, or a nursing home' (Zaviršek and Fischbach, 2023: 100). Notably, the material interests driving the construction of new residential institutions for social care resemble those driving imprisonment – as Ben-Moshe (2020: 12) points out, institutionalised disabled people are commodified in similar ways to prisoners.

In essence, the Independent Living initiatives in most European countries have included small groups of activists opposing large national and international networks of much better resourced welfare 'experts', academics, and disability charities with vested interests in maintaining and extending extant relations of biopower. As a result, deinstitutionalisation reforms in Europe have been sluggish, half-hearted, and have often resulted in reinstitutionalising solutions:

> We have received numerous reports of plans to replace large residential institutions with small group homes and similar residential facilities, as well as with foster care for disabled adults. While these services may be located in the community, they perpetuate the segregation and social exclusion of disabled people by failing to provide disabled people with the opportunity 'to choose their

> place of residence and where and with whom they live on an equal basis with others' [as stipulated in Article 19 (b) of the CRPD]. ENIL is also concerned that Member States are not using ESI [European Structural and Investment] Funds to invest in mainstream services, such as housing, employment or inclusive education. (Bulic Cojocariu and Kokic, 2018: 7)

Deinstitutionalisation in Bulgaria could serve as a representative example. Financially supported by European Structural and Investment Funds, the reform has essentially amounted to moving disabled people from large institutions to 'small group homes' and 'centres for family-type accommodation' (CIL, 2012). Although the living conditions in these newly created residential settings have been materially better than the conditions in the large facilities, the practices and relationships between the residents and the staff members have remained unchanged – disabled people have been treated as 'patients' and as a homogeneous group, their everyday lives have been subjected to constant surveillance, their opportunities to choose have been determined by the preferences and schedules of the staff, their personal spaces have been systematically violated, and their participation in the lives of the local communities has remained minimal or symbolic (CIL, 2012; Deneva and Petrov, 2016). (For similar observations on the conditions in the institutions created under 'deinstitutionalisation' programmes in Slovenia, see Zaviršek and Fischbach, 2023.) In essence, the approach of paternalist care has been transferred from the old to the newly created settings:

> The large institution in the small village turns into a small institution in the big town; the space of the large institution (bedrooms, kitchen, dining room, living rooms) turns into the same rooms but within two separate buildings – the bedrooms, kitchen and dining room, into the CFTA [centre for family-type accommodation], the living room and another dining room – into the day-care centre [DC]. The users are 'socially included' by being moved in the morning from the CFTA into the DC, and back in the evening – that is, if there are transport and attendants available. The result – more funding and more jobs are provided, but the effect on the clients is limited to materially improved facilities. (Deneva and Petrov, 2016: 7–8)

The persistent misframing of deinstitutionalisation as renovation of the old institutions or as relocation of residents to newly created smaller settings such as group homes has been particularly prominent in the postsocialist countries of CEE because of the weaker Independent Living traditions there, combined with the heavier reliance on institutional care inherited from the state socialist social policy (Chapter 3). In addition to the Bulgarian case discussed above, other examples include deinstitutionalisation reforms in Croatia, the Czech Republic, Estonia, Hungary, Romania, Latvia, Lithuania, Serbia, Slovakia, and Slovenia, where EU funds have consistently been used to maintain institutional care in a more or less 'facelifted' form (Bulic Cojocariu and Kokic, 2018: 9–10; ENIL, 2022a: 13–15; Parker and Bulic Cojocariu, 2016; Zaviršek and Fischbach, 2023). If, for example, in the US today, 'one would be hard-pressed to hear a doctor order the institutionalization of someone with I/DD [intellectual and/or developmental disability] as an infant' (Ben-Moshe, 2020: 67), physicians continue to advise parents to send their children to residential institutions in present-day Bulgaria (Mladenov and Dimitrova, 2023).

That said, investment in group homes and clustered housing, particularly for people with intellectual and psychosocial impairments, has also been routinely made in Western and Southern European countries characterised by conservative welfare regimes like Austria, Germany, Italy, Malta, and Spain (ENIL, 2022a: 13–18; ENIL, 2022c). Moreover, reinstitutionalising deinstitutionalisation – or reinstitutionalisation, in cases where deinstitutionalisation had already progressed – has also happened in European countries with social democratic or borderline-liberal welfare regimes and strong Independent Living traditions such as Norway, Scotland, and Sweden (Altermark, 2018; ENIL, 2022a: 14).[2]

For example, Altermark's (2018: 92–99) analysis of group homes in Sweden uncovers more or less subtle ways of controlling or micro-managing their residents. The support workers interviewed by Altermark routinely misrepresent independence as self-sufficiency and, accordingly, exercise their professional judgement and power to make the residents more self-sufficient by trying to teach residents do things on their own, without support. In addition, residents are subjected to continuing surveillance and their actions and choices are meticulously recorded (while they are denied access to these recordings). The support workers frequently make ableist assumptions about the capacity of the residents to choose, which leads to nudging the residents towards making 'good' choices. Soft forms of power are exercised in the guise of 'motivational work'. There are also hard and clear restrictions 'concerning how many cups of coffee tenants are allowed to have, what days they are permitted to eat sweets, what kinds of stuff they are allowed to spend their money on' (Altermark, 2018: 102). Restrictions on eating (e.g., staff deciding what is served), sexual activity (e.g., involuntary administration of birth control pills), and movement (e.g., locked doors) are particularly straightforward and blunt (Altermark, 2018: 103). In essence, professional power is reasserted in small institutions – to which the residents (legitimately) respond with frustration and anger due to 'a sense of being controlled and watched over' (Altermark, 2018: 98).

Another example of reinstitutionalising deinstitutionalisation in a Western European context is a recent initiative in Scotland that addressed remote placements and delayed hospital discharges of people with intellectual impairments and complex support needs (Scottish Government, 2022). Although the government report framing the initiative referenced Independent Living and the CRPD, the ideas and practices promoted by the policy makers contradicted both the Independent Living paradigm and Article 19. Let me provide some details.

The report defines the term 'institution' vaguely, and the definition implies that if an institution is closer to home, smaller in size, and providing quality care, it is an acceptable form of support (Scottish Government, 2022: 22). The document also mentions that £20 million have been invested in facilitating hospital discharges and relocating disabled people back to Scotland through a Community Living Change Fund. However, the provision that 'the Fund should not be used to develop institutional services which lack connection with the community and do not allow for people to live a full and rewarding life' (Scottish Government, 2022: 51) implies that funding institutions located in the community is appropriate. And indeed, the policy explicitly promotes clustered housing and shared accommodation: 'it is likely that a bespoke solution in the form of an individual dwelling or some arrangement of shared accommodation or core and cluster provision is likely to be most appropriate' (Scottish Government, 2022: 31). At the same time, disabled people have been hermeneutically marginalised in the development of the policy, as reflected in the composition of the working group drafting the report: 'The expertise of the group was primarily made up of learning disability sector specialists and family carers of people with learning disabilities' (Scottish Government, 2022: 16).

The publication of the report elicited a strongly critical response from the Scottish Independent Living movement, as expressed in a letter of concern to the Scottish government that was signed by more than 20 disability rights organisations (Stakeholder Submission on Common Concerns, 2022). Non-participation was a key complaint:

> Despite stating 'genuine allyship is key, staying true to *nothing about us without us*' (pg.5) and referencing a Human Rights Based Approach and the PANEL Principles (the P standing for participation) (pg.6), there was *no* involvement of people with learning disabilities and/or autistic people, or Disabled People's Organisations in the drafting of this report. (Stakeholder Submission on Common Concerns, 2022, original emphases)

Research on congregated support solutions such as clustered housing and group homes has shown that even if small-scale, better resourced, and/or placed within communities, such settings nevertheless tend to reproduce key features of institutional care (Altermark, 2018; Deneva and Petrov, 2016; Fylkesnes, 2021). But although the relations of biopower in small institutions often recreate the disciplining of bodies and minds in large institutions, the language of 'deinstitutionalisation', including terms and concepts coined and promoted by Independent Living advocates, have been routinely used to present recurrence as progress, as the Bulgarian, Swedish, and Scottish examples discussed above testify. This misuse of terminology has not only been criticised by the members of the Independent Living movement including ENIL (Angelova-Mladenova, 2017; Jolly, 2009), but has also been addressed by the Committee on the Rights of Persons with Disabilities, the body overseeing the implementation of the CRPD. In its General Comment No. 5 on Article 19, the Committee (2017: para. 16) has stated that neither large-scale institutions nor smaller group homes can be called 'independent living arrangements' if they deprive their residents of choice and control in their everyday lives through rigid routines, block treatment, surveillance, and other practices characteristic of institutional care. Furthermore,

> no new institutions may be built by States parties, nor may old institutions be renovated beyond the most urgent measures necessary to safeguard residents' physical safety. Institutions should not be extended, new residents should not enter when others leave and 'satellite' living arrangements that branch out from institutions, i.e., those that have the appearance of individual living (apartments or single homes) but revolve around institutions, should not be established. (Committee on the Rights of Persons with Disabilities, 2017: para. 49)

To avoid reinstitutionalising deinstitutionalisation in Europe, it has been imperative (although far from straightforward) to include smaller but more critical disabled people's organisations in the monitoring of deinstitutionalisation programmes (Parker *et al.*, 2017). As a network of such organisations, ENIL has insisted that European Structural and Investment Funds should only be used to promote Independent Living and inclusion in the community (Bulic Cojocariu and Kokic, 2018), and that this requires establishing appropriate community-based supports. I now turn to these advocacy efforts.

ENIL's advocacy for deinstitutionalisation

ENIL's advocacy for deinstitutionalisation in Europe has been guided by its understanding of the reform as 'a political and a social process, which provides for the shift from institutional care and other isolating and segregating settings to independent living' (ENIL, n.d.-b). This understanding has informed a number of initiatives. To begin with, since 2008, ENIL has managed the European Coalition for Community Living (ECCL) – a Europe-wide initiative that has promoted community-based services as alternatives to institutional care (Parker and Bulic, 2010). ENIL has also been an active member of the European Expert Group on the Transition from Institutional to Community-based Care (EEG) – a coalition of advocacy organisations, international bodies, and service providers established in 2009 by Vladimír Špidla, then European Commissioner for Employment, Social Affairs and Equal Opportunities, and supported by the European Commission to guide deinstitutionalisation in the EU. As part of this collaboration, ENIL has led the development of two highly influential reports on deinstitutionalisation that have had a significant impact on deinstitutionalisation policies at EU level (EEG, 2012, 2014).

ENIL has also monitored the use of European Structural and Investment Funds (ESIFs) for projects ostensibly committed to deinstitutionalisation in EU countries. ESIFs have been the main financial instrument used by the European Commission to help and/or nudge EU member states towards developing their economies and welfare systems in sustainable and socially just ways (European Commission, n.d.). ENIL has monitored the use of ESIFs by collecting and assessing country-specific information on deinstitutionalisation reforms, which has resulted in a number of reports and policy briefings (e.g., Parker and Bulic, 2010, 2013; Parker *et al.*, 2016).

When gathering evidence for these monitoring activities, ENIL has prioritised the testimonies of disabled people and their local organisations, in line with the organisation's democratic constitution discussed in Chapter 2. Thus, rather than confining its monitoring to legal and policy analysis, ENIL has relied heavily on evidence generated on the ground by its members and stemming from the lived experiences of disabled people. This has been a defining feature of ENIL's monitoring and has differentiated its policy work from that of other international organisations that have relied on expert fact-checking missions to develop their reports. Since 2016, ENIL has been doing this work in the framework of its EU Funds for Our Rights campaign, financially supported by the Open Society Foundations (Bulic Cojocariu and Kokic, 2018; Parker *et al.*, 2017).

A more recent initiative has included ENIL's participation in the Global Coalition on Deinstitutionalisation – an international partnership of eight disability rights organisation that emerged from the work on the COVID-19 Disability Rights Monitor (Brennan *et al.*, 2020; also discussed in Chapter 2). In 2022, the Global Coalition on Deinstitutionalisation facilitated the involvement of disabled people and their organisations from around the world in drafting the new *Guidelines on Deinstitutionalisation, Including in Emergencies* (Committee on the Rights of Persons with Disabilities, 2022). Currently, the efforts of the partners are focused on the global dissemination and promotion of these guidelines (ENIL, 2023f).

A critical theorist would approach sceptically these examples of ENIL's engagement with mainstream policy making at the EU and international levels, despite its grounding in local concerns and voices. A critical reading of ENIL's high-level advocacy for deinstitutionalisation would suspect tokenistic involvement and even (inadvertent) legitimising of practices that are contrary to the organisation's mission. As argued in Chapter 2, research on social movements has suggested that the closer the activists get to formal power-holders, the more difficult it becomes to criticise the status quo – a mechanism known as the 'paradox of institutionalisation' (Stammers, 2009). Worse still, ENIL's engagement with global governance might signal co-option into structures of neoliberal governmentality and neo-colonialism (e.g., Altermark, 2018; McGrogan, 2021).

Indeed, ENIL's reports sometimes over-rely on juridical–administrative (although certainly not therapeutic) language that is highly specialised, technical, and expert-centred. Such a discourse maintains the dominance in policy making of lawyers and officials with expertise in EU law and governance, while marginalising the activists: 'if special expertise or highly educated "experts" are needed to even talk about human rights then emancipatory knowledge may remain inaccessible to those who most need it' (Petri *et al.*, 2017: 11). Moreover, the juridical–administrative discourse tends to be self-serving and self-referential by creating its own code, which also gives rise to a demand for the specific expertise needed for the code's decoding and reproduction. At that, the grassroots – in the name of which the discourse is articulated in the first place – are sidelined at the expense of reaching out to EU bureaucrats. Technical language, self-referentiality, and EU targeting threaten to depoliticise ENIL's initiatives.

ENIL's leadership and management have recognised these issues and have responded to them by strengthening the organisation's work with the activists at the grassroots level (Chapter 2). It has also mediated between the activists on the ground and the bureaucrats in Brussels by helping the activists to interact with the civil servants (see, for example, *ENIL's Guide to Advocating for Independent Living in the European Parliament* [ENIL, 2020]) and by informing the latter about the activists' demands (see, for example, *ENIL's Proposal for the EC Guidance on Independent Living and Being Included in the Community*' [ENIL, 2023d]). Still, such mediations inevitably generate internal contradictions. The paradox of institutionalisation affects every activist initiative that seeks to create an impact through participation in mainstream policy making.

A more generous reading of ENIL's campaigning and monitoring activities would also uncover at their heart a fierce epistemic struggle over the meaning of deinstitutionalisation, itself an element of the fight of Independent Living advocates for the meaning of independence (Chapter 1). As already noted, deinstitutionalisation reforms in Europe have overwhelmingly been channelled by the most powerful stakeholders in the process (service providers, policy makers, trade unions, big disability charities) towards reinstitutionalising ends. But although the new settings have reproduced key features of institutional life, the stakeholders have claimed creating 'independent living' solutions, thus appropriating the language of Independent Living. This strategy of maintaining the status quo has been deployed in all welfare regimes considered so far. In a position paper drafted for ENIL, the British Independent Living activist Debbie Jolly (2009: 5) has described it in the following way:

> Such organisations do not work within the framework of the independent living movement to benefit disabled people; rather they use these terms to profit financially and politically. In fact residential institutions can use these terms to claim that their institutions are 'independent living institutions', they and the non-residential day centres can develop terms like 'independent living' skills which may consist of learning tasks which relieve staff of some activities for example doing up buttons on clothing. While residential institutions cannot be called independent living institutions or centres neither can those working in them be claimed to provide 'personal assistant services'.

It is therefore hardly surprising that ENIL's epistemic struggle over the meaning of deinstitutionalisation has been a central aspect of its monitoring of deinstitutionalisation reforms in Europe. The organisation has repeatedly asserted that according to EU regulations, guidelines, and reports, European Structural and Investment Funds should not be invested in building new residential institutions or renovating existing ones, except in life-threatening circumstances and as part of ongoing efforts at deinstitutionalisation (Parker *et al.*, 2016: 43). To rectify the hermeneutical marginalisation of disabled people in interpreting and assessing deinstitutionalisation initiatives, ENIL has advocated for the inclusion of disabled people's organisations in the monitoring of deinstitutionalisation programmes at the national and European levels (Parker *et al.*, 2017).

The next section focuses on personal assistance (PA), which has been yet another site of fierce epistemic struggle for the campaigners from ENIL. The advocacy for PA in Europe has encountered similar misuse and misappropriations as the advocacy for deinstitutionalisation.

ENIL's advocacy for personal assistance

The provision of support for hiring and managing personal assistants has been among the original priorities of CIL–Berkeley (Zukas, 1975) and has eventually become a defining feature of its European heirs, including ENIL (Hunt, 2019: Ch. 8; Ratzka, 2004). Article 19 (b) of the CRPD explicitly includes PA among the community services that the States Parties should develop to enable disabled people to live independently and be included in the community, and PA is discussed extensively in General Comment No. 5 of the Committee on the Rights of Persons with Disabilities (2017). Currently, most European countries have publicly funded PA schemes (ENIL, 2022a: 3).

However, as with deinstitutionalisation, with PA the devil is in the details. Whereas properly resourced, user-led, and user-controlled PA is key for Independent Living, provider-controlled and/or restrictive one-on-one support billed as PA may hinder self-determination and lead to institutionalisation at home. Ratzka (2019: 10–11) makes the point clear:

> The transition from institutional to community living is not automatically accompanied by higher degrees of independence and self-determination for the person who requires assistance. Depending on the number of assistance hours, the organizational structure of the service provider and the resulting division of power over services between staff and client, the individual user – although living by him- or herself in an ordinary apartment – might in effect not have more self-determination than someone who lives in an institution of brick and mortar. Not being in charge of important functions, such as recruitment, training, scheduling, supervision of your assistants can turn your home into an institution.

Independent Living activists have created and promoted detailed definitions of PA to prevent such mis-provision of PA or misuse of the term. A prominent example is the model of PA described by Ratzka (2004) and explored in detail in Chapter 4, in the discussion of the convergences and divergences between psychopower and Independent Living. Drawing on this work, ENIL (n.d.-g) has defined PA as 'a tool which allows for independent living', characterised by funding through cash allocations (direct payments), provision on the basis of individual needs and circumstances, rates of pay that ensure adequate salaries for the assistants and cover additional expenses (e.g., employer contributions, administration, and peer support), and, perhaps most importantly, the ability of the PA users to recruit, train, and manage their assistants. This definition is also in line with the detailed definition of PA provided by the Committee on the Rights of Persons with Disabilities (2017: para. 16) in its General Comment No. 5.

ENIL's definition of PA challenges provider-led interpretations which have presented as 'personal assistance' support that is available only in kind and/or covering only a limited set of needs, with inadequate rates of pay and other restrictions – in essence, support that deprives its users of choice and control over recruitment, training, and management of their assistants. Independent Living activists have insisted that provider-led, limited, conditional, and/or inflexible support schemes may amount to home care, or nursing, or companionship, but not PA (Westberg, 2010; Mladenov *et al.*,

2023). By making such distinctions possible, ENIL's definition of PA has been yet another vehicle for the advancement of epistemic justice in the disability policy area – it has provided hermeneutically marginalised people with a means to challenge interpretations of individually provided support that may restrict disabled people's self-determination under the guise of maximising it.

Notwithstanding such definitional efforts, ENIL's monitoring of PA programmes in Europe has consistently highlighted the significant variability of support identified (sometimes misleadingly) as PA in different countries (ENIL, 2013, 2015, 2022a; Mladenov *et al.*, 2019). At the beginning of the 2010s, ENIL conducted a study of PA that included desk research of existing national legislative provisions, as well as a survey among disability experts from 22 European countries about the availability and the characteristics of PA schemes provided in their countries (ENIL, 2013). In this study, experts from 14 of the countries in the sample reported on the availability of relevant legislation, but the characteristics of the services provided under the heading of PA varied widely and, in many cases, these characteristics were in contradiction with ENIL's definition of PA. This analysis was updated in a follow-up study conducted in 2015 that identified lack of progress or deterioration of existing PA services:

> The challenges that PA users throughout Europe meet nowadays have not changed much since 2013. Disabled people are still fighting to receive more hours of assistance, better salaries for their assistants and access to PA regardless of the type of their impairment. One of the main reasons for these challenges is financial, but not less important is the difficult transition from the medical to the social model of disability. Changing the mindset of society and decision makers is a challenge that needs to be tackled persistently. (ENIL, 2015)

More recently, in 2018, while working as a researcher at ENIL, I co-produced with my colleagues a monitoring tool that we called 'PA Checklist' and that was mentioned in Chapters 4 and 5 (Mladenov, 2020b). The PA Checklist was then applied by Independent Living experts and PA users in eight European countries (Mladenov *et al.*, 2019). Based on their assessments, each PA scheme achieved an overall score, indicating the degree to which the scheme enabled or hindered users' choice and control. In addition to the overall scores, mean scores were calculated for five different dimensions of PA. Table 6.1 summarises the results – more detailed information about the study is presented in Mladenov *et al.* (2019), where the PA Checklist is also included as an appendix. It should be noted that the specific information provided by the experts in their assessments has not been cross-checked or further verified, so it must be taken with caution.

Table 6.1 PA Checklist – summary (reprinted from Mladenov *et al.*, 2019)

Country, region	PA scheme (in local language in brackets)	Coverage*	Overall mean score	Mean score by dimension				
				Context	Funding	Needs assessment	Provision	Working conditions
Belgium, Flanders	Personal Following Budget (PVB Persoonvolgende budget)	regional	0.30	–0.23	1.05	0.89	–0.94	0.73
Bulgaria, Sofia†	Assistant for Independent Living (Асистент за независим живот)	local	–0.71/ –0.91	–0.69/ –1.30	–1.87/ –1.87	0.23/ 0.20	–0.05/ –0.24	–1.19/ –1.33
Ireland	Health Service Executive Scheme	national	–0.61	–1.60	0.06	–1.32	–0.18	–0.03
Serbia	Personal Assistance Service (Usluga personalne asistencije)	national	1.13	1.98	–1.14	1.41	1.43	1.97
Slovenia	Independent Living (Neodvisno življenje)	national	1.03	0.88	–1.14	1.73	2.05	1.64
Spain, Andalucía	Pilot Project of Independent Living (Proyecto piloto Vida Independiente)	regional	0.03	0.76	–1.87	0.52	0.98	–0.23
Sweden	Personal Assistance Direct Payment (Assistansersättning)	national	1.34	0.64	1.87	0.18	2.08	1.96
United Kingdom§	Direct Payment – Personal Budget	national (local funding)	–0.42	–1.33	–0.43	–0.43	–0.02	0.10

Notes

*All of the PA schemes included in the sample are publicly funded, although levels (national, regional, local) and forms of funding vary (i.e., they can be annual, project-based, social insurance based, requiring users' contributions, including charity contributions).

†Two assessments were completed in Bulgaria by two experts who assessed the same PA scheme independently of each other. Therefore, the corresponding cells of the table contain two values for mean score each.

§The UK assessment concerns the national policy of providing 'direct payments' for PA as a whole, rather than any particular version of the policy implemented by a particular local authority.

The results from the application of the PA Checklist confirmed a key finding reported in the previous two studies of PA implemented by ENIL (2015, 2013) about the variability of support schemes identified as PA in different European countries. Thus, the checklist provided a quantifiable way of assessing and comparing support schemes presented as PA, and it did so from the hermeneutically marginalised position of the Independent Living paradigm. The mean scores given in Table 6.1 allowed judging at a glance whether a PA scheme conformed to a definition of PA created and supported by the members of the Independent Living movement in Europe. Thus, for example, the PA schemes available on the national level in Sweden and Serbia were assessed as highly compatible with this definition, whereas the PA schemes available at the local level in Bulgaria and at the national level in Ireland were assessed as incompatible. Similar to reinstitutionalising deinstitutionalisation, restrictive and/or provider-controlled PA deprives the people who use the support of their independence. The Bulgarian and Slovenian case studies presented in Chapter 5 also evidence this point.

ENIL has continued the work of monitoring PA schemes by launching its first Independent Living Survey in June 2020 (ENIL, 2022a). The survey contained general questions about Independent Living and more specific questions about PA that draw on its previous two studies (ENIL, 2015, 2013) and the PA Checklist (Mladenov *et al.*, 2019). It covered 43 European countries, receiving a total of 143 responses from disabled people (including PA users) and disabled people's organisations (ENIL, 2022a). The results (updated in 2022) iterate the findings from the previous surveys, including that 'many of the schemes/policies described [by the respondents] do not fulfil some or many of the criteria listed in the definition of PA' (ENIL, 2022a: 6). Overall, all but one of the PA schemes reported in the survey were assessed by the respondents as 'inadequate' or 'requiring improvement' (ENIL, 2022a: 22). Widespread problems identified by the respondents included decentralised funding (that leads to a 'postcode lottery' of support), restrictions on PA tasks and timing, insufficient funding (to cover all needs), unavailability of direct payments, discrimination against persons with certain impairments and/or older people, restricted national or transnational portability of PA, medicalised assessments of needs, and lack of peer support (ENIL, 2022a).

The research efforts mentioned in this section have also amounted to policy interventions that have sought to advance epistemic justice in disability policy making by asserting an interpretation of PA grounded in the experiences of disabled people who use support from others on an everyday basis.

Concluding remarks

This chapter explored ENIL's advocacy for deinstitutionalisation in the context of transitioning from institutional to community-based support in Europe. I discussed the tendency to misuse Independent Living vocabulary and grammar by presenting the refurbishment of old institutions and/or the building of new ones as a shift from institutional care to 'living independently and being included in the community' (Article 19 of the CRPD). I identified this misuse as a case of epistemic injustice which ENIL has struggled to rectify by exposing the understanding of deinstitutionalisation embraced by the dominant stakeholders as false. In its advocacy, ENIL has sought to overcome the hermeneutical marginalisation of disabled people in negotiating the meaning of deinstitutionalisation by formulating and promoting an understanding of the reform grounded in the Independent Living paradigm. According to this (still) marginalised understanding, effective deinstitutionalisation requires access to housing in the community, mainstream services, peer support, and adequate PA, among other supports.

The analysis of the epistemic struggles of Independent Living activists amidst deinstitutionalisation reforms has been enabled by the concept of 'reinstitutionalising deinstitutionalisation'. This helps unmask the facelifting of old institutions and the building of new (usually smaller) ones as recurrence presented as progress and increasingly legitimised with reference to Article 19 of the CRPD. I argued that reinstitutionalising deinstitutionalisation is most conspicuous in the postsocialist countries of CEE. There, the reform targeted the 'total institutions' inherited from state socialist disability policy – large, grim, prison-like, geographically remote, materially neglected during post-1989 neoliberalisation, but still deeply embedded in local economies (themselves devastated by the neoliberal transformations). Against this background, it has been relatively easy to present as 'deinstitutionalisation' any improvements in the living conditions of the residents.

I also argued that reinstitutionalising deinstitutionalisation has been widespread in conservative, liberal, and social democratic regimes as well. There, the recurrence of institutional care has been presented by the dominant stakeholders as progress towards community-based support in policies specifically targeted at people with psychosocial and intellectual impairments, and/or those with complex support needs. Notably, these are the groups that have been most strongly entangled in relations of biopower in all welfare state regimes. In essence, reinstitutionalising deinstitutionalisation reflects the sheer resilience of biopower, conspicuous in postsocialist countries but also characteristic of other welfare regimes. In other words, reinstitutionalising deinstitutionalisation evidences the difficulty of transforming biopower into either psychopower or genuine empowerment in contemporary European disability policy.

In Chapter 4, I argued that PA – a prominent element of deinstitutionalisation that has always been a priority for Independent Living activists – may at first sight appear as enabling the shift from biopower to psychopower, or from (statist) societies of discipline to (marketised) societies of control. However, when analysed in detail, the PA promoted by the Independent Living movement is revealed as crowding out psychopower by prioritising self-determination over self-exploitation. In this chapter, I considered another critique of PA – when organised in restrictive ways, PA approximates home care and becomes a vehicle of institutionalisation at home. Familialist models of PA are a major enabler of this recurrence of institutionalisation in a domesticated form. They maintain relations of familial power and paternalist care, and as such are particularly prominent in conservative welfare regimes, but also in the increasingly retraditionalising postsocialist societies of CEE (Chapter 5).

In the final part of the chapter, I discussed the ways in which ENIL has sought to overcome such distortions of PA, as understood by the Independent Living activists. The organisation has done this by monitoring PA programmes in Europe, including through checklists detailing 'good PA' and grounded in the experiences and visions of Independent Living activists and PA users (Mladenov *et al.*, 2019). These monitoring activities have helped expose flawed PA in the same way in which ENIL's monitoring of deinstitutionalisation has helped expose flawed transitioning to 'living independently and being included in the community' as recurrence masked as progress (drawing on Ratzka, Elder-Woodward [2023] has used the more suggestive term 'fake PA').

In conclusion, ENIL's work reflects the essence of Independent Living advocacy, as identified in the preceding chapters of this book. The Independent Living paradigm simultaneously criticises and defends the state, the market, and the family. At that, each of these principles of the organisation of social welfare may be mobilised by the activists against the others. Thus, ENIL's critique of the state, implied in the organisation's monitoring of publicly funded yet *re*institutionalising deinstitutionalisation in Europe, is enabled by the promotion of quasi-marketisation through PA based on direct payments. ENIL's critique of the market is implied in the organisation's advocacy for public funding for PA, which is itself underpinned by ENIL's qualified but still family-friendly promotion of *inter*dependence. Finally, ENIL's critique of the family is implied in the organisation's criticisms of institutionalisation at home and the attendant questioning of familialist and/or restrictive PA. In all these critical interventions, ENIL has fought for epistemic justice by striving to overcome the hermeneutical marginalisation of the Independent Living activists in defining institutional care, deinstitutionalisation, and PA.

Notes

1 Ben-Moshe (2020: 3) provides data on deinstitutionalisation in the US, where the process has similarly been reduced to the relocation of residents from big to small institutions. Thus, while the number of people with intellectual impairments living in large institutions in the US decreased by 80 per cent in the period 1977–2015, the number of residents in 'small residences (six or fewer people)' increased by more than 1,900 per cent over the same period (Ben-Moshe, 2020: 3). Hence, the analysis in this chapter would apply to the US context as well.

2 Another manifestation of reinstitutionalisaiton is making recourse to imprisonment as a substitute for residential care. Analysts who condemn imprisonment sometimes highlight this form of incarceration to criticise the closure of social care institutions as an injustice inflicted on people with psychosocial impairments by neoliberal welfare-state retrenchment (e.g., Wacquant, 2009: 72–73). From the perspective of Independent Living, this diagnosis is correct (lack of support enhances imprisonment), but the implied treatment (rebuilding social care institutions) is flawed. Ben-Moshe (2020: 11–12) explains the substitutions of institutionalisation with imprisonment in the US with neoliberalisation because it combined welfare state retrenchment (disinvestment in social support) with law-and-order entrenchment (investment in punishment). However, instead of defending residential care from neoliberal cuts, the Independent Living paradigm suggests that advocacy should focus on securing public support for community-based and user-led alternatives to institutional care. One promising approach is to highlight the parallels between peer support for 'desistance' (Maruna, 2017) and peer support for Independent Living. Similar to the mutual help among disabled people who seek to escape confinement, desistance approaches to criminal justice aim at transcending 'professionally-centric, individual-level and sustaining co-production modalities, towards the advance of user-led, group and collective forms' (McCulloch, 2021: 421–422). Indeed, McCulloch (2021: 422) explicitly mentions the Independent Living movement as epitomising the approach of peer support that has eventually been embraced by the desistance movement: 'It is this kind of user-led, collective, rights-based, paradigm-changing, empowered, empowering and advocacy-oriented construction of peer support that is relevant to our discussion here.'

7

Independent Living and other critical positions

There are considerations that are highly relevant to Independent Living but that have remained marginal or insufficiently theorised in the preceding chapters of the book. They include mental capacity, de/coloniality, and technology. On the one hand, considering these broad topics through a critical-theoretical lens has the potential to strengthen Independent Living's conceptual foundations. On the other hand, exploring capacity, de/coloniality, and technology from an Independent Living perspective could enhance extant critical-theoretical analyses in these areas. Moreover, support with decision-making (capacity) and access to assistive technology are major 'pillars' of Independent Living, as explained in the Introduction – therefore, their analysis has a strong practical and policy relevance.

Considering de/coloniality has important meta-theoretical implications when approaching Independent Living as a historically, culturally, and materially grounded epistemology. Indeed, throughout this book, I have consistently emphasised the rootedness and context-dependence of the Independent Living paradigm – for example, by historicising it and by discussing the details of the movement's interactions with various welfare regimes. Engaging with a meta-theoretical analysis of the type produced by critiques of de/coloniality is also imperative, considering that a key concept driving the discussion in the preceding chapters has been epistemic in/justice.

What does a 'capacity' to reason entail? Does Independent Living presuppose mental capacity? How can one exercise 'choice and control' if one's decision making is impaired? How 'colonial' is the Independent Living paradigm? Does it marginalise Indigenous knowledges about disability, thus reproducing a trans-cultural epistemic injustice, while trying to overcome an intra-cultural one? Is there a sense in which Independent Living helps 'decolonise' people? What does the disability perspective suggest about prevailing criticisms of modern technology? What is the impact of new technologies on disabled people's opportunities to live independently in their communities? These are the questions that will be explored below, hoping to fill in some of the gaps left by the preceding analysis. I start with capacity, then consider critiques of coloniality and decoloniality, finishing with a brief overview of technology.

Independent Living and critique of capacity

The concept of mental capacity resonates with the foundational assumptions of liberalism. In its influential Kantian version, it is asserted that human beings are at their best when they make autonomous use of their reason, as explained in Chapter 1. Tellingly, Kant (1991a: 54) uses the metaphor of 'walk[ing] unaided' (in German: *allein zu gehen*) to explain his idea of autonomous reasoning. In disability studies, the praise of unsupported walking has been exposed as manifesting a cultural politics of disablement (Oliver, 1993). It overvalues self-sufficiency and is associated with the intersectional norm of the adult, non-disabled, property-owning man. Women, children, salaried workers, and disabled people are excluded from the Kantian model of full citizenship because they are perceived as non-autonomous. The metaphor of 'walking unaided' indicates that for classical liberalism, compulsory able-bodiedness has always been underpinned by compulsory able-mindedness. One is a full ('mature') human being only when one can reason without external support or influence.

As repeatedly emphasised throughout this book, the Independent Living paradigm provides a solid ground for rejecting self-sufficiency as a measure of human worth. Moreover, Independent Living helps reject self-sufficiency as an existential-ontological claim as well. From the perspective of Independent Living, self-sufficiency is an optical illusion generated by taken-for-granted or familiar (hence invisible) social constructs that prioritise certain groups while marginalising or oppressing others. In reality, no one is self-sufficient. The Kantian embodiment of autonomous reasoning – the adult, non-disabled, property-owning man – is *enabled* by his parents, wife, workers, assistants, infrastructures, and wider legal and cultural norms to exercise his autonomy. As an alternative to self-sufficiency, the Independent Living paradigm foregrounds a qualified defence of *inter*-dependence. Importantly, the latter concerns not only one's capacity to act (or 'walk' in the Kantian example) but also and essentially one's capacity to think (or 'reason').

This means that the Independent Living paradigm rejects the policy of 'guardianship' and the attendant denial of legal capacity. Dismantling these mechanisms of paternalist care is an essential condition for effective deinstitutionalisation, which 'includes an end to substitute decision-making, including guardianship, and to forced treatment (including in the community)' (ENIL, 2023d: 15). At first sight, it may seem that rejecting substitute decision making is commensurate with Kant's liberal-individualist vision of 'maturity' as the ability to think unaided:

> The guardians who have kindly taken upon themselves the work of supervision will soon see to it that by far the largest part of mankind (including the entire fair sex) should consider the step forward to maturity not only as difficult but also as highly dangerous. Having first infatuated their domesticated animals, and carefully prevented the docile creatures from daring to take a single step without the leading-strings to which they are tied, they next show them the danger which threatens them if they try to walk unaided. (Kant, 1991a: 54)

Indeed, guardianship empowers another to make decisions in one's stead. As such, guardianship has been a key driver of the institutional confinement of disabled people. In contexts with established traditions in institutionalisation and poorly developed community-based supports – for example, in the postsocialist countries of CEE – guardianship has been used to keep disabled people locked up in remote and prison-like facilities, including by appointing the managers of these facilities as the residents' guardians.[1] But guardianship has also enabled institutionalisation in contexts with well-developed community support structures such as the UK – for example, by preventing people with intellectual impairments from accessing direct payments (Morris, 2004: 431), or by facilitating delayed hospital discharges and remote placements (Stakeholder Submission on Common Concerns, 2022).

However, instead of rejecting interference with decision making, Independent Living advocates insist on a shift towards interference that enables self-determination. From the perspective of Independent Living, a person's (presumed) lack of mental capacity cannot be used as an argument for restricting the person's self-determination by limiting their legal capacity (People First Scotland, n.d.). This argument stems from the relational or distributed understanding of agency discussed in Chapter 1, rather than from the liberal-individualist approach promoted by Kant. Accordingly, Independent Living advocates defend a shift from substitute to supported decision making. The underpinning assumption is that mental capacity, understood as capacity to make decisions, is socially constructed, relational, and contextual. It is a function of upbringing, experience, available supports, relationships, hierarchies, and cultural norms: 'not only is the person's ability to think and act affected by where the person lives and how the person is treated but the people who assess capacity also do that differently depending on where they live and the rules they live under' (People First Scotland, n.d.: 12). This position is also in line with Article 12 of the CRPD on 'equal recognition before the law' and the accompanying

General Comment No. 1 of the Committee on the Rights of Persons with Disabilities (2014).

Some disability studies scholars have challenged the distinction between substitute and supported decision making. In Chapter 4, I mentioned Altermark's (2018: 86) criticism that instead of disrupting liberal-individualist models of agency, supported decision making (indirectly and insidiously) reasserts this model by creating a softer version of substitute decision making. This is a healthy scepticism that could help prevent misuses of the concept like the misuses of 'Independent Living', 'deinstitutionalisation', and 'personal assistance' discussed in the preceding chapters. But there is no need to abandon the concept as inherently reproducing liberal-individualist exclusions. Genuine supported decision making has the potential to be truly emancipatory for those who have access to it. This is the view of Independent Living organisations of people with intellectual impairments such as JAG (2011) and People First Scotland (n.d.). They understand mental capacity in a distributed, socially constructed way. That said, it may sometimes be difficult to distinguish genuine support with decision making from one that merely masks substitute decision making. This is particularly the case when soft forms of power (or psychopower) are used to nudge or 'motivate' people to make specific decisions, as often happens in small institutions:

> You constantly need to guide them in their self-determination and decisions. It is about informing and pointing out why certain things are important [to think about when choosing]. Sometimes, it is not possible, but oftentimes you can argue with them. It is never about forcing, because we are not allowed to do that. (staff member in a group home, quoted in Altermark, 2018: 96)

This example suggests that the context of the support with decision making is as important as the intentions of those providing such support. It makes a difference if support with decision making is provided in a group home by caring professionals, or at one's own home by peers. Altermark (2018: 97, original emphasis) makes the point that in the group home 'we are not dealing with regular advice giving like you would find in most relationships between friends or siblings. Motivation is not presented as input into the decision-making process of people with intellectual disabilities but as a measure that seeks to produce the *correct* decisions.' In the group home, there is an underlying hierarchy structured along the lines of professional power that invokes paternalistic attitudes: 'motivational work presumes a hierarchy, where the support worker doing the motivating perceives their own viewpoint as superior' (Altermark, 2018: 98). Genuine deinstitutionalisation is, therefore, essential for genuine supported decision making. Accordingly, reinstitutionalising deinstitutionalisation (Chapter 6) turns supported decision making into a tool for psychopolitical control.

Another point to consider is that, by being socially constructed, mental capacity is also profoundly intersectional. When full citizenship is understood as requiring self-sufficiency, and self-sufficiency is perceived as founded on unsupported and abstracted use of reason, then the adult, non-disabled, property-owning man – who is also usually an urban resident of the metropole, of a majority-ethnic background, heterosexual, and of working age – inevitably emerges as an intersectional ideal. One of the prominent critiques of the Independent Living paradigm has been that it has prioritised physically impaired middle-class males (e.g., Ferguson, 2007: 398; Williams, 1983: 1005). This charge highlights the issue of persisting impairment hierarchies within the wider disabled people's movement (Griffiths, 2019), but also the widespread misrepresentation of the Independent Living movement as promoting self-sufficiency.

Independent Living organisations such as ENIL have responded to such criticisms with an intersectional turn (Chapter 2). The latter has entailed an increasing attention to the specific forms of marginalisation experienced by people with intellectual and psychosocial impairments (including psychiatric survivors), autistic people, young and older disabled people, and disabled women. The evidence considered in the preceding chapters of this book suggests that in the work of ENIL, Independent Living has manifested as a cross-impairment and gender-sensitive approach to disability. I will briefly revisit here the version of personal assistance (PA) promoted by ENIL because it clearly demonstrates an understanding of mental capacity as socially constructed, thus enabling intersectional alliances.

As argued in Chapter 6, ENIL's understanding of PA has drawn heavily on the model described by Ratzka (2004). This model presupposes a distributed understanding of agency by stipulating that to enable self-determination, the decision making exercised by disabled people in managing their assistance needs to be underpinned by various supports (Mladenov, 2012). Thus, children and people with intellectual and psychosocial impairments may need to be enabled by 'third persons' in using PA (Ratzka, 2004: 3). The model complements this claim with a redistributive demand – the delegation of agency through involvement of third persons should be publicly funded: 'The costs of such support need to be covered by the policy, if necessary, by higher payments for the average assistance hour' (Ratzka, 2004: 3, n. 4).

Ratzka (2004: 3) also renders assistance-related choices as socially constructed by requiring 'information, counselling and other support' in addition to delegation of decision-making power. Moreover, decision-making capacity entails skills that are acquired through experience and socialisation – the model envisions that people can 'try assistance solutions with varying degrees of user responsibility and, step by step, at their own pace,

… develop the skills required to take on more control over their services' (Ratzka, 2004: 3, n. 3). Last but not least, by emphasising the significance of peer support for effective management of PA, the model described by Ratzka incorporates a collective aspect that further contextualises capacity: 'In all contacts with the funding agency's staff regarding needs assessment, appeals or other administrative issues assistance users can utilize the counsel and support of third persons of their choice, in particular, other personal assistance users' (Ratzka, 2004: 5). Peer support is also considered essential in information, training, and advocacy activities (Ratzka, 2004: 4), and its costs should be covered by the scheme (Ratzka, 2004: 7), which articulates yet another redistributive demand.

Based on this analysis, in an article published in 2012 I argued that for Independent Living activists

> to be fully human does not mean to be autonomous in any material and/or ideal sense. Neither the objectively delimited 'healthy' body nor the subjectively delimited 'sovereign' mind can serve as ultimate existential-ontological reference points for proposing social policy solutions to disability-related problems. … Without being determinable in any case, free choice and subject-centred control are nevertheless *mediated* by choice-facilitating practices in which humans engage in their being-in-the-world. This might seem puzzling, but only if we stick to an understanding of 'independence' as 'autonomy' in the liberal-individualist way. On the other hand, if we understand 'independence' as a *particular type of inter-dependence* (as suggested above), the empuzzlement dissolves. (Mladenov, 2012: 252, original emphases)

A decade later, I still affirm this view. Its significance for the 'capacity' debate outlined above is obvious. People's decision-making ability is socially constructed. Therefore, a presumed lack of mental capacity cannot justify a denial of legal capacity. Instead, any identified deficiencies in mental capacity need to be addressed by providing additional supports and adapting the environment so that people's opportunities to make choices and be in control are maximised. Supported decision-making models such as the one developed by the disabled people's organisation People First Scotland (n.d.) are designed to enable people's self-determination instead of confining them at home or in an institution via guardianship. They are underpinned by a relational or distributed understanding of agency, as is the model of PA described by Ratzka (2004) and embraced by ENIL: 'all forms of substitute decision-making should be abolished and replaced by supported decision-making arrangements, recognizing disabled people's right to make their own decisions' (Angelova-Mladenova, 2017: 6).

It is also worth mentioning that the ideas of distributed agency in managing PA towards self-determination have been realised in practice. A prominent example is the work of the Swedish Independent Living organisation

JAG (2011) – a cooperative of PA users with intellectual impairments.[2] The supportive decision maker in JAG's model of PA is a 'legal proxy' who is designated by the court and 'is able to interpret needs, wishes and communication' (JAG, 2011: 6) of the PA user. The latter is also helped by a 'service guarantor', who supervises the assistant/s (JAG, 2011: 10–12). This support with managing PA is crucial and displays the minute details of the distributed agency embraced by the Independent Living paradigm:

> The service guarantor is under contract with JAG and responsible for the continuity, security and quality of the assistance. Included in the service guarantor's tasks are recruiting and supervising the JAG member's assistants, guaranteeing that the members get their granted assistance and that it is of good quality as defined under LSS [the Swedish Act Concerning Support and Service for Persons with Certain Functional Impairments of 1993] and by JAG's aims. The responsibility to adhere to labour market legislation and union agreements is delegated to the service guarantor. (Westberg, 2010: 62)

That said, the practices described above are organisation-based rather than nationwide. As far as policy is concerned, ENIL (2023d: 18) has recently reported that, currently, 'there are no EU countries which comply with the UN CRPD in terms of ending substitute decision-making, involuntary detention in psychiatric hospitals and forced treatment on the basis of disability'. The critique of capacity from the perspective of Independent Living is still in its infancy, as are the policies implementing supported decision making, notwithstanding the widespread adoption of the CRPD. The impending mainstreaming of the concept is likely to be accompanied by fierce epistemic struggles like the ones waged by Independent Living activists around 'independence', 'deinstitutionalisation', and 'personal assistance'.

Independent Living and critique of coloniality

Since the beginning of the 2010s, decolonial scholars have been increasingly vocal in their call for a 'paradigm shift' in disability studies (e.g., Grech, 2009; Meekosha, 2011; Meekosha and Soldatic, 2011; Soldatic, 2013). This has been imagined as a complex transformation involving the substitution of the methodologically national, metropolitan, and desomatised understandings of disability, characterising mainstream and essentially Northern disability studies, with methodologically transnational, Indigenous, and appropriately somatised concepts and frameworks fit for the purpose of understanding and fighting disablement in the Global South contexts. The advocacy for this profound epistemic change has targeted the 'methodological nationalism' (Mladenov, 2016: 1236), 'cultural imperialism' (Goodley *et al.*, 2019: 978), and 'somatophobic' tendencies (Hughes, 2009: 686) of mainstream disability studies. A key insight of the decolonial turn has been that only the transnational perspective can account for the damages that capitalist globalisation and imperialism have inflicted on the subaltern people's bodies and minds.

The decolonial approach has also opposed the silencing of subaltern people's voices. To this end, it has challenged the dominant concepts and frameworks created in the affluent and consumerist Global North, including the Independent Living paradigm. It its stead, scholars and activists have been summoned to prioritise local, presumably more communal but subjugated knowledges and practices (Soldatic, 2013). Accordingly, decolonial analyses have emphasised the need to deconstruct assumptions about the universality of ideas originating in Northern contexts (Grech, 2009) – a charge seemingly striking at the very heart of Independent Living, since the latter 'is often seen as a "western" concept, promoting an individualistic and atomistic view of people' (Angelova-Mladenova, 2017: 14; see also Smith and Routel, 2009). From the decolonial perspective, claims for universality cannot help but miss the point, misrepresent half-truths and vested interests as incontrovertible axioms, perpetuate hermeneutical marginalisation, and justify colonial violence. The decolonial approach has thus been part of the wider poststructuralist turn of contemporary critical disability studies that has emphasised the inextricable tie between knowledge and power.

Like the critique of capacity, the critique of coloniality in disability studies has targeted an intersectional norm – the adult, middle-class male with physical impairments, residing in North American or Western European big cities. As argued in the preceding section, the Independent Living paradigm has been attacked for prioritising this same group of people. Such a prioritisation obscures the fact that most disabled people reside in the Global South, and that only a fraction of them are middle-class males – a survey conducted by the World Health Organization (WHO) in 2002–2004 estimated that across 59 of the countries covered, 'women, those in the poorest wealth quintile, and older people had higher prevalences of disability. For all these groups the rate was higher in developing countries' (WHO, 2011: 27). It follows that disability studies and advocacy need locally specific and intersectionally sensitive models to respond to the issues on the ground. Of note is that Independent Living organisations like ENIL have heeded this call, as evidenced by ENIL's intersectional turn and its emphasis on listening to the grassroots (Chapter 2).

The decolonial perspective would have the social model of disability augmented (or discarded) by embracing the body as a legitimate focus of disability theorising – a transnational understanding of disability suggests that most impairments in the Global South (and therefore, most impairments in the world) result from the structural violence of (neo)colonialism and neoliberal globalisation (Soldatic, 2013). As far as Independent Living is concerned, decolonial analysis has emphasised that the collectivism of many Southern societies is incompatible with the individualism (allegedly) underpinning the Independent Living paradigm (Smith and Routel, 2009). Moreover, Independent Living's emphasis on formal (contractual) support arrangements has been at odds with the centrality of informal (family- and community-based) supports in the lives of many disabled people from the Global South, but also from the North as well:

> While formal organized support services and programmes for people with disabilities are common in high-income countries, they are a fairly new concept in many low-income and middle-income countries. But even in countries with well-developed systems of support, informal care and support from families and friends predominates, being indispensable and cost-efficient. In all countries family support is essential. Across high-income countries families meet around 80% of the support needs of older people. (WHO, 2011: 142–143)

Finally, when physical survival is at stake – as is the case for most disabled people in the majority world who experience extreme poverty and lack of basic welfare-state provisions (Ghai, 2002) – self-determination inevitably takes the back seat: 'The key debates around disability and impairment, independent living, care and human rights are often irrelevant to those whose major goal is survival' (Meekosha, 2011: 670).

The human rights agenda, of which Independent Living is a part, has also been exposed by decolonial disability scholars as serving colonial ends (Meekosha and Soldatic, 2011) – a charge echoing critical-theoretical analyses of rights (McGrogan, 2021). The critics have recognised the significance of the social model of disability and the Independent Living paradigm for the emancipation of disabled people in the North but have pointed out that these frameworks are out of touch with the situation in the South. That said, the CRPD has been regarded by prominent decolonial scholars approvingly, as 'a major achievement for disability communities around the world' (Meekosha, 2011: 679). Moreover, the CRPD's emergence on the initiative of a Southern nation (Mexico) has been highlighted as an indication of its subversive potential (Meekosha and Soldatic, 2011: 1394–1395; Soldatic, 2013: 245). This endorsement of a key pillar of the global rights discourse (Degener, 2016) suggests that the advocacy for disabled people's rights – and with it, the social model of disability and Independent Living that have been embedded in the CRPD (Harpur, 2012: 3; Gooding, 2018: 34) – has sometimes exceeded the (active) North versus (passive) South binary.

The last point reflects a different take on human rights – not as obscure legal norms coined in the colonial metropole and perpetuating its cultural hegemony, but as social constructs emerging out of the emancipatory struggles of social movements on the ground (Stammers, 2009). This has certainly been the case with disabled people's rights codified in the CRPD that have been articulated with the active involvement of disabled people (Moriarity and Dew, 2011), including people from the Global South (Meekosha and Soldatic, 2011).

Moreover, the subsequent (and undeniable) appropriation of rights by the legal and administrative elites has never been total. Once articulated, the meaning of rights – including the meaning of the CRPD's provisions – cannot be unilaterally imposed by the North on the South but remains unstable and continuously recreated by communities of interpretation that engage in fierce definitional fights at the international, national, and local levels (Mladenov, 2013). The rights discourse has even been appropriated to serve the ends of exclusion – as in neighbourhoods resisting projects for housing disabled people by claiming the right of the community to be safe and quiet; or in the case of parents defending the right of their children to be institutionalised and thus protected from the pressures and risks of community living (Ben-Moshe, 2020: Ch. 5 and 6). A feature of the rights discourse that makes such appropriations possible – particularly with regard to the liberal-individualist concept of choice, in other words, when rights are reduced to civil rights – is that it obscures relations of power and hierarchy. Notably, one cannot properly choose in an unequal, epistemologically unjust, hierarchical context – choosing requires a level playing field.

The detailed General Comments issued by the CRPD Committee constitute authoritative instances of a grassroots-informed interpretative work on the meaning of the CRPD's provisions, but even they are unable to arrest the ongoing process of interpretation – hence ENIL's continuing struggle for epistemic justice. Another important instance of interpretation of the CRPD is its translation between languages – local disability rights groups and organisations have been heavily involved in this form of epistemic struggle (Mladenov, 2013).

In more general terms, the decolonial perspective offers existential-ontological insights that are of specific interest to Independent Living studies and advocacy. This is because, at its best, the decolonial agenda helps rearticulate what it means to be human by questioning dominant standards of functioning, capacity, and productivity (Meekosha, 2011). Historically, such norms have been imposed by the colonial centres in the North on the peripheries in the South as part of the efforts to create hierarchies that subjugate southern majorities and appropriate value. The extraction and accumulation of capital has entailed defining human functioning and capacity in ways that enhance the self-determination of the owners in the centre, while denying it to the propertyless in the periphery. Existential-ontological invalidation has therefore been an integral part of colonial expansion – as Fanon (1969) has famously argued, colonialism operates by devaluing the very being of colonised peoples. By being rendered as less capable, productive, and/or intellectually 'mature', the subaltern subject endures ontological disablement in addition to having its body and mind materially injured by the empire.

The existential-ontological prong of the decolonial critique expands the understanding of 'independence' in ways that resonate with the Independent Living paradigm reconstructed in this book. Understanding independence as a specific type of *inter*dependence is in concert with the decolonial assertion of communal and collectivist forms of living in the name of peripheral self-determination (Musengi, 2023) and as alternatives to the liberal-individualist ones usually associated with the colonial centres of power (Meekosha, 2011). The more inclusive, structural-collectivist understanding of Independent Living asserted on the basis of the foregoing evidence and analysis is therefore in tune with the existential-ontological decolonising of disability. Unfortunately, the latter has tended to reduce Independent Living to a liberal-individualist, marketised, and colonial version of disability emancipation (e.g., Ben-Moshe, 2020: 79), which has prevented mutually beneficial encounters between decolonial analysis and the movement. A closer engagement with the Independent Living paradigm – of the type advanced on the pages of this book – would reveal multiple points of agreement revolving around a resolute deconstruction of the dominant notions of independence, functioning, capacity, and productivity.

In sum, many of the arguments put forward by the decolonial scholars are convincing, insightful, and useful for Independent Living thinkers and activists. Moreover, Independent Living advocacy would certainly benefit from adopting a transnational perspective and emphasising the international solidarity of the oppressed. The transnational approach and solidarity have been major considerations in the founding of ENIL (Chapter 2) and are reflected in ENIL's monitoring of deinstitutionalisation and PA programmes in the EU (Chapter 6). From a purely strategic perspective, the hard-won struggles against the forces of statism, radical marketisation, and familialism at the local and national levels (e.g., direct payments schemes adopted by certain countries or municipalities) remain fragile without their expansion and internationalisation. The Swedish cooperative JAG has expressed this point eloquently: 'We are afraid that Swedish politicians will pull back the standards and freedoms that we have unless the rest of Europe has the same human rights and opportunities as us. *For our own sake, we must improve the world!*' (JAG, 2011: 3, emphasis added).

Independent Living's embrace of *inter*dependence is also in sync with decolonial analyses, especially if self-determination is identified as a core value that helps distinguish good from bad *inter*dependence (or paternalist from egalitarian care). Moreover, it is impossible to explain the imperative to empower or emancipate the South without making recourse to (some form of) self-determination. That said, I doubt that Independent Living's promotion of quasi-marketisation and consumerism would appeal to decolonial scholars, even when complemented by the activists' strong emphasis on collective organising and peer support. Nevertheless, it is worth recalling that the consumerism originally underpinning the Independent Living paradigm has been a strategy for combating professional power rather than a narcissistic self-indulgence through overconsumption of commodities, which is the usual understanding of the word.

And as far as the question of the body is concerned, at first sight, Independent Living seems as 'somatophobic' as its kindred framework, the social model of disability. For example, in his seminal article on Independent Living, DeJong (1979: 443) has pointed out that according to this paradigm, the 'locus of the problem is not the individual but the environment that includes not only the rehabilitation process but also the physical environment and the social control mechanisms in society-at-large'. However, at closer look, Independent Living advocacy has also recognised the social production of impairments by highlighting the damage done by institutionalisation on people's bodies and minds – damages that come on top of restricting self-determination (EEG, 2012: 10; ENIL, 2023e, 2022c).

Moreover, in many cases the harms of institutionalisation have been transnationally produced and rooted in colonial violence – consider, for example, the genealogy of leper colonies: 'The segregation practices of the 19th century included the exile of people with leprosy to islands or otherwise isolated areas, in the context of nations states and colonization' (Devlieger, 2017: n.p.). The same point applies to the various detention facilities and other confinement regimes created by the Global North to manage the mobility of people from the Global South (Adams, 2023; Besteman, 2019). Colonial violence has always already been a violence of institutionalisation. The globalisation of the Independent Living paradigm should therefore be regarded not in terms of cultural imperialism, but in terms of a critical response to the global spread of segregation and institutional confinement, itself a cause and consequence of the global production of impairments.

Independent Living and critique of decoloniality

The decolonial approach is not without its flaws and internal contradictions. To begin with, reflecting its poststructuralist and critical-theoretical roots, it has been formulated in a largely inaccessible and strikingly Northern academic idiom that has been in tension with its professed prioritisation of local/Indigenous knowledges. Moreover, it has tended to deprive the 'colonised' of agency at the level of content as well – the 'attribution to colonial causation of many practices and processes comes from an absolutisation of colonialism and its supposedly almost undefeatable capacity to bend the will of the colonised' (Táíwò, 2022: 7). However, as Táíwò (2022: 7) also observes, the 'colonised' may find some of the ideas and practices of the 'colonisers' worthy and subsequently appropriate and reshape them to serve their own ends (which is what decolonial scholars have effectively done in some of their best analyses). Indigenous peoples are neither passive nor inherently pacifist – to maintain the latter would be to reproduce their epistemological and political marginalisation (Reid, 2023).

Moreover, some of the allegedly 'colonising' ideas and practices have themselves been *imported* in the metropole from the South. This has been the case, for example, with the social model of disability – a main target of decolonial critique whose genealogy, ironically, points towards a Southern origin. To iterate the point already made in Chapter 1, the elaboration of the social model is grounded in the anti-apartheid struggles in South Africa through the experiences of its conceptual founder, Vic Finkelstein (2005).

In the same vein, the North versus South binary asserted by many decolonial scholars obscures the experiences of those who are neither 'colonisers' nor 'colonised'. These are the people and contexts that remain in the middle – for example, people who have lived in the region formerly known as the 'second world' (Suchland, 2011: 837), which includes the postsocialist societies in CEE. The embrace of Independent Living in the 'poor North' (Tlostanova, 2012) of postsocialism complicates the decolonial critique of this paradigm. My experience in the Centre for Independent Living–Sofia (CIL–Sofia; see also the Introduction) suggests that Independent Living can be – and, actually, has been – owned, reconstructed, and enhanced by local actors in geopolitically and epistemically marginalised contexts to suit our cultural, legislative, and political-economic realities.

At CIL–Sofia, we did a lot of work that, from a decolonial perspective, may look like importing ideas from the Global North, and by extension, as perpetuating cultural imperialism. For example, in 2002, I and a colleague were sent by the organisation on a study visit to Washington DC to learn about the Independent Living movement in the US and the work of the CILs there. We visited the National Council on Independent Living (an umbrella organisation representing US CILs – see ncil.org), as well as several local CILs. We also met with the late Judy Heumann, a pioneer of the Independent Living movement and a former deputy director of CIL–Berkeley. Later in the 2000s, I was commissioned by CIL–Sofia to translate Adolf Ratzka's (2004) PA model into Bulgarian. The subsequent publication

(CIL, 2004) was used by the organisation in its campaigning for PA. My colleagues also invited Ratzka to come to Bulgaria and speak about PA and Independent Living to disabled people and policy makers.

However, we did not take what we saw, heard, and read uncritically. The CILs in the US that we visited were strongly engaged in service provision, whereas CIL–Sofia emphasised advocacy (although it also provided services), which we considered at that time to be the proper role of an Independent Living organisation. My understanding of Independent Living developed further as I conducted a study of a public campaign for the promotion of a pilot PA programme administered by CIL–Sofia and supported by a foreign funder (Mladenov, 2004). For this study, I interviewed PA users, policy makers, and journalists, and I conducted content analysis of media reports on PA. Exploring how Independent Living ideas were perceived by the local actors was a revelatory experience. Thus, my understanding of Independent Living was influenced by the pioneers of the movement from the Global North but was grounded in local discourses and practices.

The significance and meaning of Independent Living can only be revealed when one realises the ubiquity of paternalist care and confinement (both in institutions and at home), as well as the profound transformation that people experience when they overcome their confinement. This transformative experience was beautifully expressed at the time by Borislav Vachkov, one of the participants in the CIL–Sofia's PA programme:

> Do you know the happiness I experienced at the very start of the programme – I had just started to go out more often. We were at the NDK [the National Palace of Culture, located in the centre of Sofia], it was summer, and a hard rain started falling, a summer one, of the kind with the big drops that make bubbles on the asphalt. I was sitting under the rain – I was so happy and joyful. And then I thought what a big thing it is to be able to let the rain fall on you. In brief, if I were at home, if the programme did not exist, I would not even be able to get wet by the rain. (Borislav Vachkov, cited in Mladenov, 2004: 18)

In the mid-2000s, CIL–Sofia developed a draft ordinance for providing PA that was inspired by Ratzka's work (Mladenov, 2017b). However, the scheme was essentially based on the organisation's previous experience with the already mentioned foreign-funded PA project (Dakova, 2004), thus reconstructing Ratzka's (2004) model in a contextually specific way. For example, people at CIL–Sofia were at that time reluctant to advocate for direct payments in Bulgaria because we did not think that most disabled Bulgarians were structurally and culturally prepared to act as employers. In addition, there were (and still are) significant legal barriers to using direct payments to employ personal assistants related to Bulgarian employment legislation. The ordinance was eventually adopted by the Metropolitan Municipal Council and has been implemented by the Sofia Municipality since 2007, providing disabled residents of the capital with access to PA. However, the scheme eventually evolved into a conditional, workfare programme, which prompted its originator, CIL–Sofia, to criticise the amended version as distorting the Independent Living principles (Mladenov, 2017b).

In essence, the understanding of Independent Living developed in CIL–Sofia has been an inextricable hybrid between 'imported' frameworks and 'local' notions and experiences. Such a hybrid is not well represented by the North versus South binary of decolonial scholarship. Moreover, I argue that at CIL–Sofia we also made our own, original contributions to the Independent Living paradigm, as reflected in the organisation's many publications, public engagement activities, legislative proposals, campaigns, and media appearances. I consider this book as an offshoot of these epistemic and advocacy efforts. ENIL has also been influenced by having Kapka Panayotova as its president for almost a decade. Thanks to influences like these, that also include the work of disability activists and researchers from other countries in the region (e.g., Modic *et al.*, 2023; Ružičić-Novković, 2020; Zaviršek and Fischbach, 2023), the Independent Living paradigm has been enriched and has gone beyond the original insights of the pioneers from the Global North.

Independent Living and critique of technology

Many contemporary critical theorists have been techno-pessimist, highlighting modern technology's entanglement with the circuits of cybernetic control and neoliberal government. For Martin Heidegger (1977), cinema (akin to television) has been 'a pernicious manifestation of technological enframing' (Sinnerbrink, 2006: 27). More recently, Jonathan Crary (2014: 1) has asserted that the only possible 'livable and shared future' for humanity would be offline, 'decoupled from the world-destroying systems and operations of 24/7 [techno-]capitalism'. Byung-Chul Han's (2017: 57–58) critique of present-day psychopolitics has been equally techno-pessimist: 'The soul of the second Enlightenment is data totalitarianism, or data fetishism.' Undeniably, there is a strong link between quantification, performance management, big data, and the 24/7 (self-)exploitation engendered by the internet, social media, and the smartphone, 'the devotional objects of the Digital' (Han, 2017: 12). The transition from the societies of discipline to the ones of control has arguably been enabled by digitalisation and networking (Deleuze, 1992).

What is the place of technology in the Independent Living paradigm? Most obviously, having access to appropriate assistive devices has been identified by the activists as a major pillar of Independent Living, as discussed in the Introduction. However, what 'assistive technology' means and what it does are far from straightforward. I argue that Independent Living is neither a purely techno-optimist nor a radically techno-pessimist paradigm. This is reflected in the fact that technology is considered as just one among many other pillars of Independent Living – some of them material, but most of them deeply relational. Independent Living does not regard technology as a *panacea* – instead, thinking of technology as a *pharmakon* would be a better approximation of the movement's attitude. As explained by Stiegler (2010: 194, n. 15), the concept 'is theorized by Jacques Derrida ("Plato's Pharmacy," in *Dissemination*) through commentary on Plato's *Phaedra*, in which Plato writes that writing itself is a *pharmakon*, at once what remedies the failures of memory and what weakens memory'.

A *pharmakon* is thus both a remedy and a poison. Technologies like writing can be illuminating and enable people's self-determination, but they can also create illusions, substitute truth with appearances, mislead, misguide, and confuse: 'the book can just as likely suspend the reader in immaturity – starting with the writer as first reader – to "replace understanding," in which case the auto-capture of attention can become auto-alienation of the writer by the book itself, which writes him' (Stiegler, 2010: 24).

Another point to make about technology is that it would be misleading to regard it in purely instrumental terms in the same way in which it would be misleading to regard personal assistants in purely instrumental terms (Shakespeare *et al.*, 2017). As the 'new materialists' among science and technology studies (STS) scholars have argued, technological 'things' have 'agency' that is (partly) independent from the intentions of humans. For example, Bruno Latour (2005: 39) has pointed out that to understand non-human entities (including technological supplements), one should regard them as 'mediators' that 'translate' or transform meanings, as opposed to mere 'intermediaries' that 'transport' meanings without changing them. This approach has been influenced by Heidegger's (1971: 181) philosophy, and in particular by his insight that things do a work of *thinging*, which means that they *shape* the field of human possibilities rather than just enabling intentional action: 'The thing things world.' When a thing things, humans become 'the be-thinged, the conditioned ones' (Heidegger, 1971: 181).

For Bernard Stiegler (2010: 69), only by paying attention to this conditioning – or to the state of being 'be-thinged' – can humans transform psychotechnologies of control into nootechnologies of self-determination: 'this is not a question of rejecting psychotechnologies or cultural industries but of transforming them into technologies of mind, into nootechnologies'. As explained by STS scholars, disability makes a person attentive to the minutest details of techno-material mediation in relation to issues of everyday living, and particularly in relation to personal autonomy (Moser and Law, 1999; Winance, 2006). The Independent Living paradigm is the quintessence of such an enhanced awareness of the conditioning of self-determination by relational and technological *inter*dependence. Moreover, Independent Living reveals a truth about freedom-as-independence that concerns everyone and not only disabled people.

Third-wave feminists, inspired by the pioneering work of Donna Haraway (1991), have used the 'cyborg' metaphor to challenge the binary opposition between the 'natural' (associated with femininity) and the 'technological' (associated with masculinity). Binary oppositions tend to be hierarchical, and hierarchical binaries tend to be inflected by sexist, ableist, productivist, racist, ageist, heteronormative, and other oppressive imaginaries. Non-oppressive and non-oppressed humanity would be reflexively non-binary – that is, as much natural as artificial or technological. To imagine all humans – and not only disabled people – as reliant on other humans and non-human entities is yet another way to universalise *inter*dependence and negate self-sufficiency. This is the spirit of Davis's (2002: 30) critique of liberal-individualist independence: 'As the quadriplegic is incomplete without the motorized wheelchair and the controls manipulated by the mouth or tongue, so the citizen is incomplete without information technology, protective legislation, and globalized forms of security ordering and peace.'

The Independent Living paradigm embraces this insight. However, this is only part of the story. In Heideggerian terms, the essence of technology is not something technological (Heidegger, 1977: 4).[3] The embeddedness of technology into state-, market-, or family-based assemblages (themselves intersecting with ableism, racism, sexism, ageism, heteronormativity, etc.) suggests that technology is not a neutral mediator. The state, the market, and the family help people communicate or enable their mobility towards the ends of maintaining order, increasing productivity, making profit, raising workers, or transmitting capital between generations.

Low-cost flights enable transnational mobility but damage the environment and facilitate the transmission of cheap yet stigmatised (and therefore exploitable) labour from the poor to the rich regions of the world. Countable 'likes' and 'reads' on social networks enable instantaneous and quantifiable feedback but breed conformism and competition, while crowding out deep and critical thinking. Assistive technology is similarly enabling and disabling (Roulstone, 2016). It both enables disabled people's self-determination and suppresses it – for example, by being overwhelmingly medicalised, ableist, and expert-defined. It may be wrong to regard technology in purely instrumental terms. However, as with PA, the way technological entities are designed has an impact on Independent Living. Recall that Independent Living requires *inter*dependence to be organised in such a way that people's opportunities for self-determination are maximised. Not all *inter*dependence is enabling – far from it.

Thus, although assistive technology is one of the pillars of Independent Living, this does not preclude critique of technology, nor of the instrumentalisation of being. Independent Living criticises various forms of disablement (statist, market-based, familial), and this includes exposing disablement's embeddedness in technological 'things'. But the Independent Living paradigm is certainly not a radically techno-pessimist epistemology. It is more in line with Stiegler's (2010: 180) qualified techno-optimist assertion that technologically enabled psychopower is or can be positive – 'a nootechnique in the sense of a technique for the formation and development of the psyche *as* noetic (that is, spiritual) and not simply sensory or nutritive (that is, reactive)'. There is no logocentrism at the foundations of Independent Living, no assertion that (natural) speech is more authentic than (technological) writing – or that a non-aided body/mind is inherently freer than a cyborgian one.

In terms of policy and practice, it is not enough to have access to appropriate assistive technology in order to live independently. In the technological field, Independent Living requires non-instrumental, personalised, non-stigmatising, de-medicalised, and non-exceptionalising technologies that may be achieved through what Graham Pullin (2019) has called a 'super normal design for extraordinary bodies'. In terms of politics, Independent Living requires democratisation and decolonialisation of the design of the 'things' that help people be and do – in the same way in which it requires democratisation and decolonialisation of the caring relationships.

Concluding remarks

In this chapter, I considered some critical positions that have remained undertheorised in the preceding chapters of the book. I started with an overview of mental capacity, highlighting the differences between liberal-individualist understanding of the term and the Independent Living paradigm. I argued that Independent Living constructs capacity in relational and collectivist terms, and I supported this assertion by revisiting the model of personal assistance described by Ratzka (2004). In the field of social policy, the relational understanding of capacity has found expression in advocacy for supported (as opposed to substitute) decision making.

I then looked into the critique of coloniality, providing a brief overview of key arguments put forward by decolonial disability studies scholars. Independent Living has been vulnerable to decolonial criticism because of its Global North origins, but also because of the continuing misrepresentation of the movement as defending self-sufficiency and liberal individualism. Independent Living activists' qualified support for quasi-marketisation and consumerism, as well as Independent Living's allegiance to the 'desomatised' politics of the social model of disability, have also helped target the movement as colonial. In response, I highlighted Independent Living's qualified embrace of *inter*dependence, as well as the movement's embodied critique of institutionalisation. Ultimately, the globalisation of Independent Living is a response to the colonial violence of institutional confinement.

I then explored the relevance for Independent Living of some critical responses to the decolonial approach. In particular, I argued that Independent Living ideas have not been merely imposed on passive Indigenous peoples but have been actively embraced and reshaped by local actors. As evidence, I discussed my own experience of collaborating with CIL–Sofia. This also enabled me to highlight the position of those regions that fall in the gap opened by the binary distinction between the colonising North and the colonised South – in particular, the postsocialist region of CEE. This part of the analysis drew on a recent paper by Dimitrova and Mladenov (2023).

Finally, I considered contemporary critiques of technology. I charted the uneasy relations between techno-pessimist and techno-optimist renderings of technology, and I situated Independent Living advocacy between the two. Drawing on Heideggerian insights, I pointed out that technology actively shapes human possibilities for doing and being, and I also emphasised technology's embeddedness in larger disempowering frames. Against this theoretical background, I argued that Independent Living navigates the muddy waters between techno-pessimism and techno-optimism by highlighting the technological conditioning of self-determination, but also by calling for democratising and decolonising the design of assistive 'things' as necessary for genuine self-determination.

Notes

1 The confinement of Rusi Stanev (also mentioned in Chapter 3), who sued the Bulgarian state in the European Court of Human Rights for his involuntary detention in an institution for people with intellectual and psychosocial impairments, could serve as a representative example: 'On an unspecified date in 2000, at the request of the applicant's two relatives, the Ruse regional prosecutor applied to the Ruse Regional Court (Окръжен съд) for a declaration of

total legal incapacity in respect of the applicant. In a judgment of 20 November 2000, the court declared the applicant to be partially incapacitated on the grounds that he had been suffering from simple schizophrenia since 1975, and that his ability to manage his own affairs and interests and to realise the consequences of his own acts had been impaired' (*Stanev v. Bulgaria*, no. 36760/06, §10, ECHR, 2012). 'On 9 September 2005 the applicant's lawyer requested the Rila Municipal Council to appoint a guardian for her client. In a letter dated 16 September 2005, she was informed that the Municipal Council had decided on 2 February 2005 to appoint the Director of the Pastra social care home as the applicant's guardian' (*Stanev v. Bulgaria*, no. 36760/06, §17, ECHR, 2012).

2 PA users' cooperatives have been regarded by Independent Living advocates as providing a strong collective base that makes the movement more inclusive: 'Considering that not every disabled [person] will have the right level of education, experience, or skills needed to deal with the tasks involved in being an employer, Centers for Independent Living (CILs) and user co-operatives play an important role in making sure that personal assistance is accessible to everyone. In a user cooperative (see ULOBA in Norway, or STIL in Sweden), disabled people who employ personal assistants come together as employers and delegate the tasks such as training, recruitment, the paying of salaries and taxes to the co-operative. The co-operative can also support disabled people who employ personal assistants in the day-to day supervision of a PA, time management, and any other administrative task. User cooperatives are funded by personal assistance employers with the funding they receive for administration (i.e. for managing of their personal assistance)' (ENIL, 2022b: 23). See also the work of Graby (2018).

3 'Everywhere we remain unfree and chained to technology, whether we passionately affirm or deny it. But we are delivered over to it in the worst possible way when we regard it as something neutral; for this conception of it, to which today we particularly like to do homage, makes us utterly blind to the essence of technology' (Heidegger, 1977: 4). For Heidegger, the essence of technology is the totalising instrumentalisation characterising modernity (itself enabled by modern technology), or what Heidegger (1977: 19) calls technological 'Enframing'. The latter 'demands that nature be orderable as standing-reserve' (Heidegger, 1977: 23), that is, be approached as a usable resource. 'Technological Enframing' is a critique of instrumental reason (Schecter, 2010), with the provision that Heideggerian instrumentalisation is more than 'rationality' – technological Enframing is a way of being.

Conclusion

The notion of freedom-as-independence and, by association, the Independent Living movement have been criticised by disability studies scholars for their liberal-individualist and ableist underpinnings. In their stead, social-constructionist analyses of disability have promoted alternative frameworks informed by concepts such as vulnerability, care, and *inter*dependence (e.g., Altermark, 2018; Ben-Moshe, 2020; Davis, 2002; Hughes *et al.*, 2005; Watson *et al.*, 2004). However, if we understand vulnerability as essentially social, rather than reducing it to bodily/mental frailty; if we advocate for egalitarian rather than paternalist care; and if we promote *inter*dependence that enables self-determination rather than one that reinforces confinement, we may transform the critique of Independent Living into an affirmation of its fundamental principle. In this book, I suggested that this principle has to do with remaking our meaning-engendering and life-sustaining worlds into worlds that promote disabled people's freedom. In other words, I argued that Independent Living is not about individual self-sufficiency but about socially enabled self-determination.

It may be the case that social enablement of self-determination is just another term for allo-exploiting biopower or, in the context of 'advanced' techno-capitalist societies, for auto-exploiting psychopower. The poststructuralist approach of framing power as omnipresent may suggest that genuine self-determination is impossible, but this bears the risk of depoliticising the analysis, sidelining activism, and normalising oppression. The version of critical theorising embraced in this book asserts that elements of both biopower and psychopower can be appropriated to serve emancipatory ends – or transformed into vehicles of liberation. But how to know the difference between oppression and emancipation? Using Kant's 'maturity' as a litmus test by following Bernard Stiegler's approach risks reaffirming self-sufficiency and making freedom impossible for people who are deemed to lack mental capacity.

Moreover, all these distinctions are precarious and unstable. Worse still, one of the terms may mask the continuing dominance of the other, like a Trojan horse that harbours more danger than an open confrontation. Thus, the discourse of social vulnerability may (inadvertently) strengthen representations of people as passive victims of their circumstances; branding care as egalitarian could be used as a convenient excuse for reaffirming paternalism; and *inter*dependence that purports to enable self-determination might turn out to be a form of institutional confinement, even when happening in one's own home. It is doubtful that biopower has shown its emancipatory face in group homes; it is likely that psychopower has been enhanced with the transformation of social care institutions into community support programmes; and it is possible that peer support has generated psychopolitical control – for example, as a consequence of peer pressure.

In the book, I explored the ways in which the Independent Living movement and analytic paradigm have been grappling with, and thereby shining an 'organically intellectual' critical-theoretical light on, all these issues. Thus, I rendered Independent Living as a living and breathing, bottom-up, grassroots epistemology, preserved and developed in the work of activist organisations like ENIL. Independent Living has not been static – since its emergence in the 1960s, it has responded to changes in policies and regulations, some of which have been driven by the movement itself. These changes have included the spread of deinstitutionalisation programmes, the adoption and implementation of antidiscrimination legislation, the ratification and incorporation of the CRPD, the emergence of personal assistance programmes in different countries around the world, the globalisation of neoliberal marketisation, and more recent retraditionalising trends. The movement has also been affected by changes in thinking about disability, including the emergence and evolution of the social model of disability, intersectional analysis, advances in feminist thought, developments in decolonial critique, and recent advances in thinking and policy around mental capacity.

I also regarded Independent Living as responding and adapting to variations between welfare regimes. To do this, I used Esping-Andersen's typology as a point of departure, but I went beyond it by engaging with postsocialist scholarship and feminist theorising on welfare. The analysis suggested that liberal and social democratic regimes have historically been more hospitable to Independent Living than conservative and post/socialist ones. However, the movement has struggled with all three organising principles of welfare – with the market under liberal and postsocialist residualism; with the state under social democratic and state socialist welfarism; and with the family under conservative and postsocialist traditionalism. Independent Living advocates have drawn on the countervailing forces of decommodification, deétatisation, and defamilialisation to overcome regime-specific barriers to disabled people's self-determination.

In recent decades, the global spread of neoliberal marketisation has enhanced the need to advocate for decommodification, as reflected in the anti-austerity campaigning of ENIL and other Independent Living organisations. However, the continuing institutionalisation (often in the form of reinstitutionalising deinstitutionalisation) has kept deétatisation initiatives high on the list of Independent Living's priorities. In addition, the need to advocate for both decommodification and deétatisation has increased due to the multiplication of personal assistance programmes engendering institutionalisation at home. In familialist contexts, flawed personal assistance has nudged Independent Living advocates towards demanding defamilialisation. At the epistemic level, the Independent Living movement has promoted decommodification, deétatisation, and defamilialisation by trying to overcome the hermeneutical marginalisation of disabled people in defining key terms such as 'independence', 'deinstitutionalisation', and 'personal assistance'. To clarify these points, I discussed in detail ENIL's advocacy and some local Independent Living mobilisations.

The analysis was further complicated by suggesting that decommodification, deétatisation, and defamilialisation have themselves sometimes been in tension with Independent Living. When underpinned by productivism (understood here as biopolitical or psychopolitical pressure to engage in paid work), these strategies have distorted Independent Living, making the movement exclusive towards people unable or unwilling to work (under the prevailing conditions on the labour market), and/or to people deemed to lack mental capacity. Productivism has also devalued caregiving and enhanced gender inequalities, as gender-sensitive analyses of the welfare regimes have shown. I suggested that a 'universal caregiver/care-receiver' model of organising welfare to achieve gender/disability equity is best suited to Independent Living advocacy. Such a model is also able to reconcile (at least some of) the tensions between Independent Living and the feminist critique of androcentrism.

To make matters even more complicated, the Independent Living movement has not been internally homogeneous. Its idiosyncratic mixture of socialist, liberal, and communitarian ideas has made it appealing to people with varying ideological commitments. There has also been a strong libertarian undercurrent informing many of the movement's interactions with the state, the market, and the family. The reconstruction of the Independent Living paradigm in this book has been done from social-democratic and left-libertarian perspectives, but they are far from the only valid or possible ones when exploring Independent Living. Still, they fit ENIL's work, which I used to ground my reflections in policy and practice.

On this basis, I asserted that Independent Living is a transformative rather than affirmative approach to in/justice, using Nancy Fraser's distinction between 'affirmation' and 'transformation'. Independent Living's practical approach to achieving social change has been of a 'non-reformist reform' (Gorz, 1967) type. To convey this point, I explored in detail the transformative potential of reforms that introduce genuine deinstitutionalisation and personal assistance. I also discussed the emancipatory power of peer support, self-organising, supported decision making, and assistive technology, although some of the pillars of Independent Living remained outside the scope of the analysis. For example, I did not consider inclusive education, and I did not pay specific attention to the relevance of the Independent Living paradigm for disabled children. Of note is that most of the discussions and concepts mobilised in the book would apply to education and children as well, although there are specifics that require a separate analysis.

Instead of conclusion, I will identify some of the issues likely to shape the Independent Living agenda in the future. The mainstreaming of the CRPD is bound to intensify the conflicts over the interpretations of its key terms. This means that in addition to fighting neoliberal residualism, Independent Living activists will have to reinforce their critique of reinstitutionalising deinstitutionalisation and flawed personal assistance. Increased public funding for the transition to community-based support does not mean better opportunities for Independent Living, as the postsocialist experience with deinstitutionalisation programmes testifies. On the contrary, flawed deinstitutionalisation and personal assistance could cement the status quo of paternalist care.

These intensifying struggles over definitions come on top of the chronic deficiency of accessible and affordable housing in the community, increasing poverty and inequality amidst austerity, transnational migration, creeping retraditionalisation, and right-wing populism. The latter threatens to undermine the human rights paradigm and, by extension, the fragile achievements of the CRPD and other international human rights instruments. Against this background, Independent Living campaigning and analysis will inevitably become increasingly intersectional and transnational. The emerging critique of capacity is also likely to occupy centre stage within the movement – without it, Independent Living risks becoming increasingly irrelevant in the face of the prevailing forms of ableism and disablement in societies of control.

I would like to conclude by emphasising the importance of practice and struggle. The best critical theorising often happens outside the medium of academic articles and books. The latter's institutionalised and therefore highly prescriptive manner of expression contradicts the radical critique of reason and sovereignty characterising most contemporary critical theory. Some of the arguments put forward by critical theorists would be non-contradictory only if expressed in poetry, dance, song, or action – an empowering peer support meeting, a well-working personal assistance relationship, a case of successful deinstitutionalisation, a bold intervention in a discussion with the powerholders, a loud protest march.

References

Abberley, P. (1998) 'The spectre at the feast: disabled people and social theory', in T. Shakespeare (ed.) *The Disability Reader: Social Science Perspectives*. London: Continuum, 79–93.

Abrams, T. (2016) *Heidegger and the Politics of Disablement*. London: Palgrave.

Adams, C. (2023) 'Barge to house 500 male migrants off Dorset coast, says government', *BBC News*, 5 April 2023. https://web.archive.org/web/20231107092556/https://www.bbc.co.uk/news/uk-65193446 (accessed 7 November 2023).

Agamben, G. (2005) *State of Exception*, trans K. Attell. Chicago, IL: University of Chicago Press.

Agamben, G. (1998) *Homo Sacer: Sovereign Power and Bare Life*, trans D. Heller-Roazen. Stanford, CA: Stanford University Press.

Aidukaite, J. (2009) 'Old welfare state theories and new welfare regimes in Eastern Europe: challenges and implications', *Communist and Post-Communist Studies*, 42, 23–39. DOI: 10.1016/j.postcomstud.2009.02.004

Alliance for Protection against Gender Based Violence, Bulgarian Centre for Not-for-Profit Law, Centre for Inclusive Education, Center for Independent Living–Sofia, and Validity Foundation–Mental Disability Advocacy Centre (2018) 'NGO and DPO joint submission for consideration at the 20th Session of the United Nations Committee on the Rights of Persons with Disabilities and the First Periodic of Bulgaria: list of issues'. https://web.archive.org/web/20231107093858/https://cil.bg/wp-content/uploads/2020/03/NGOs-answers.pdf (accessed 7 November 2023).

Altermark, N. (2018) *Citizenship Inclusion and Intellectual Disability: Biopolitics Post-Institutionalisation*. London: Routledge.

Angelova-Mladenova, L. (2017) *The Right to Live Independently and be Included in the Community. Addressing Barriers to Independent Living across the Globe*. Online publication. Brussels: European Network on Independent Living. https://web.archive.org/web/20231107094150/https://enil.eu/wp-content/uploads/2022/03/The-right-to-live-independently_FINAL.pdf (accessed 7 November 2023).

Antov, P. (1950) *Trudat na ogranicheno rabotosposobnite v SSSR i u nas*. [*The Labour of Those with Limited Ability to Work in the USSR and in Our Country*]. Sofia: Saiuz na postradalite ot voynite i fashizma.

Bagenstos, S. R. (2000) 'Subordination, stigma, and "disability"', *Virginial Law Review*, 86:3, 397–534. DOI: 10.2307/1073960

Barnes, C. (2007) 'Direct payments and their future: an ethical concern?' *Ethics and Social Welfare*, 1:3, 348–354. DOI: 10.1080/17496530701603095

Barnes, C. (2004) 'Independent living, politics and implications', online publication. https://web.archive.org/web/20231110175631/https://disability-studies.leeds.ac.uk/wp-content/uploads/sites/40/library/Barnes-Janes-paper.pdf (accessed 10 November 2023).

Barnes, C. and Oliver, M. (1995) 'Disability rights: rhetoric and reality in the UK', *Disability & Society*, 10:1, 111–116. DOI: 10.1080/09687599550023769

Barnes, M., Brannelly, T., Ward, L., and Ward, N. (2015) 'Introduction: the critical significance of care', in M. Barnes, T. Brannelly, L. Ward, and N. Ward (eds) *Ethics of Care: Critical Advances in International Perspective*. Bristol: Policy, 3–19.

Bauman, Z. (1992) *Intimations of Postmodernity*. London: Routledge.

Begum, N. (1992) 'Disabled women and the feminist agenda', *Feminist Review*, 40:1, 70–84. DOI: 10.2307/1395278

Bell, C. M. (ed.) (2011) *Blackness and Disability: Critical Examinations and Cultural Interventions*. Münster: LIT.

Ben-Moshe, L. (2020) *Decarcerating Disability: Deinstitutionalization and Prison Abolition*. Minneapolis: University of Minnesota Press.

Beresford, P. (2005) 'Social work and a social model of madness and distress: developing a viable role for the future', *Social Work & Social Sciences Review*, 12:2, 59–73. DOI: 10.1921/17466105.12.2.59

Beresford, P., Nettle, M., and Perring, R. (2010) *Towards a Social Model of Madness and Distress? Exploring What Service Users Say*. York: Joseph Rowntree Foundation. https://web.archive.org/web/20231107095212/https://www.jrf.org.uk/sites/default/files/jrf/migrated/files/mental-health-service-models-full.pdf (accessed 7 November 2023).

Berghs, M. J., Atkin, K. M., Graham, H. M., Hatton, C., and Thomas, C. (2016) 'Implications for public health research of models and theories of disability: a scoping study and evidence synthesis', *Public Health Research*, 4:8. DOI: 10.3310/phr04080

Berlant, L. (2011) *Cruel Optimism*. Durham, NC: Duke University Press.

Besteman, C. (2019) 'Militarized global apartheid', *Current Anthropology*, 60:S19, S26–S38. DOI: 10.1086/699280

Bezmez, D. and Porter, T. (2022) 'Disabled women's care experiences in Turkey: intimacy, dependency, independent living', *Scandinavian Journal of Disability Research*, 24:1, 54–67. DOI: 10.16993/sjdr.852

Boyle, D. and Harris, M. (2009) 'The challenge of co-production. How equal partnerships between professionals and the public are crucial to improving public services', discussion paper. London: NESTA. https://web.archive.org/web/20240624090538/http://www.camdencen.org.uk/Resources/Public%20services/The_Challenge_of_Co-production.pdf (accessed 10 November 2023).

Brennan, C. S., Allen, S., Arnold, R., Bulic Cojocariu, I., Milovanovic, D. C., Gurbai, S., Hardy, A., Kawano-Chiu, M., Kokic, N., Mgijima-Konopi, I., Rosenthal, E., and Youssefian, E. (2020) *Disability Rights During the Pandemic. A Global Report on Findings of the COVID-19 Disability Rights Monitor*. https://web.archive.org/web/20231107100016/https://covid-drm.org/assets/documents/Disability-Rights-During-the-Pandemic-report-web.pdf (accessed 7 November 2023).

Brennan, C., Traustadóttir, R., Anderberg, P., and Rice, J. (2016) 'Are cutbacks to personal assistance violating Sweden's obligations under the UN Convention on the Rights of Persons with Disabilities?', *Laws*, 5:23, 1–15. DOI: 10.3390/laws5020023

Brisenden, S. (1986) 'Independent living and the medical model of disability', *Disability, Handicap & Society*, 1:2, 173–178. DOI: 10.1080/02674648666780171

Brown, W. (2006) 'American nightmare: neoliberalism, neoconservatism, and de-democratization', *Political Theory*, 34:6, 690–714. DOI: 10.1177/0090591706293016

Buğra, A. and Keyder, Ç. (2006) 'The Turkish welfare regime in transformation', *Journal of European Social Policy*, 16:3, 211–228. DOI: 10.1177/0958928706065593

Bulic Cojocariu, I. and Kokic, N. (2018) *Briefing on the Use of EU Funds for Independent Living*. Online publication. Brussels: European Network on Independent Living. https://web.archive.org/web/20231107100432/https://enil.eu/wp-content/uploads/2022/03/EU-Funds-Briefing_web0903.pdf (accessed 7 November 2023).

Butler, J. (2004) *Precarious Life: The Powers of Mourning and Violence*. London: Verso.

Campbell, B. (2014) 'After neoliberalism: the need for a gender revolution', *Soundings*, 56:17, 10–26. DOI: 10.3898/136266214811788736

Campbell, J. and Oliver, M. (1996) *Disability Politics: Understanding Our Past, Changing Our Future*. London: Routledge.

Carel, H. and Kidd, I. J. (2017) 'Epistemic injustice in medicine and healthcare', in I. J. Kidd, J. Medina, and G. Pohlhaus Jr. (eds) *The Routledge Handbook of Epistemic Injustice*. New York: Routledge, 336–346.

Chambers, S. A. (2001) 'Language and politics: agonistic discourse in The West Wing', *CTheory*. https://web.archive.org/web/20240219050921/https://journals.uvic.ca/index.php/ctheory/article/view/14591/5443 (accessed 23 November 2023).

Charlton, J. (1998) *Nothing About Us Without Us. Disability Oppression and Empowerment*. Berkeley: University of California Press.

CIL (2018) 'Stanovishte na TsNZh po Zakonoproekta za lichna pomosht, razraboten or Ombudsmana na Republika Balgariya Maya Manolova' ['CIL's position on the Personal Assistance Bill drafted by the Ombudsman of the Republic of Bulgaria Maya Manolova'], online publication. Sofia: Center for Independent Living–Sofia. https://web.archive.org/web/20231108142325/https://cil.bg/blog/stanovishte-na-cil-po-zakonoproekta-za-lichna-pomosht-na-maja-manolova/ (accessed 8 November 2023).

CIL (2012) *Reinstitutsionalizirashta deinstitutsionalizatsiya* [*Reinstitutionalizing deinstitutionalization*]. Sofia: Center for Independent Living–Sofia. https://web.archive.org/web/20231108142648/https://cil.bg/wp-content/uploads/2020/03/DIK_final.pdf (accessed 8 November 2023).

CIL (2004) *Nezavisim zhivot i lichna pomosht v Shvetsiya* [*Independent Living and Personal Assistance in Sweden*]. Sofia: Center for Independent Living–Sofia. https://web.archive.org/web/20240624154012/https://cil.bg/wp-content/uploads/2020/03/sweden_2005.pdf (accessed 10 November 2023).

Clifford Simplican, S. (2015) *The Capacity Contract: Intellectual Disability and the Question of Citizenship*. Minneapolis: University of Minnesota Press.

Committee on the Rights of Persons with Disabilities (2022) *Guidelines on Deinstitutionalization, Including in Emergencies*. CRPD/C/5. Geneva: United Nations. www.ohchr.org/en/documents/legal-standards-and-guidelines/crpdc5-guidelines-deinstitutionalization-including (accessed 8 November 2023).

Committee on the Rights of Persons with Disabilities (2017) *General Comment No. 5 (2017) on Living Independently and Being Included in the Community*. CRPD/C/GC/5. Geneva: United Nations. www.ohchr.org/en/hrbodies/crpd/pages/gc.aspx (accessed 8 November 2023).

Committee on the Rights of Persons with Disabilities (2014) *General Comment No. 1 (2014) – Article 12: Equal Recognition Before the Law*. CRPD/C/GC/1. Geneva: United Nations. www.ohchr.org/en/hrbodies/crpd/pages/gc.aspx (accessed 8 November 2023).

Cooper, M. (2017) *Family Values: Between Neoliberalism and the New Social Conservatism*. New York: Zone.

Corker, M. and Shakespeare, T. (eds) (2002) *Disability/Postmodernity: Embodying Disability Theory*. London: Continuum.

Council of Europe (2020) *Report to the Bulgarian Government on the Visit to Bulgaria Carried Out by the European Committee for the Prevention of Torture and Inhuman or Degrading Treatment or Punishment (CPT) from 10 to 21 August 2020*. Strasbourg: Council of Europe. https://web.archive.org/web/20240624121426/https://rm.coe.int/1680a090b7 (accessed 10 November 2023).

Crary, J. (2014) *24/7: Late Capitalism and the Ends of Sleep*. London: Verso.

Crenshaw, K. (1991) 'Mapping the margins: intersectionality, identity politics, and violence against women of colour', *Stanford Law Review*, 43:6, 1241–1299. DOI: 10.2307/1229039

Cruickshank, J. (2016) 'Putting business at the heart of higher education: on neo-liberal interventionism and audit culture in UK universities', *Open Library of Humanities*, 2:1, 1–33. DOI: 10.16995/olh.77

Dakova, V. (2004) *Za chinovnitsite i horata* [*Of Officials and People*]. Sofia: Center for Independent Living–Sofia. https://web.archive.org/web/20240624155132/https://cil.bg/wp-content/uploads/2020/03/za_chinovnitsite_i_horata_1_2004.pdf (accessed 10 November 2023).

Dale, G. (2011) 'Introduction: The transition in Central and Eastern Europe' in G. Dale (ed.) *First the Transition, Then the Crash. Eastern Europe in the 2000s*. London: Pluto, 1–20.

Daly, M. (2022) 'The resilience of maternalism in European welfare states', *Contemporary Social Science*, 17:4, 313–325. DOI: 10.1080/21582041.2022.2061042

Davies, W. (2014) 'Neoliberalism: a bibliographic review', *Theory, Culture & Society*, Think-Pieces, 7 March 2014. DOI: 10.1177/0263276414546383

Davis, A. (2003) *Are Prisons Obsolete?* New York: Seven Stories.

Davis, K. and Woodward, J. (1981) 'DIAL UK: The development of the National Disablement Information and Advice Services', in A. Brechin, P. Liddiard and J. Swain (eds) *Handicap in a Social World*. Milton Keynes: Open University Press.

Davis, L. (2021) 'In the time of pandemic, the deep structure of biopower is laid bare', *Critical Inquiry*, 47:S2, S138–S142. DOI: 10.1086/711458

Davis, L. (2002) *Bending over Backwards: Disability, Dismodernism, and other Difficult Positions*. New York: New York University Press.

Deeming, C. (2017) 'The lost and the new "liberal world" of welfare capitalism: a critical assessment of Gøsta Esping-Andersen's *The Three Worlds of Welfare Capitalism* a quarter century later', *Social Policy and Society*, 16:3, 405–422. DOI: 10.1017/s1474746415000676

Degener, T. (2016) 'Disability in a human rights context', *Laws*, 5:3, 1–24. DOI: 10.3390/laws5030035

DeJong, G. (1979) 'Independent Living: from social movement to analytic paradigm', *Archives of Physical Medicine and Rehabilitation*, 60:10, 435–446.

DeJong, G., Batavia, A. I., and McKnew, L. B. (1992) 'The independent living model of personal assistance in national long-term-care policy', *Generations: Journal of the American Society on Aging*, 16:1, 89–95. DOI: 10.4324/9781315227634-20

Deleuze, G. (1992) 'Postscript on the societies of control', *October*, 59, 3–7.

Deleuze, G. and Guattari, F. (2004 [1980]) *A Thousand Plateaus: Capitalism and Schizophrenia*, trans. B. Massumi. London: Continuum.

Deneva, N. and Petrov, R. (2016) *Zhivot na volya ili po chuzhda volya! Politikata na t. nar. "deinstitutsionalizatsiya" (DI) v Balgariya i posleditsite za pravoto na nezavisimiya zhivot na horata, s uvrezhdaniya, koito sa obekt na tazi politika* [*Living at will or by another's will! The policy of the so-called 'deinstitutionalization' (DI) in Bulgaria and its consequences for the right to independent living of people with disabilities who are subject to this policy*]. Sofia: Center for Independent Living–Sofia. https://web.archive.org/web/20231108165532/https://cil.bg/wp-content/uploads/2020/03/Report-DI-Final.pdf (accessed 8 November 2023).

de Shazer, S. (1994) *Words Were Originally Magic*. New York: Norton.

Devlieger, P. (2017) 'Leprosy, heritage, and art: histories of exile in a world perspective', *Public Disability History*, 15 June 2017. https://web.archive.org/web/20230330121941/https://www.public-disabilityhistory.org/2017/06/leprosy-heritage-and-art-histories-of.html (accessed 8 November 2023).

Dimitrova, I. (2020) 'Impasses of disability alliance-building in Bulgaria: successful phantom activism and toxic grassroots mobilization', in A. Carey, J. M. Ostrove, and T. Fannon (eds) *Disability Alliances and Allies: Opportunities and Challenges Vol: 12*. Bingley: Emerald, 67–86.

Dimitrova, I. (2019) 'Disability in the world of work: representations of productivism and cruel promises', *Sociological Problems*, 51:1, 79–100.

Dimitrova, I. and Mladenov, T. (2023) 'Decolonising disability in contexts of illiberalism and social abandonment: the case for a double-edged critique from the postsocialist margins', *Critical Sociology*, 50:3, 499–515. DOI: 10.1177/08969205231191651

Disability Rights UK (n.d.) 'Independent Living. Disability Rights UK Factsheet F38', online publication. London: Disability Rights UK. https://web.archive.org/web/20231108170115/https://www.disabilityrightsuk.org/resources/independent-living (accessed 8 November 2023).

ECHR (2012) *Case of Stanev v. Bulgaria*. Application no. 36760/06. Strasbourg: ECHR. https://web.archive.org/web/20240624115902/https://www.escr-net.org/sites/default/files/caselaw/decision_on_stanev_v._bulgaria_0.pdf (accessed 10 November 2023).

EEG (2014) *Toolkit on the Use of European Union Funds for the Transition from Institutional to Community-based Care*. Brussels: European Expert Group on the Transition from Institutional to Community-Based Care. https://web.archive.org/web/20240308171226/https://deinstitutionalisationdotcom.files.wordpress.com/2017/07/toolkit-10-22-2014-update-web.pdf (accessed 10 November 2023).

EEG (2012) *Common European Guidelines on the Transition from Institutional to Community-based Care*. Brussels: European Expert Group on the Transition from Institutional to Community-Based Care. https://web.archive.org/web/20240305021445/https://deinstitutionalisationdotcom.files.wordpress.com/2017/07/guidelines-final-english.pdf (accessed 10 November 2023).

Elder-Woodward, J. (2023) 'Personal assistance in Scotland: a postcolonial perspective', *International Journal of Disability and Social Justice*, 3:1, 114–120. DOI: 10.13169/intljofdissocjus.3.1.0114

Elder-Woodward, J. (2016) 'Disabled people's Independent Living Movement in Scotland: a time for reflection', *Ethics and Social Welfare*, 10:3, 252–266. DOI: 10.1080/17496535.2016.1193760

Elder-Woodward, J. (2014) 'Epistemic displacement: a particular wrong', paper presented at the 23rd International Rehabilitation World Congress, Edinburgh. https://web.archive.org/web/20240308172405/https://www.academia.edu/109863423/Epistemic_Displacement_draft_Note_page (accessed 23 November 2023).

Elder-Woodward, J. (2001) 'Making sense of community care', paper presented at the Community Care Providers Scotland Conference, September 2001, Hilton Dunblane Hydro. https://web.archive.org/web/20231110101653/https://disability-studies.leeds.ac.uk/wp-content/uploads/sites/40/library/elderwood-CCPS-paper3-Times12.pdf (accessed 10 November 2023).

ENIL (2023a) 'Amendments of the European Network on Independent Living to the Draft Council Conclusions on the transition of care systems throughout life towards holistic, person-centred and community-based models (11993/23, SOC 549, EMPL 387, GENDER 167)', online publication. Brussels: ENIL. https://web.archive.org/web/20231110101901/https://enil.eu/amendments-of-the-european-network-on-independent-living/ (accessed 10 November 2023).

ENIL (2023b) 'ENIL's Members Mailing #51: December 2022 – January 2023', online publication. Brussels: European Network on Independent Living. https://web.archive.org/web/20231110102052/https://mailchi.mp/enil/enil-members-mailing-no51?e=82d0403629 (accessed 10 November 2023).

ENIL (2023c) 'ENIL's position on the new UN Resolution for the International Day for Care and Support', online publication. Brussels: European Network on Independent Living. https://web.archive.org/web/20231110102238/https://enil.eu/enils-position-on-the-new-un-resolution-for-the-international-day-for-care-and-support/ (accessed 10 November 2023).

ENIL (2023d) 'ENIL's Proposal for the EC Guidance on Independent Living and being included in the community', online publication. Brussels: European Network on Independent Living. https://web.archive.org/web/20231110102937/https://enil.eu/wp-content/uploads/2023/05/ENIL_Proposal-to-the-Guidance-on-Independent-Living.docx (accessed 10 November 2023).

ENIL (2023e) 'Institutions in Europe, models of good practice?', online publication. Brussels: European Network on Independent Living. https://web.archive.org/web/20231110103809/https://enil.eu/institutions-in-europe-models-of-good-practice/ (accessed 10 November 2023).

ENIL (2023f) 'The Global Coalition on Deinstitutionalisation meets in Mexico to discuss next steps', online publication. Brussels: European Network on Independent Living. https://web.archive.org/web/20231110104141/https://enil.eu/the-global-coalition-on-deinstitutionalisation-meets-in-mexico-to-discuss-next-steps/ (accessed 10 November 2023).

ENIL (2022a) *Independent Living Survey. Summary Report, December 2022.* Online publication. Brussels: European Network on Independent Living. https://web.archive.org/web/20231110104303/https://enil.eu/wp-content/uploads/2022/03/IL-Survey_Summary-report_Dec2020.pdf (accessed 10 November 2023).

ENIL (2022b) *Myth Buster on Personal Assistance*. Brussels: European Network on Independent Living. https://web.archive.org/web/20231110105315/https://enil.eu/wp-content/uploads/2023/06/Myths-Buster_Personal-assistance_web_low-res-1.pdf (accessed 10 November 2023).

ENIL (2022c) *Shadow Report on the Implementation of the UN Convention on the Rights of Persons with Disabilities in the EU*. Brussels: European Network on Independent Living. https://web.archive.org/web/20231110105613/https://enil.eu/wp-content/uploads/2022/03/ShadowReport_EU_Final_140222.pdf (accessed 10 November 2023).

ENIL (2020) *ENIL's Guide to Advocating for Independent Living in the European Parliament*. Online publication. Brussels: European Network on Independent Living. https://web.archive.org/web/20231110105849/https://enil.eu/wp-content/uploads/2022/03/ENIL_EPGuide_Sept2020-1.docx (accessed 10 November 2023).

ENIL (2015) *Personal Assistance Services in Europe 2015*. Online publication. Brussels: European Network on Independent Living. https://web.archive.org/web/20231110110116/https://enil.eu/wp-content/uploads/2022/03/Personal-Assistance-Service-in-Europe-Report-2015.pdf (accessed 10 November 2023).

ENIL (2014) *European Network on Independent Living: 2014 Manifesto*. Online publication. Dublin: European Network on Independent Living. https://web.archive.org/web/20231110111011/https://enil.eu/wp-content/uploads/2022/03/ENIL-Manifesto.pdf (accessed 10 November 2023).

ENIL (2013) *Personal Assistance Services in Europe*. Dublin: European Network on Independent Living. Available online at: https://web.archive.org/web/20231110111318/https://enil.eu/wp-content/uploads/2022/03/European-Survey-on-Personal-Assistance-Final.pdf (accessed 10 November 2023).

ENIL (n.d.-a) 'About ENIL', online publication. Brussels: European Network on Independent Living. https://web.archive.org/web/20231110111447/https://enil.eu/about-enil/ (accessed 10 November 2023).

ENIL (n.d.-b) 'Deinstitutionalisation', online publication. Brussels: European Network on Independent Living. https://web.archive.org/web/20231110114701/https://enil.eu/deinstitutionalisation/ (accessed 10 November 2023).

ENIL (n.d.-c) 'Family planning project', online publication. Brussels: European Network on Independent Living. https://web.archive.org/web/20231110111647/https://enil.eu/project/family-planning-project/ (accessed 10 November 2023).

ENIL (n.d.-d) 'Independent Living', online publication. Brussels: European Network on Independent Living. https://web.archive.org/web/20231110111810/https://enil.eu/independent-living/ (accessed 10 November 2023).

ENIL (n.d.-e) 'Join ENIL', online publication. Brussels: European Network on Independent Living. https://web.archive.org/web/20231110112824/https://enil.eu/join-enil/ (accessed 10 November 2023).

ENIL (n.d.-f) 'Our people', online publication. Brussels: European Network on Independent Living. https://web.archive.org/web/20231110113137/https://enil.eu/about-enil/our-people/ (accessed 10 November 2023).

ENIL (n.d.-g) 'Personal assistance', online publication. Brussels: European Network on Independent Living. https://web.archive.org/web/20231110112327/https://enil.eu/personal-assistance/ (accessed 10 November 2023).

ENIL (n.d.-h) 'Projects', online publication. Brussels: European Network on Independent Living. https://web.archive.org/web/20231110113734/https://enil.eu/our-projects/ (accessed 10 November 2023).

Erevelles, N. (2011) *Disability and Difference in Global Contexts: Enabling a Transformative Body Politic*. New York: Palgrave Macmillan.
Esping-Andersen, G. (1999) *Social Foundations of Postindustrial Economies*. Oxford: Oxford University Press.
Esping-Andersen, G. (1990) *The Three Worlds of Welfare Capitalism*. Cambridge: Polity.
Esping-Andersen, G. (1985) *Politics against Markets. The Social Democratic Road to Power*. Princeton, NJ: Princeton University Press.
European Commission (2021) *Union of Equality: Strategy for the Rights of Persons with Disabilities 2021–2030*. COM(2021) 101 final. Brussels: European Commission. https://web.archive.org/web/20231110115939/https://eur-lex.europa.eu/legal-content/EN/TXT/PDF/?uri=CELEX:52021DC0101 (accessed 10 November 2023).
European Commission (2010) *European Disability Strategy 2010–2020: A Renewed Commitment to a Barrier-Free Europe*. COM(2010) 636 final. Brussels: European Commission. https://web.archive.org/web/20231110120134/https://eur-lex.europa.eu/LexUriServ/LexUriServ.do?uri=COM:2010:0636:FIN:en:PDF (accessed 10 November 2023).
European Commission (n.d.) 'European structural and investment funds', online publication. Brussels: European Commission. https://web.archive.org/web/20231110120352/https://commission.europa.eu/funding-tenders/find-funding/funding-management-mode/2014-2020-european-structural-and-investment-funds_en (accessed 10 November 2023).
Evans, J. (2002) 'Independent Living Movement in the UK', online publication. Leeds: Disability Archive UK. Available online at: https://web.archive.org/web/20231110120434/https://disability-studies.leeds.ac.uk/wp-content/uploads/sites/40/library/evans-Version-2-Independent-Living-Movement-in-the-UK.pdf (accessed 10 November 2023).
Fanon, F. (1969 [1961]) *The Wretched of the Earth*, trans. C. Farrington. Harmondsworth: Penguin.
Ferge, Z. (1997) 'Women and social transformation in Central-Eastern Europe: the "Old Left" and the "New Right"', *Sociologický časopis* [*Czech Sociological Review*], 5:2, 159–178. DOI: 10.13060/00380288.1997.33.12.05
Ferguson, I. (2007) 'Increasing user choice or privatizing risk? The antinomies of personalization', *British Journal of Social Work*, 37:3, 387–403. DOI: 10.1093/bjsw/bcm016
Finkelstein, V. (2005) 'Reflections on the Social Model of Disability: the South African connection', online publication. https://web.archive.org/web/20231110121056/https://disability-studies.leeds.ac.uk/wp-content/uploads/sites/40/library/finkelstein-Reflections-on-the-Social-Model-of-Disability.pdf (accessed 10 November 2023).
Finkelstein, V. (1980) *Attitudes and Disabled People: Issues for Discussion*. New York: World Rehabilitation Fund.
Foucault, M. (1991 [1975]) *Discipline and Punish: The Birth of the Prison*, trans. A. Sheridan. London: Penguin.
Foucault, M. (1988 [1984]) 'Technologies of the self', in L. H. Martin, H. Gutman and P. H. Hutton (eds) *Technologies of the Self: A Seminar with Michel Foucault*. Amherst: University of Massachusetts Press, 16–49.
Foucault, M. (1980) *Power/Knowledge: Selected Interviews and Other Writings, 1972–1977*. New York: Pantheon.

Foucault, M. (1978 [1976]) *The History of Sexuality, Volume 1: An Introduction*, trans. R. Hurley. New York: Pantheon.

Fraser, N. (2022) *Cannibal Capitalism: How Our System is Devouring Democracy, Care, and the Planet – and What We Can Do about It*. London: Verso.

Fraser, N. (2013) *Fortunes of Feminism: From State-Managed Capitalism to Neoliberal Crisis*. London: Verso.

Fraser, N. (2005) 'Reframing justice in a globalizing world', *New Left Review*, 36, 1–19.

Fraser, N. (2003) 'From discipline to flexibilization? Rereading Foucault in the shadow of globalization', *Constellations*, 10:2, 160–171. DOI: 10.1111/1467-8675.00321

Fraser, N. (1997) *Justice Interruptus: Critical Reflections on the 'Postsocialist' Condition*. London: Routledge.

Fraser, N. (1996) 'Social justice in the age of identity politics: redistribution, recognition and participation', The Tanner Lectures on Human Values, Stanford University, April 30–June 2. https://web.archive.org/web/20231110121621/https://tannerlectures.utah.edu/_resources/documents/a-to-z/f/Fraser98.pdf (accessed 10 November 2023).

Fraser, N. (1987) 'Women, welfare and the politics of need interpretation', *Hypatia*, 2:1, 103–121. DOI: 10.1111/j.1527-2001.1987.tb00855.x

Fraser, N. and Gordon, L. (1994) 'A genealogy of dependency: tracing a keyword of the U.S. welfare state', *Signs*, 19:2, 309–336. DOI: 10.1086/494886

Fraser, N. and Honneth, A. (2003) *Redistribution or Recognition? A Political-Philosophical Exchange*. London: Verso.

Fricker, M. (2007) *Epistemic Injustice – Power and the Ethics of Knowing*. Oxford: Oxford University Press.

Fylkesnes, I. (2021) 'Institutional talk and practices: a journey into small group-homes for intellectually disabled children', *Disability & Society*, 36:6, 999–1020. DOI: 10.1080/09687599.2020.1779037

Gal, J. (2010) 'Is there an extended family of Mediterranean welfare states?', *Journal of European Social Policy*, 20:4, 283–300. DOI: 10.1177/0958928710374374

Gamble, A. (1996) *Hayek: The Iron Cage of Liberty*. Cambridge: Polity.

Garland-Thomson, R. (1997) *Extraordinary Bodies: Figuring Physical Disability in American Culture and Literature*. New York: Columbia University Press.

Ghai, A. (2002) 'Disability in the Indian context: post-colonial perspectives', in M. Corker and T. Shakespeare (eds) *Disability/Postmodernity: Embodying Disability Theory*. London: Continuum, 88–100.

Giddens, A. (1994) *Beyond Left and Right: The Future of Radical Politics*. Cambridge: Polity.

Goffman, E. (1974 [1961]) *Asylums: Essays on the Social Situation of Mental Patients and Other Inmates*. Harmondsworth: Penguin.

Golemanov, H. and Popov, M. (1976) *Social Welfare in the People's Republic of Bulgaria*, trans. D. Lambrinov. Sofia: Sofia Press.

Gooding, P. (2018) 'The right to independent living and being included in the community: lessons from the United Nations', *International Journal of Mental Health and Capacity Law*, 24, 32–54. DOI: 10.19164/ijmhcl.v2018i24.747

Goodley, D. (2017) *Disability Studies: An Interdisciplinary Introduction*. 2nd edition. London: SAGE.

Goodley, D., Lawthom, R., Liddiard, K., and Runswick-Cole, K. (2019) 'Provocations for Critical Disability Studies', *Disability & Society*, 34:6, 972–997. DOI: 10.1080/09687599.2019.1566889

Goodley, D., Lawthom, R., and Runswick-Cole, K. (2014) 'Dis/ability and austerity: beyond work and slow death', *Disability & Society*, 29:6, 980–984. DOI: 10.1080/09687599.2014.920125

Gorz, A. (1967) *Strategy for Labor: A Radical Proposal*. Boston, MA: Beacon.

Graby, S. D. (2018) *Personal Assistance: The Challenge of Autonomy*. PhD thesis. University of Leeds.

Gramsci, A. (1971) *Selections from the Prison Notebooks*. New York: International.

Grech, S. (2009) 'Disability, poverty and development: critical reflections on the majority world debate', *Disability & Society*, 24:6, 771–784. DOI: 10.1080/09687590903160266

Griffiths, M. (2019) '"These days are ours." Young disabled people's experiences of activism and participation in social movements', in M. Bergh, T. Chataika, Y. El-Lahib, and K. Dube (eds) *The Routledge Handbook of Disability Activism*. New York: Routledge, 57–70.

Hahn, H. (1990 [1988]) 'Can disability be beautiful?', in M. Nagler (ed.) *Perspectives on Disability. Text and Readings on Disability*. Palo Alto, CA: Health Markets Research, 310–319.

Hall, S. (2011) 'The neo-liberal revolution', *Cultural Studies*, 25:6, 705–728. DOI: 10.1080/09502386.2011.619886

Han, B.-C. (2017) *Psychopolitics: Neoliberalism and New Technologies of Power*. London: Verso.

Haraway, D. (1991) *Simians, Cyborgs, and Women. The Reinvention of Nature*. London: Free Association.

Harpur, P. (2012) 'Embracing the new disability rights paradigm: the importance of the Convention on the Rights of Persons with Disabilities', *Disability & Society*, 27:1, 1–14. DOI: 10.1080/09687599.2012.631794

Harry, B. and Klingner, J. (2006) *Why Are So Many Minority Students in Special Education? Understanding Race and Disability in Schools*. New York: Teachers College Press.

Hartblay, C. (2014) 'A genealogy of (Post-)Soviet dependency: disabling productivity', *Disability Studies Quarterly*, 34:1. DOI: 10.18061/dsq.v34i1.4015

Harvey, D. (2005) *Brief History of Neoliberalism*. Oxford: Oxford University Press.

Hasler, F. (1993) 'Developments in the disabled people's movement', in J. Swain, V. Finkelstein, S. French, and M. Oliver (eds) *Disabling Barriers – Enabling Environments*. London: SAGE, 278–284.

Hayek, F. A. (2001 [1944]) *The Road to Serfdom*. London: Routledge.

Heidegger, M. (1977) *The Question Concerning Technology, and Other Essays*, trans. W. Lovitt. New York: Harper & Row.

Heidegger, M. (1971) *Poetry, Language, Thought*, trans. A. Hofstadter. New York: Harper & Row.

Heidegger, M. (1962 [1927]) *Being and Time*, trans. J. Macquarrie and E. Robinson. Oxford: Blackwell.

Holliday, I. (2000) 'Productivist welfare capitalism: social policy in East Asia', *Political Studies*, 48:4, 706–723. DOI: 10.1111/1467-9248.00279

Hughes, B. (2009) 'Disability activism: social model stalwarts and biological citizens', *Disability & Society*, 24:6, 677–688. DOI: 10.1080/09687590903160118

Hughes, B. (2007) 'Being disabled: towards a critical social ontology for disability studies', *Disability & Society*, 22:7, 673–684. DOI: 10.1080/09687590701659527

Hughes, B. and Paterson, K. (1997) 'The social model of disability and the disappearing body: towards a sociology of impairment', *Disability & Society*, 12:3, 325–340. DOI: 10.1080/09687599727209

Hughes, B., McKie, L., Hopkins, D., and Watson, N. (2005) 'Love's labours lost? Feminism, the Disabled People's Movement and an ethic of care', *Sociology*, 39:2, 259–275. DOI: 10.1177/0038038505050538

Hunt, J. (2019) *No Limits. The Disabled People's Movement – A Radical History*. Manchester: TBR Imprint. https://gmcdp.com/sites/gmcdp.com/files/No%20Limits_%20Judy%20Hunt_%20book%20(12ptTimesRoman_%20270pg).pdf (accessed 14 July 2024).

Iarskaia-Smirnova, E. (2011) '"A girl who liked to dance": life experiences of Russian women with motor impairments', in M. Jäppinen, M. Kulmala and A. Saarinen (eds) *Gazing at Welfare, Gender and Agency in Post-socialist Countries*. Newcastle upon Tyne: Cambridge Scholars, 104–124.

Ife, J., Soldatic, K., and Briskman, L. (2022) *Human Rights and Social Work. Towards Rights-based Practice*. 4th edition. Cambridge: Cambridge University Press.

ILI (n.d.) 'What is Independent Living', online publication. Stockholm: Independent Living Institute. https://web.archive.org/web/20231110125823/https://www.independentliving.org/indexen.html (accessed 10 November 2023).

Illich, I. (2013 [1975]) *Limits to Medicine: Medical Nemesis – The Expropriation of Health*. London: Marion Boyars.

Institute for Bulgarian Language (n.d.) 'Грижа' ['Care'], online entry. Sofia: Institute for Bulgarian Language. https://ibl.bas.bg/rbe/lang/bg/грижа/ (accessed 10 November 2023).

JAG (2011) *The "JAG-model". Personal Assistance with Self-Determination*. Stockholm: The JAG Association. https://web.archive.org/web/20231110130140/https://enil.eu/wp-content/uploads/2022/03/Pa-manual_ENG.pdf (accessed 10 November 2023).

Johnson, M. (2003) *Make Them Go Away: Clint Eastwood, Christopher Reeve and the Case against Disability Rights*. Louisville, KY: Advocado.

Jolly, D. (2009) 'ENIL Position Paper 2009/02. Personal Assistance and Independent Living: Article 19 of the UN Convention on the Rights of Persons with Disabilities', online publication. Brussels: European Network on Independent Living. https://web.archive.org/web/20231110131627/https://www.mcgill.ca/humanrights/files/humanrights/enil-position-paper_personal-assistance-independent-living.pdf (accessed 10 November 2023).

Kant, I. (1991a [1784]) 'An answer to the question: What is Enlightenment?', in H. S. Reiss (ed.) *Kant: Political Writings*, trans. H. B. Nisbet. Cambridge: Cambridge University Press, 54–60.

Kant, I. (1991b [1793]) 'On the common saying: "This may be true in theory but it does not apply in practice"', in H. S. Reiss (ed.) *Kant: Political Writings*, trans. H. B. Nisbet. Cambridge: Cambridge University Press, 61–91.

Katzman, E. and Kinsella, E. A. (2018) '"It's like having another job": the invisible work of self-managing attendant services', *Disability & Society*, 33:9, 1436–1459. DOI: 10.1080/09687599.2018.1497949

Kay, P. (2003) 'Trying on the emperor's new clothes? Concertación, corporatism and neoliberal restructuring in the semiperiphery', *Bulletin of Latin American Research*, 22:3, 291–318. DOI: 10.1111/1470-9856.00079

Keane, J. (1984) 'Introduction', in C. Offe *Contradictions of the Welfare State*. Ed. by J. Keane. London: Hutchinson, 11–34.

Kirkwood, R. (1970) 'The ideology of casework and professionalism', *Case-Con*, 3, 3–8. https://web.archive.org/web/20231110132343/https://files.libcom.org/files/3CaseCon_0.pdf (accessed 10 November 2023).

Kittay, E. (2018) 'Disability studies and an ethics of care: partners or antagonists?', paper presented at the Euro-Mediterranean Conference on Disability Studies and Disability Activism, Department of Disability Studies, University of Malta, 2–4 May 2018, Victoria Hotel, Sliema, Malta.

Kittay, E. (1999) *Love's Labor: Essays on Women Equality, and Dependency*. New York: Routledge.

Kolářová, K. (2014) 'The inarticulate post-socialist crip: on the cruel optimism of neoliberal transformations in the Czech Republic', *Journal of Literary & Cultural Disability Studies*, 8:3, 257–274. DOI: 10.3828/jlcds.2014.22

Kolářová, K. (2011) 'How Sam became a father, became a citizen: scripts of neoliberal inclusion of disability', in M. Castro Varela, N. Dhawan and A. Engel (eds) *Hegemony and Heteronormativity: Revisiting 'The Political' in Queer Politics*. London: Routledge, 121–142.

Kolářová, K. and Winkler, M. (eds) (2021) *Re/imaginations of Disability in State Socialism*. Frankfurt: Campus.

Krantz, O., Melander, S., and Bahner, J. (2023) 'The personal is political – and then what? Ideology, representation, and legitimacy in a Swedish disability organisation', *Scandinavian Journal of Disability Research*, 25: 1, 198–211. DOI: 10.16993/sjdr.1001

Latour, B. (2005) *Reassembling the Social: An Introduction to Actor-Network-Theory*. Oxford: Oxford University Press.

Leece, J. (2006) '"It's not like being at work": a study to investigate stress and job satisfaction in employees of direct payment users', in J. Leece and J. Bornat (eds) *Developments in Direct Payments*. Bristol: Policy, 189–205.

Leitner, S. and Lessenich, S. (2007) '(In-)Dependence as dependent variable: conceptualising and measuring "de-familization"', in J. Clasen and N. A. Siegel (eds) *Investigating Welfare State Change. The 'Dependent Variable Problem' in Comparative Analysis*. Cheltenham: Edward Elgar, 244–260.

Lemke, T. (2002) 'Foucault, governmentality, and critique', *Rethinking Marxism*, 14:3, 49–64. DOI: 10.1080/089356902101242288

Lenin, V. I. (1964) *Collected Works*, Vol. 25, trans. and ed. S. Apresyan and J. Riordan. Moscow: Progress.

Lewis, S. (2022) *Abolish the Family. A Manifesto for Care and Liberation*. London: Verso.

Lister, R. (1994) '"She has other duties" – women, citizenship and social security', in S. Baldwin and J. Falkingham (eds) *Social Security and Social Change: New Challenges to the Beveridge Model*. New York: Harvester Wheatsheaf, 31–44.

Mackenzie, C. and Stoljar, N. (eds) (2000) *Relational Autonomy: Feminist Perspectives on Autonomy, Agency and the Social Self*. Oxford: Oxford University Press.

Manji, K. (2018) '"It was clear from the start that [SDS] was about a cost cutting agenda." Exploring disabled people's early experiences of the introduction of Self-Directed Support in Scotland', *Disability & Society*, 33:9, 1391–1411. DOI: 10.1080/09687599.2018.1498767

Mansell, J., Knapp, M., Beadle-Brown, J., and Beecham, J. (2007) *Deinstitutionalisation and Community Living – Outcomes and Costs: Report of a European Study. Volume 2: Main Report*. Canterbury: Tizard Centre, University of Kent. https://web.archive.org/web/20231110143258/https://research.kent.ac.uk/tizard/wp-content/uploads/sites/2302/2019/01/DECLOC_Volume_2_Report.pdf (accessed 10 November 2023).

Marinova, E. (2018) 'Maykite na detsa s uvrezhdaniya gotvyat novi efektivni protesti' ['The mothers of disabled children plan new effective protests'], online publication. *Investor.BG*. https://web.archive.org/web/20231110143647/https://www.investor.bg/a/332-ikonomika-i-politika/268644-maykite-na-detsa-s-uvrezhdaniya-gotvyat-novi-efektivni-protesti (accessed 10 November 2023).

Martin, L. H., Gutman, H., and Hutton, P. H. (1988) 'Introduction', in L. H. Martin, H. Gutman, and P. H. Hutton (eds) *Technologies of the Self: A Seminar with Michel Foucault*. Amherst: University of Massachusetts Press, 3–8.

Maruna, S. (2017) 'Desistance as a social movement', *Irish Probation Journal*, 14:1, 5–20.

Marx, K. (1978) 'Critique of the Gotha Program', in R. C. Tucker (ed.) *The Marx-Engels Reader*. London: W. W. Norton, 525–541.

Mathieu, S. (2016) 'From the defamilialization to the "demotherization" of care work', *Social Politics*, 23:4, 576–591. DOI: 10.1093/sp/jxw006

McCulloch, T. (2021) 'Co-producing desistance? The role of peer support', in E. Loeffler and T. Bovaird (eds) *The Palgrave Handbook of Co-Production of Public Services and Outcomes*. London: Palgrave Macmillan, 409–426.

McGrogan, D. (2021) *Critical Theory and Human Rights: From Compassion to Coercion*. Manchester: Manchester University Press.

McRuer, R. (2006) *Crip Theory: Cultural Signs of Queerness and Disability*. New York: New York University Press.

McRuer, R. (2002) 'Compulsory able-bodiedness and queer/disabled existence', in S. L. Snyder, B. J. Brueggemann, and R. G. Thomson (eds) *Disability Studies: Enabling the Humanities*, Volume 1. New York: Modern Language Association of America, 88–99.

Meekosha, H. (2011) 'Decolonising disability: thinking and acting globally', *Disability & Society*, 26:6, 667–682. DOI: 10.1080/09687599.2011.602860

Meekosha, H. and Shuttleworth, R. (2009) 'What's so "critical" about critical disability studies?', *Australian Journal of Human Rights*, 15:1, 47–75. DOI: 10.1080/1323238x.2009.11910861

Meekosha, H. and Soldatic, K. (2011) 'Human Rights and the Global South: the case of disability', *Third World Quarterly*, 32:8, 1383–1398. DOI: 10.1080/01436597.2011.614800

Michalko, R. (2002) *The Difference that Disability Makes*. Philadelphia, PA: Temple University Press.

Mitchell, D. T. and Snyder, S. L. (2015) *The Biopolitics of Disability: Neoliberalism, Ablenationalism, and Peripheral Embodiment*. Ann Arbor: University of Michigan Press.

Mladenov, T. (2021a) 'Disability assessment under state socialism', in K. Kolářová and M. Winkler (eds) *Re/imaginations of Disability in State Socialism*. Frankfurt: Campus, 91–116.

Mladenov, T. (2021b) 'Gender, sexuality, and disability in postsocialist Central-Eastern Europe', in K. Fábián, J. E. Johnson and M. Lazda (eds) *The Routledge*

Handbook of Gender in Central-Eastern Europe and Eurasia. London: Routledge, 530–537.

Mladenov, T. (2021c) 'The social model of disability, the independent living and the idea of "care"', *Critique and Humanism Journal*, 55:2, 9–24.

Mladenov, T. (2020a) 'Performativity and the disability category: solving *The Zero Theorem*', *Critical Sociology*, 46:1, 51–64. DOI: 10.1177/0896920518796904

Mladenov, T. (2020b) 'What is good personal assistance made of? Results of a European survey', *Disability & Society*, 30:1, 1–24. DOI: 10.1080/09687599.2019.1621740

Mladenov, T. (2018) *Disability and Postsocialism*. London: Routledge.

Mladenov, T. (2017a) 'From state socialist to neoliberal productivism: disability policy and invalidation of disabled people in the postsocialist region', *Critical Sociology*, 43: 7–8, 1109–1123. DOI: 10.1177/0896920515595843

Mladenov, T. (2017b) 'Governing through personal assistance: a Bulgarian case', *Scandinavian Journal of Disability Research*, 19:2, 91–103. DOI: 10.1080/15017419.2016.1178168

Mladenov, T. (2016) 'Disability and social justice', *Disability & Society*, 31:9, 1226–1241. DOI: 10.1080/09687599.2016.1256273

Mladenov, T. (2015a) *Critical Theory and Disability: A Phenomenological Approach*. New York: Bloomsbury.

Mladenov, T. (2015b) 'Neoliberalism, postsocialism, disability', *Disability & Society*, 30:3, 445–459. DOI: 10.1080/09687599.2015.1021758

Mladenov, T. (2013) 'The UN Convention on the Rights of Persons with Disabilities and its interpretation', *ALTER – European Journal of Disability Research*, 7:1, 69–82. DOI: 10.1016/j.alter.2012.08.010

Mladenov, T. (2012) 'Personal assistance for disabled people and the understanding of human being', *Critical Social Policy*, 32:2, 242–261. DOI: 10.1177/0261018311430454

Mladenov, T. (2004) *Za horata i horata. Izsledvane, posveteno na kampaniyata v podkrepa na uslugata 'asistent za nezavisim zhivot' na TsNZh – Sofia*. [*Of People and People: Analysis of the "Assistant for Independent Living" Campaign of CIL – Sofia*]. Sofia: Center for Independent Living–Sofia. https://web.archive.org/web/20240624154652/https://cil.bg/wp-content/uploads/2020/03/za_horata_i_horata_2004.pdf (accessed 10 November 2023).

Mladenov, T. and Brennan, C. (2021) 'Social vulnerability and the impact of policy responses to COVID-19 on disabled people', *Sociology of Health and Illness*, 42:9, 2049–2065. DOI: 10.1111/1467-9566.13379

Mladenov, T. and Dimitrova, I. (2023) 'Epistemic injustice as a bridge between medical sociology and disability studies', *Sociology of Health and Illness*, 45:6, 1146–1163. DOI: 10.1111/1467-9566.13479

Mladenov, T. and Petri, G. (2019) 'Independent living in Central and Eastern Europe? The challenges of postsocialist deinstitutionalisation', in I. Fylling, L. Baciu, and J. Breimo (eds) *EU Social Inclusion Policies in Post-Socialist Countries: Top-Down and Bottom-Up Perspectives on Implementation*. London: Routledge, 16–34.

Mladenov, T., Bulic Cojocariu, I., Angelova-Mladenova, L., Kokic, N., and Goungor, K. (2023) 'Independent Living in Europe and beyond: past, present, and future', *International Journal of Disability and Social Justice*, 3:1, 4–23.

Mladenov, T., Pokern, Y., and Cojocariu, I. B. (2019) *PA Checklist – A Tool for Assessing Personal Assistance Schemes*. Brussels: European Network on Independent Living. https://web.archive.org/web/20231110153618/https://enil.eu/wp-content/uploads/2022/03/Mladenov_Pokern_Bulic-PA_Checklist.pdf (accessed 10 November 2023).

Modic, K., Pečarič, E., and Retelj, D. (2023) *Personal Assistance: Handbook for Understanding Independent Living*. Ljubljana: YHD. https://web.archive.org/web/20231110153739/https://yhd-drustvo.si/wp-content/uploads/2023/06/OA-PRIROCNIK_e-izdaja_ANGLESKA-VERZIJA_14_06_2023_KONCNA-VERZIJA-ZA-OBJAVO.pdf (accessed 10 November 2023).

Moore, P. and Robinson, A. (2016) 'The quantified self: what counts in the neoliberal workplace', *New Media & Society*, 18:11, 2774–2792. DOI: 10.1177/1461444815604328

Moriarity, L. and Dew, K. (2011) 'The United Nations Convention on the Rights of Persons with Disabilities and participation in Aotearoa, New Zealand', *Disability & Society*, 26:6, 683–697. DOI: 10.1080/09687599.2011.602861

Morris, J. (2011) 'Rethinking disability policy', online publication. London: Joseph Rowntree Foundation. https://web.archive.org/web/20231110154212/https://www.jrf.org.uk/sites/default/files/jrf/migrated/files/disability-policy-equality-summary.pdf (accessed 10 November 2023).

Morris, J. (2006) 'Independent living: the role of the disability movement in the development of government policy', in C. Glendinning and P. A. Kemp (eds) *Cash and Care: Policy Challenges in the Welfare State*. Bristol: Policy, 235–248.

Morris, J. (2004) 'Independent living and community care: a disempowering framework', *Disability & Society*, 19:5, 427–442. DOI: 10.1080/0968759042000235280

Morris, J. (1993a) 'Gender and disability', in J. Swain, V. Finkelstein, S. French and M. Oliver (eds) *Disabling Barriers – Enabling Environments*. London: SAGE, 85–92.

Morris, J. (1993b) *Independent Lives? Community Care and Disabled People*. Basingstoke: Palgrave Macmillan.

Moser, I. and Law, J. (1999) 'Good passages, bad passages', *Sociological Review*, 47:S1, 196–219. DOI: 1 10.1111/j.1467-954x.1999.tb03489.x

Mouffe, C. (2013) *Agonistics: Thinking the World Politically*. London: Verso.

Müller, M. (2007) 'What's in a word? Problematizing translation between languages', *Area*, 39:2, 206–213. DOI: 10.1111/j.1475-4762.2007.00731.x

Murrell, P. (1993) 'What is shock therapy? What did it do in Poland and Russia?' *Post-Soviet Affairs*, 9:2, 111–140. DOI: 10.1080/1060586x.1993.10641362

Musengi, M. (2023) 'Decolonizing disability rights policies through indigenous theorization: the case of Zimbabwe', in S. Robinson and K. R. Fisher (eds) *Research Handbook on Disability Policy*. Cheltenham: Edward Elgar, 256–268.

Nasir, M. A. (2017) 'Biopolitics, thanatopolitics and the right to life', *Theory, Culture & Society*, 34:1, 75–95.

Negri, A. (2014) *Factory of Strategy: Thirty-Three Lessons on Lenin*, trans. A. Bove. New York: Columbia University Press.

Norberg, I. (2022) 'Austerity as bureaucratic violence: understanding the impact of (neoliberal) austerity on disabled people in Sweden', *Sociology*, 56:4, 655–672. DOI: 10.1177/00380385211051210

Obinger, H. and Schmitt, C. (2011) 'Guns and butter? Regime competition and the welfare state during the Cold War', *World Politics*, 63:2, 246–270. DOI: 10.1017/s0043887111000025

Offe, C. (1984) *Contradictions of the Welfare State*. Ed. by John Keane. Cambridge, MA: MIT Press.

Oliver, M. (2009) *Understanding Disability: From Theory to Practice*. 2nd edition. Basingstoke: Palgrave Macmillan.

Oliver, M. (1996) *Understanding Disability: From Theory to Practice*. London: Macmillan.

Oliver, M. (1994) 'Moving on: from welfare paternalism to welfare citizenship', *Journal of the Centre for Social Action*, 2:1.

Oliver, M. (1993) 'What's so wonderful about walking?', inaugural professorial lecture, 9 February 1993. London: University of Greenwich. https://web.archive.org/web/20231110162503/https://disability-studies.leeds.ac.uk/wp-content/uploads/sites/40/library/Oliver-PROFLEC.pdf (accessed 10 November 2023).

Oliver, M. (1992a) 'Changing the social relations of research production?', *Disability, Handicap & Society*, 7:2, 101–114. DOI: 10.1080/02674649266780141

Oliver, M. (1992b) 'Intellectual masturbation: a rejoinder to Söder and Booth', *European Journal of Special Needs Education*, 7:1, 20–28. DOI: 10.1080/0885625920070103

Oliver, M. (1990) *The Politics of Disablement*. London: Macmillan.

Oliver, M. (1981) 'A new model of the social work role in relation to disability', in J. Campling (ed.) *The Handicapped Person: A New Perspective for Social Workers?* London: RADAR. https://web.archive.org/web/20240624101259/https://disability-studies.leeds.ac.uk/wp-content/uploads/sites/40/library/Campling-handicppaed.pdf (accessed 10 November 2023).

Oliver, M. and Barnes, C. (2012) *The New Politics of Disablement*. Basingstoke: Palgrave Macmillan.

Oliver, M. and Zarb, G. (1992) *Greenwich Personal Assistance Schemes: An Evaluation*. London: Greenwich Association of Disabled People's Centre for Independent Living.

Orloff, A. S. (2009) 'Gendering the comparative analysis of welfare states: an unfinished agenda', *Sociological Theory*, 27:3, 317–343. DOI: 10.1111/j.1467-9558.2009.01350.x

Outhwaite, W. and Ray, L. (2005) *Social Theory and Postcommunism*. Oxford: Blackwell.

Parker, C. and Bulic Cojocariu, I. (2016) *European Structural and Investment Funds and People with Disabilities in the European Union*. Online publication. Brussels: European Parliament. https://web.archive.org/web/20231110163705/https://enil.eu/wp-content/uploads/2022/03/COMMITTEES_PETI_2016_11-09_Study-EUFunds-Disabilities.pdf (accessed 10 November 2023).

Parker, C. and Bulic, I. (2013) *Briefing on Structural Funds Investments for People with Disabilities: Achieving the Transition from Institutional Care to Community Living*. Dublin: European Network on Independent Living – European Coalition for Community Living. https://web.archive.org/web/20231110163811/https://enil.eu/wp-content/uploads/2022/03/Structural-Fund-Briefing-final-WEB.pdf (accessed 10 November 2023).

Parker, C. and Bulic, I. (2010) *Wasted Time, Wasted Money, Wasted Lives … A Wasted Opportunity? A Focus Report on How the Current Use of Structural Funds Perpetuates the Social Exclusion of Disabled People in Central and Eastern Europe by Failing to Support the Transition from Institutional Care to Community-based Services*. London: European Coalition for Community Living.

https://web.archive.org/web/20231110164103/https://enil.eu/wp-content/uploads/2022/07/Wasted-opportunity.pdf (accessed 10 November 2023).

Parker, C., Angelova-Mladenova, L., and Bulic, I. (2016) *Working Together to Close the Gap Between Rights and Reality. A report on the action needed to ensure that European Structural and Investment Funds promote, not hinder, the transition from institutional care to community living*. Brussels: European Network on Independent Living – European Coalition for Community Living. https://web.archive.org/web/20231110162819/https://enil.eu/wp-content/uploads/2022/07/Briefing-June-2016.pdf (accessed 10 November 2023).

Parker, C., Bulic, I., and Kokic, N. (2017) *European Union Structural and Investment Funds and the Transition from Institutional Care to Community Living: Towards a More Effective Monitoring and Complaints System*. Brussels: European Network on Independent Living. https://web.archive.org/web/20231110164604/https://enil.eu/wp-content/uploads/2022/03/OurRightsCampaign-Briefing_FINAL.pdf (accessed 10 November 2023).

Paterson, K. and Hughes, B. (1999) 'Disability studies and phenomenology: the carnal politics of everyday life', *Disability & Society*, 14:5, 597–610. DOI: 10.1080/09687599925966

People First Scotland (n.d.) *Supported Decision-Making: A Framework*. Edinburgh: People First Scotland. https://web.archive.org/web/20231108201708/https://peoplefirstscotland.org/wp-content/uploads/2019/02/Framework-Final.compressed.pdf (accessed 8 November 2023).

Petri, G., Beadle-Brown, J., and Bradshaw, J. (2017) '"More honoured in the breach than in the observance" – self-advocacy and human rights', *Laws*, 6:26, 1–20. DOI: 10.3390/laws6040026

Phillips, S. D. (2010) *Disability and Mobile Citizenship in Postsociallist Ukraine*. Bloomington: Indiana University Press.

Phillips, S. D. (2009) '"There are no invalids in the USSR!": A missing Soviet chapter in the new disability history', *Disability Studies Quarterly*, 29:3. DOI: 10.18061/dsq.v29i3.936

Phillips, S. D., Herasymova, T., and Pcholkina, U. (2023) 'Women with disabilities, and communities of care in wartime Ukraine: Conversations with disability and women's rights activists about feminist and disability solidarities', *Women's Studies International Forum*, 98, 1–9. DOI: 10.1016/j.wsif.2023.102740

Polanyi, K. (2001 [1944]) *The Great Transformation. The Political and Economic Origins of Our Time*. Boston, MA: Beacon.

Popova, G. (2011) 'Preodolyavaneto na pola prez parvoto desetiletie sled 9 septemvri 1944 g. – utopichnata kulminatsiya na marksistkiya feminizam' ['Overcoming gender in the first decade after 9 September 1944 – the utopian climax of Marxist feminism'], in K. Daskalova and T. Kmetova (eds) *Pol i prehod: 1938–1958* [*Gender and Transition: 1938–1958*]. Sofia: Tsentar za izsledvaniya i politiki za zhenite.

Priestley, M., Riddell, S., Jolly, D., Pearson, C., Williams, V., Barnes, C., and Mercer, G. (2010) 'Cultures of welfare at the front line: implementing direct payments for disabled people in the UK', *Policy & Politics*, 38:2, 307–324. DOI: 10.1332/030557309x477956

Puar, J. (2017) *The Right to Maim: Debility, Capacity, Disability*. Durham, NC: Duke University Press.

Pullin, G. (2019) 'Super normal design for extraordinary bodies: a design manifesto', in K. Ellis, R. Garland-Thomson, M. Kent, and R. Roberson (eds) *Manifestos for the Future of Critical Disability Studies*. Volume 1. New York: Routledge, 166–176.

Rasell, M. and Iarskaia-Smirnova, E. (eds) (2014) *Disability in Eastern Europe and the Former Soviet Union: History, Policy and Everyday Life*. London: Routledge.

Ratzka, A. (2019) 'What is personal about personal assistance: the difference between personal assistance and other community-based services. A personal comment on personal assistance', *Fukushi-Rodo*, No. 162, Gendai Shokan, Tokyo. www.ratzka.se/lectures-in-english/ (accessed 10 November 2023).

Ratzka, A. (2012) 'Beyond the social model of disability', keynote at Disability Studies Conference, Lancaster University, UK, 7–9 September 2010. https://web.archive.org/web/20230624105403/https://www.lancaster.ac.uk/fass/events/disabilityconference_archive/2010/keynote.htm (accessed 10 November 2023).

Ratzka, A. (2004) 'Model national personal assistance policy', online publication. Stockholm: Independent Living Institute. https://web.archive.org/web/20231110165919/https://www.independentliving.org/docs6/ratzka200410a.pdf (accessed 10 November 2023).

Ratzka, A. (1996) 'STIL, the Stockholm Cooperative for Independent Living', online publication. Stockholm: Independent Living Institute. https://web.archive.org/web/20231110170022/https://www.independentliving.org/docs3/stileng.html (accessed 10 November 2023).

Ratzka, A. (1993) 'The user cooperative model in personal assistance: the example of STIL, the Stockholm Cooperative for Independent Living', online publication. Stockholm: Independent Living Institute. https://web.archive.org/web/20231110170118/https://www.independentliving.org/docs5/ratzka199301.html (accessed 10 November 2023).

Reclaiming Our Futures Alliance (2018) 'Independent living for the future', online publication. London: Reclaiming Our Futures Alliance. https://web.archive.org/web/20240624144005/https://www.rofa.org.uk/independent-living-future/ (accessed 10 November 2023).

Reid, J. (2023) 'Martial indigeneity: deconstructing "decolonization" in international relations', *Georgetown Journal of International Affairs*, September 2023. https://web.archive.org/web/20231110170418/https://gjia.georgetown.edu/2023/09/18/martial-indigeneity-deconstructing-decolonization-in-international-relations/ (accessed 10 November 2023).

Rogowski, S. (2015) 'From child welfare to child protection/safeguarding: a critical practitioner's view of changing conception, policies and practice', *Practice*, 27:2, 97–112. DOI: 10.1080/09503153.2015.1014337

Rose, N. (1999) *Governing the Soul: The Shaping of the Private Self*. 2nd edition. London: Free Association.

Roulstone, A. (2016) *Disability and Technology. An Interdisciplinary and International Approach*. London: Palgrave Macmillan.

Roulstone, A. and Prideaux, S. (2012) *Understanding Disability Policy*. Bristol: Policy.

Ružičić-Novković, M. M. (ed.) (2020) *Vying for A Choice: Gordana Rajkov – A Life Story*. 2nd edition, trans. J. Browne. Belgrade: Center for Independent Living Serbia. https://web.archive.org/web/20231110170738/https://www.czuns.org/wp-content/uploads/2021/01/Gordana-Rajkov-Vying-for-a-Choice-Life-Story.pdf (accessed 10 November 2023).

Ryan, F. (2019) *Crippled: Austerity and the Demonization of Disabled People*. London: Verso.

Ryan, S. and Runswick-Cole, K. (2008) 'Repositioning mothers: mothers, disabled children and disability studies', *Disability & Society*, 23:3, 199–210. DOI: 10.1080/09687590801953937

Sanden, F. (2022) 'Personal assistance for independent living for disabled people old and young', online publication. Brussels: European Network on Independent Living. https://web.archive.org/web/20231110171107/https://enil.eu/personal-assistance-for-independent-living-for-disabled-people-old-and-young/ (accessed 10 November 2023).

Schecter, D. (2010) *The Critique of Instrumental Reason from Weber to Habermas*. London: Continuum.

SCIE (2022) 'Co-production: what it is and how to do it', online publication. www.scie.org.uk/co-production/what-how (accessed 28 November 2023).

Scottish Government (2022) *Coming Home Implementation: A Report from the Working Group on Complex Care and Delayed Discharge*. Edinburgh: Scottish Government. www.gov.scot/publications/coming-home-implementation-report-working-group-complex-care-delayed-discharge/documents/ (accessed 10 November 2023).

Sépulchre, M. (2022) 'Disability, justice and freedom as non-domination', *International Journal of Disability and Social Justice*, 2:1, 11–30. DOI: 10.13169/intljofdissocjus.2.1.0011

Shakespeare, T. (2014) *Disability Rights and Wrongs Revisited*. 2nd edition. New York: Routledge.

Shakespeare, T. (2006) *Disability Rights and Wrongs*. New York: Routledge.

Shakespeare, T. (1994) 'Cultural representation of disabled people: dustbins for disavowal?', *Disability & Society*, 9:3, 283–299. DOI: 0.1080/09687599466780341

Shakespeare, T., Gillespie-Sells, K. and Davies, D. (1996) *The Sexual Politics of Disability: Untold Desires*. New York: Cassell.

Shakespeare, T., Porter, T., and Stöckl, A. (2017) *Personal Assistance Relationships: Power, Ethics and Emotions*. Report on ESRC Project ES/L007894/1. Norwich: University of East Anglia.

Sinnerbrink, R. (2006) 'A Heideggerian cinema? On Terrence Malick's *The Thin Red Line*', *Film-Philosophy*, 10:3, 26–37. DOI: 10.3366/film.2006.0027

Šiška, J. and Beadle-Brown, J. (2020) *Transition from Institutional Care to Community-Based Services in 27 EU Member States: Final report*. Brussels: European Expert Group on the Transition from Institutional to Community-Based Care. https://web.archive.org/web/20231110172055/https://www.inclusion-europe.eu/wp-content/uploads/2020/01/eeg-di-report-2020-1.pdf (accessed 10 November 2023).

Smith, P. and Routel, C. (2009) 'Transition failure: the cultural bias of self-determination and the journey to adulthood for people with disabilities', *Disability Studies Quarterly*, 30:1. DOI: 10.18061/dsq.v30i1.1012

Soldatic, K. (2013) 'The transnational sphere of justice: disability praxis and the politics of impairment', *Disability & Society*, 28:6, 744–755. DOI: 10.1080/09687599.2013.802218

Spectrum CIL (n.d.) '"Rights not Charity" – 12 Basic Rights', online publication. Southampton: Spectrum CIL. https://web.archive.org/web/20231110172314/https://spectrumcil.co.uk/wp-content/uploads/2015/04/SPECTRUM-12-Basic-Rights-2013.pdf (accessed 10 November 2023).

Stakeholder Submission on Common Concerns (2022) *Coming Home Implementation: A Report from the Working Group on Complex Care and Delayed*

Discharge. Stakeholder Submission on Common Concerns. July 2022. https://web.archive.org/web/20231110154933/https://inclusionscotland.org/wp-content/uploads/2022/08/Coming-Home-Implementation-Report-submission-August-2022-with-signatures.pdf (accessed 10 November 2023).

Stammers, N. (2009) *Human Rights and Social Movements*. London: Pluto.

Stammers, N. (1999) 'Social movements and the social construction of human rights', *Human Rights Quarterly*, 21:4, 980–1008. DOI: 10.1353/hrq.1999.0054

Stiegler, B. (2010 [2008]) *Taking Care of Youth and the Generations*, trans. S. Barker. Stanford, CA: Stanford University Press.

Stone, D. (1984) *The Disabled State*. London: Macmillan.

Stoyanova, T. and Stoynova, D. (2018) 'Dostoen zhivot za detsata si poiskaha protestirashtite mayki, obedineni pod mototo "Sistemata ni ubiva"' ['Dignified living for their children demanded protesting mother, unified by the slogan "The system kills us"'], online publication. *BNR*. https://web.archive.org/web/20190319081130/http://bnr.bg/post/101001838/zapochna-nacionalnoto-protestno-shestvie-na-maikite-na-deca-s-uvrejdania (accessed 10 November 2023).

Suchland, J. (2011) 'Is postsocialism transnational?', *Signs*, 36:4, 837–862. DOI: 10.1086/658899

Sumskiene, E. and Orlova, U. L. (2015) 'Sexuality of "dehumanized people" across post-Soviet countries: patterns from closed residential care institutions in Lithuania', *Sexuality & Culture*, 19:2, 369–387. DOI: 10.1007/s12119-014-9262-1

Szarota, M. (2023) *Nothing (About Us) Without Us. Activism of Women-led Disability Civil Society Organisations in Post-socialist Poland*. PhD thesis. Lancaster University.

Szasz, T. (2001) 'The therapeutic state. The tyranny of pharmacracy', *The Independent Review*, 5:4, 485–521.

Szasz, T. (1991 [1969]) *Ideology and Insanity: Essays on the Psychiatric Dehumanization of Man*. Syracuse, NY: Syracuse University Press.

Szelényi, I. (2009) 'Janos Kornai: from socialism to capitalism', *Czech Sociological Review*, 45:3, 611–615.

Táíwò, O. (2022) *Against Decolonization: Taking African Agency Seriously*. London: Hurst.

Thatcher, M. (1981) 'Mrs Thatcher: the first two years', an interview, *Sunday Times*, 1 May 1981. https://web.archive.org/web/20231110173021/https://www.margaretthatcher.org/document/104475 (accessed 10 November 2023).

Thomas, C. (1999) *Female Forms: Experiencing and Understanding Disability*. Buckingham: Open University Press.

Tierney, T. (2016) 'Toward an affirmative biopolitics', *Sociological Theory*, 34:4, 358–381. DOI: 10.1177/0735275116678998

Titmuss, R. M. (1974) *Social Policy: An Introduction*. Ed. by B. Abel-Smith and K. Titmuss. London: George Allen and Unwin.

Tlostanova, M. (2012) 'Postsocialist ≠ postcolonial? On post-Soviet imaginary and global coloniality', *Journal of Postcolonial Writing*, 48:2, 130–142. DOI: 10.1080/17449855.2012.658244

Tobis, D. (2000) *Moving from Residential Institutions to Community-Based Social Services in Central and Eastern Europe and the Former Soviet Union*. Washington, DC: World Bank.

Tremain, S. (ed.) (2005) *Foucault and the Government of Disability*. Ann Arbor: University of Michigan Press.

Tronto, J. C. (1993) *Moral Boundaries: A Political Argument for an Ethic of Care.* New York: Routledge.

United Nations (n.d.) 'Convention on the Rights of Persons with Disabilities (CRPD)', online publication. New York: United Nations. https://web.archive.org/web/20240624095846/https://social.desa.un.org/issues/disability/crpd/convention-on-the-rights-of-persons-with-disabilities-crpd (accessed 10 November 2023).

UPIAS (1976a) *Fundamental Principles of Disability.* London: Union of the Physically Impaired against Segregation and the Disability Alliance. https://web.archive.org/web/20231110173315/https://disability-studies.leeds.ac.uk/wp-content/uploads/sites/40/library/UPIAS-fundamental-principles.pdf (accessed 10 November 2023).

UPIAS (1976b) *Policy Statement.* London: Union of the Physically Impaired against Segregation. https://web.archive.org/web/20231110173434/https://disability-studies.leeds.ac.uk/wp-content/uploads/sites/40/library/UPIAS-UPIAS.pdf (accessed 10 November 2023).

Verdery, C. (1995) 'What was Socialism, and why did it fall?', in D. Orlovsky (ed.) *Beyond Soviet Studies.* Washington, DC: Woodrow Wilson Center, 27–46.

Wacquant, L. (2009) *Punishing the Poor: The Neoliberal Government of Social Insecurity.* Durham, NC: Duke University Press.

Watson, N., McKie, L., Hughes, B., Hopkins, D., and Gregory, S. (2004) '(Inter) dependence, needs and care: the potential for disability and feminist theorists to develop an emancipatory model', *Sociology*, 38:2, 331–350. DOI: 10.1177/0038038504040867

Walby, S. (2020) 'Varieties of gender regimes', *Social Politics*, 27:3, 414–431. DOI: 10.1093/sp/jxaa018

Westberg, K. (2010) *Personal Assistance in Sweden*, trans. S. Berg. Stockholm: Independent Living Institute. https://web.archive.org/web/20231110173659/https://www.independentliving.org/files/Personal_Assistance_in_Sweden_KW_2010.pdf (accessed 10 November 2023).

WHO (2011) *World Report on Disability.* Geneva: World Health Organization.

Williams, F. (2002) 'The presence of feminism in the future of welfare', *Economy and Society*, 31:4, 502–519. DOI: 10.1080/03085140220000020652

Williams, G. (1983) 'The movement for Independent Living: an evaluation and critique', *Social Science and Medicine*, 17:15, 1003–1010. DOI: 10.1016/0277-9536(83)90403-3

Winance, M. (2006) 'Trying out the wheelchair: the mutual shaping of people and devices through adjustment', *Science, Technology & Human Values*, 31:1, 52–72. DOI: 10.1177/0162243905280023

Witcher, S. (2014) *My Choices: A Vision of Self-directed Support. Action Research Report.* Glasgow: Glasgow Disability Alliance.

Woodin, S. (2017) 'Research with disabled people: a health action research project with people with learning difficulties', in *Sage Research Methods Cases* Part 2. London: SAGE. DOI: 10.4135/9781526421050

Woolham, J., Norrie, C., Samsi, K., and Manthorpe, J. (2019) 'The employment conditions of social care personal assistants in England', *Journal of Adult Protection*, 21:6, 296–306. DOI: 10.1108/jap-06-2019-0017

World Bank (2003) *Social Development in Europe and Central Asia Region: Issues and Directions*. Washington, DC: World Bank. https://web.archive.org/web/20240624145934/https://documents1.worldbank.org/curated/en/858001468250263597/pdf/642530WP0Socia00BOX353803B00Public0.pdf (accessed 10 November 2023).

Zaviršek, D. and Fischbach, S. (2023) 'Independent living in post-socialist countries: between familialism, deinstitutionalisation and re-institutionalisation', *International Journal of Disability and Social Justice*, 3:1, 96–113. DOI: 10.13169/intljofdissocjus.3.1.0096

Zukas, H. (1975) *CIL History. Report of the State of the Art Conference*. Berkeley, CA: Center for Independent Living–Berkeley. https://web.archive.org/web/20231110174358/https://www.independentliving.org/docs3/zukas.html (accessed 10 November 2023).

Index

EU authorised representative for GPSR:
Easy Access System Europe, Mustamäe tee 50,
10621 Tallinn, Estonia
gpsr.requests@easproject.com

www.ingramcontent.com/pod-product-compliance
Ingram Content Group UK Ltd.
Pitfield, Milton Keynes, MK11 3LW, UK
UKHW021839100926
8556IPUK00004B/448